New Perspectives in Organizational Communication

Series Editors
Milton Mayfield, Texas A&M International University, Laredo, TX, USA
Jacqueline Mayfield, Texas A&M International University,
Laredo, TX, USA

This series will examine current, emerging, and cutting edge approaches to organizational communication. Throughout this series, authors will present new ideas in – and methods for – conducting organizational communication research. The series will present a variety of topics, giving readers an in-depth understanding of the organizational communication field to develop the skills necessary to engage in field research.

More information about this series at
http://www.palgrave.com/gp/series/16587

Linjuan Rita Men · Ana Tkalac Verčič
Editors

Current Trends and Issues in Internal Communication

Theory and Practice

palgrave
macmillan

Editors
Linjuan Rita Men
University of Florida
Gainesville, FL, USA

Ana Tkalac Verčič
University of Zagreb
Zagreb, Croatia

ISSN 2730-5333 ISSN 2730-5341 (electronic)
New Perspectives in Organizational Communication
ISBN 978-3-030-78212-2 ISBN 978-3-030-78213-9 (eBook)
https://doi.org/10.1007/978-3-030-78213-9

This Palgrave Macmillan imprint is published by the registered company Springer Nature Switzerland AG
The registered company address is: Gewerbestrasse 11, 6330 Cham, Switzerland

Preface

Nearly a century ago (1924–1932) the Hawthorne Studies of employees at Western Electric Company in Chicago revealed a then startling discovery: the *positive power* of internal communications. Worker performance was found to improve most when they felt more informed, involved, and valued in the organization—not when lighting or other environmental conditions were changed. Productivity was dependent on social issues and job satisfaction, in addition to monetary incentives and workplace conditions.

A long chain of research evidence since then underscores the importance of internal communications in organizations and the crucial roles leaders at all levels play in strategic communications. Yet, our *knowing more* about the positive power of employee communication and leadership has not been matched over the years by *doing more* to realize that power and reap the substantial benefits of enriched workplace communications and interactions.

Our hesitancy or unwillingness to seize and act upon illuminating research findings is due to many constraints. They range from blinding egos and self-interests, to sticky entrapments in long-time practices and procedures, to lack of belief in research findings, to researchers' deficiencies in communicating their findings clearly and more widely.

But the urgency to do more with what we know regarding internal communications in all types of groups and organizations has never been clearer or more urgent. The global pandemic of 2020 starkly framed these human needs and our distinct ties to each other and to group, community, and organizational success. The documented lethal effects of the pandemic reached and touched all of us, accentuating our utter connectedness as people.

Similarly, we are linked to others in our workplaces and organizations globally. Here, too, our connectedness, and the quality and integrity of our interactions and communications with each other, have everything to do with individual, team, and organizational performance. Together we have the opportunity to understand and effect positive changes in internal communication. Simply put, the power of ***doing something positive*** resides in our hands, hearts, and minds. We must but seize it.

And that is the beauty of this rich, insightful book on internal communications: it connects our research in the area to our professional practice. Edited by renowned scholars, Drs. Rita Men and Ana Tkalac Verčič, this book is a roadmap for doing something positive—clear ideas and directions for how we and our organizations can ***move from knowing*** what research and theory reveal about internal communications, ***to doing***, or putting into daily practice those crucial findings and corresponding knowledge.

The book highlights more than a dozen internal communication trends and issues, or forces affecting organizations of all kinds and their people today. These include the crucial roles of leaders as communication agents; the influences (and pitfalls) of emerging technologies on information distribution and content; measurement of internal communications; internal crises and strategic change communications; employee well-being and CSR; cross-cultural internal communications; and employee activism, voice, listening, and dialogue in the workplace.

These areas of study and practice possess the power to affect employee attitudes, engagement, productivity, trust, retention, teamwork, and policies and practices in organizations, ultimately rendering the fabric of organizational culture. Today, employees are vital communication agents and assets for organizations whose reputations and external relationships are built from within.

What distinguishes this book is the combination of excellent scholarly research with the many insights and best practices of leading professionals worldwide. The book is: (1) grounded thoroughly in empirical research by highly regarded global scholars; (2) informed by established theories; (3) enriched through interviews with or mini-cases written by leading professionals; and (4) punctuated by dozens of insightful best practices and implications.

Bottomline: This is an invaluable resource for practicing communicators, teachers, scholars, and leaders at all levels in diverse organizations. Its global scope, and topical reach and depth, inform current issues and trends in internal communications. Combined with professional insights and implications for professional tactics, strategies, and practices, the book helps us *know more* about these crucial issues and surging trends. More importantly, it arms us to *do more* to help manage and resolve such issues.

Dr. Nitin Nohria, Indian–American author and scholar, and current dean of Harvard Business School, succinctly captured this notion of *doing* when he described the relationship between communication and leadership: "Communication is the real work of leadership."

Meaningful change and improvement grow out of the combination of knowing more and then doing more. This book is the Rx for improving the health and enriching the power of internal communications. I encourage you to read and enjoy the book, learn from it, then act on your learning and make positive differences in your work, workforce, and workplace.

Bruce K. Berger, Ph.D.
Professor Emeritus
University of Alabama
Tuscaloosa, USA

Contents

Notes on Contributors

Chapter Authors

Bruce K. Berger is a professor emeritus, University of Alabama. He was founding director of The Plank Center for Leadership in PR. His research focuses on employee communications, leadership, and power relations. Previously, Berger was a corporate PR executive and worked on diverse communication projects in more than 30 countries.

Alfonsa Butera is an adjunct professor of Corporate Communication and Senior Researcher of the Centre for Employee Relations and Communication at Università IULM. She is a freelance consultant in the field of corporate communication.

Ganga S. Dhanesh (Ph.D., National University of Singapore), is an associate professor, assistant dean of Research, College of Communication and Media Sciences, Zayed University, has published on CSR and strategic communication in journals including *Business Horizons*, *Management Communication Quarterly*, *Journal of Public Relations Research*, *Journal of International Management*, and *Public Relations Review*.

Michele E. Ewing, APR, Fellow PRSA has more than 30 years of experience in public relations practice and education. She teaches public relations courses in the School of Media and Journalism at Kent State

University. Her research focuses on digital communication, fake news crises, internal communication, and leadership development. She serves on the National Public Relations Society of America's Board of Ethics and Professional Standards.

Jarim Kim (Ph.D., University of Maryland, 2014) is an assistant professor in the Department of Communication at Yonsei University, Seoul, South Korea. Her research interests include public behaviors, crisis communication, public segmentation, strategic message design, and digital media.

Arunima Krishna, Ph.D. is an assistant professor at Boston University's College of Communication. Her research examines publics' perceptions of controversial social issues, such as anti-vaccine activism, climate change, and workplace gender discrimination, and has been published in leading academic journals including *Communication Research*, *Journal of Public Relations Research*, and *Journalism and Mass Communication Quarterly*.

Yeunjae Lee (Ph.D., Purdue University, 2018) is an assistant professor in public relations and strategic communication at the University of Miami. Her research interests include relationship management, employee communication, and internal issue/crisis management.

Vibeke Thøis Madsen is a senior associate professor in organizational strategic communication at DMJX, Danish School of Media and Journalism, Denmark. Her research interests are organizational communication, communication dynamics on internal social media, and employees as strategic communicators.

Alessandra Mazzei is the director of Centre for Employee Relations and Communication at Università IULM, where she is an associate professor of Corporate Communication and Coordinator of the bachelor programme in Corporate Communication and Public Relations.

Linjuan Rita Men, Ph.D., APR is an associate professor in the Department of Public Relations at the University of Florida. Her research interests include internal communication, leadership communication, measurement and evaluation, emerging technologies, and entrepreneurial communications. She is the lead author of the book, *Excellence in Internal Communication Management* published by Business Expert Press.

Julie O'Neil, Ph.D., APR teaches and researches in public relations, strategy, and internal communication. A member of the Page Society and the Institute for Public Relations Measurement Commission, she has published and presented more than 90 peer-reviewed journal articles, proceedings, and conference papers. She is an associate editor for the *Public Relations Journal*.

Kevin Ruck is the co-founder of PR Academy and the editor and co-author of *Exploring Internal Communication: Towards Informed Employee Voice* published by Routledge.

Stacey Smith, APR, Fellow PRSA is a senior counsel and partner at Jackson Jackson & Wagner, a behavioral public relations firm. For 40 years, Stacey has helped organizations build mutually beneficial relationships with stakeholders. She sits on IPR's Measurement Commission and is co-chair of the Commission for Public Relations Education.

Krishnamurthy Sriramesh, Ph.D. is a professor of Public Relations and Director of Master of Arts in Corporate Communication at the University of Colorado, Boulder, USA. His research focuses on topics such as global public relations, the public relations and culture, public relations for development, and CSR. He has taught at universities in Asia, Australasia, Europe, and North America and received several awards for excellence in teaching and research including the prestigious 2004 Pathfinder Award from the Institute of Public Relations. He has co-edited several books (including two PRIDE award-winning volumes), published over 100 research articles and book chapters, and presented over 100 conference papers and presentations in over 35 countries.

Patrick D. Thelen is an assistant professor in the School of Journalism & Media Studies at San Diego State University. He received his Ph.D. in Mass Communication from the University of Florida in 2019. He began his professional career in Chile and worked for the multinational PR firm Hill+Knowlton Strategies.

Ana Tkalac Verčič, Ph.D. is a professor of Marketing and Public Relations at the Faculty of Economics & Business, at the University of Zagreb. Her research includes various communication topics, from marketing communication to internal communication. She has published more than 100 research papers and book chapters and has authored, co-authored and edited numerous books in public relations, marketing, and social sciences.

Dejan Verčič, Ph.D. is a professor, Head of Department of Communication and Head of Centre for Marketing and Public Relations at the University of Ljubljana, and Partner and Knowledge Director in Herman & partnerji d.o.o., Slovenia. His research interests are globalization, mediatization, reflective, and strategic communication, and future studies.

Aniisu K. Verghese, Ph.D. is an award-winning internal communications leader, author, speaker, consultant, and blogger with over 22 years of experience. The author of *Internal Communications—Insights, Practices, and Models* (Sage, 2012), he researches, teaches and speaks on internal communications, corporate social responsibility, and personal branding. He is a member of the International Association of Business Communicators.

Justin A. Walden, Ph.D. is an associate professor of organizational communication and strategic communication in the Department of Communication at North Dakota State University. Walden spent eight years total as a newspaper reporter and public relations professional before entering academia. He studies employee-organization relationships, work-life boundary navigation, and media use routines in work contexts.

Sean Williams is an assistant teaching professor at Bowling Green State University. Previously, he held senior communication positions with KeyCorp, National City Corporation, Goodyear, True Digital Communications, and his own company, Communication AMMO. He is also a member of the Institute for Public Relations Measurement Commission and the board of directors of the International PR Research Conference.

Cen April Yue, Ph.D. is an assistant professor in the Department of Communication at the University of Connecticut and research editor of the Organizational Communication Research Center at the Institute for Public Relations. Her research interest focuses on internal public relations, leadership communication, organizational change management, and relationship management.

Other Contributors

Mahul Brahma, Ph.D., D.Litt. heads Communications, CSR, and Branding at Mjunction Services Limited. A former journalist, Mahul is an award-winning communicator, a renowned luxury commentator, and an author. He is an alumnus of institutes such as Indian Institute of Management (India) and University of Cambridge (UK).

Martin Flegg Chart.PR has been an internal communication practitioner for over 20 years working in-house and as a consultant in government, financial services, legal services, and higher education. He is the 2021 Committee Chair for CIPR Inside and the founder of The IC Citizen.

Teresa Giradi is the head of internal communication at SNAM, one of the world's leading energy infrastructure operators headquartered in Italy. Her main responsibilities include planning, implementing, and directing internal communication programs.

Lasse Hoegfeldt is the head of Media and Creative at Jyske Bank and editor-in-chief of Jyske Bank TV. He is an international keynote speaker on topics like internal and external communication, brand journalism, brand Newsroom, and Social Media strategy.

Katarina is Novartis Country Communications & Engagement Head in Slovenia. She was one of the earliest practicing PR professionals in the country. Katarina has a Master's degree from the Faculty of Social Sciences in Ljubljana. She is a member of the Public Relations Society of Slovenia and the International Association of Business Communicators (IABC).

Ray Kotcher is a professor of the practice, public relations, at Boston University's College of Communication, and the former CEO and chairman of Ketchum, one of the world's largest and most awarded public relations agencies.

Alex Malouf a marketing communications executive who has spent the last 17 years in the Middle East has lived across the region, working for the public and private sectors in a variety of communications roles. He is the Corporate Communications Director for the Middle East and Africa at Schneider Electric.

Ethan McCarty is the founder and CEO of Integral, an employee activation agency. Formerly the global head of Employee and Innovation Communications for Bloomberg LP and Global Director of Social Strategy for IBM, Ethan has more than 20 years of experience leading digital communications and engagement initiatives at scale.

Kylie McQuain is the Director of Internal Communications at Airbnb, the world's leading community-driven hospitality company. Previously, she was the Director of Communications at Red Ventures for over 5 years. McQuain holds a bachelor's degree in journalism from the University of Florida.

Andrea Notarnicola is a partner of Newton, where he works as a cultural change management consultant for primary global businesses. He has been a lecturer at various universities and schools, including Università IULM. He recently (2019) authored the book *L'impresa spezzata* (*The Broken Enterprise*), focused on the recovery phase after an emergency.

Don Stanziano, MHA, APR is the chief marketing & communications officer for Geisinger, an integrated health system based in Danville, Pennsylvania, recognized as a national leader in health care innovation. Don is responsible for all marketing and communications across the Geisinger enterprise, including brand and growth marketing, internal and external communications and issues management, and digital customer and employee engagement across a robust marketing technology stack.

List of Figures

List of Tables

CHAPTER 1

Evolving Research and Practices in Internal Communication

Linjuan Rita Men

Internal communication, sometimes referred to as employee communication, internal relations, or internal public relations, has witnessed significant growth in recent decades as a discipline and profession. Globally, specialized industry associations and organizations have been established to foster research, education, and professional development in this arena, such as the Institute for Internal Communication established in 2010 in the United Kingdom, the Organizational Communication Research Center of the Institute for Public Relations created in 2012 in the United States, and the IC Kollectif, established in 2016 in Canada. In tandem, internal communication has been recognized as one of the fastest-growing specializations in public relations and communication management (Men & Bowen, 2017; Tkalac Verčič et al., 2012). Scholarship on internal communication has also soared in the past decade. According to a recent systematic review (Lee & Yue, 2020) analyzing 223 articles on internal

L. R. Men (✉)
University of Florida, Gainesville, FL, USA
e-mail: rlmen@jou.ufl.edu

L. R. Men and A. Tkalac Verčič (eds.), *Current Trends and Issues in Internal Communication*, New Perspectives in Organizational Communication, https://doi.org/10.1007/978-3-030-78213-9_1

communication published in nine communication journals from 1970 to 2019, over half of the studies appeared after 2011.

The evolvement of internal communication practice was partially prompted by the increasing recognition of employees not only as the production force but also as invaluable communication assets for organizations in today's increasingly connected, digitized, and transparent world. As organizational insiders, employees are perceived as trustworthy sources of information for external publics. What employees say publicly about the company often forms the basis for how external stakeholders view the organization. In the social media age, the role of employees as brand advocates, ambassadors, and authentic voices for the organization has become more salient than ever. As such, the line between "internal" and "external" is blurred (Mishra et al., 2014), and anything internal can easily become external. For instance, during the COVID-19 pandemic, Airbnb was lauded for its transparent, authentic, and empathetic approach to treating employees when the company announced its plan to lay off 25% of their workers. Forbes called it "a master class for empathy and compassion" (Kelly, 2020). Despite announcing a painful decision, the company's effective internal communication was not only well received by employees, but also projected an external image of a compassionate and authentic organization.

New realities in today's business environment necessitate the re-examination of how internal communication is defined and practiced, particularly from a public relations and strategic communication perspective. What do we mean by internal communication today? What key problems does internal communication address as a sub-discipline of public relations and strategic communication? Below, the definitions of internal communication are revisited, an overview of the recent developments in research and practice in this domain is provided, positioned through the lens of public relations, along with a discussion of emerging trends and issues that are shaping the practice. The chapter will end with the discussion of the vision and goals of the book and an overview of the book's structure and content.

What Is Internal Communication?

As an organizational function, internal communication has been broadly defined as "all formal and informal communication taking place internally at all levels of an organization" (Kalla, 2005, p. 304). Multidisciplinary by nature, internal communication can be positioned between public relations, human resources management and (internal) marketing. However, in practice, it is public relations and strategic communication practitioners that have the best understanding of internal stakeholders (Tkalac Verčič & Špoljarić, 2020).

Adopting a stakeholder approach, Welch and Jackson (2007) defined internal communication as "the strategic management of interactions and relationships between stakeholders within organizations" and specified interrelated dimensions that include "internal line manager communication, internal team peer communication, internal project peer communication and internal corporate communication" (p. 184). This definition can be recognized as one of the earliest definitions of internal communication from a public relations perspective. Further, this definition positions internal communication as an strategic management function beyond information exchange and acknowledges the essential role of managing "relationships" in the process, which concurs with the modern definition of public relations (c.f., Grunig et al., 2002). Likewise, grounded in public relation's excellence theory, Men and Bowen (2017) consider internal communication as a process co-created by the organization and internal stakeholders and define internal relations as "the strategic management of internal communication in managing interdependence and building mutually beneficial relationships between the organization and its employees" (p. 12). Following the relationship management paradigm and a systems theory perspective, this definition recognizes the interdependent state between the organization and its employees at various levels and aspires to a win–win situation where long-lasting quality organization–employee relationships can be cultivated. In this sense, internal communication may be understood as a means to an end and is driven by the perceived needs and wants of interacting organizations and internal stakeholders (Jiménez-Castillo, 2016; Welch, 2012). Internal stakeholders, predominantly employees, are active players in the internal communication process, who co-construct meaning with the organization and co-create the relationship as opposed to being merely passive message receivers.

In essence, internal communication is both a management function and public relations specialization. It is strategic in nature which aims to achieve specific internal communication goals that contribute to organizational effectiveness. Hence, internal communication can be more appropriately coined as "strategic internal communication," which is distinct from a similar but easily confused term, organizational communication. As a well-established field of study, organizational communication is concerned with studying all communication phenomenon inside the organization (e.g., persons and their characteristics or motivations, organizations, structure, teams, networks, discursive resources, discourse, interpretation, representation, construction of meaning, processes, etc.) (Kuhn et al., 2019) and focuses on how the organization functions, the context of organization, and communication processes (Deetz, 2001).

In practice, internal communication involves multiple dimensions: hierarchical communication (i.e., leadership communication across various levels), corporate internal communication (i.e., communication initiated by the communication department) and, horizontal/peer communication (i.e., employees as communicators, opinion leaders, or message receivers) (Men & Bowen, 2017; Whitworth, 2011). Internal communication requires a thorough understanding of how communication functions to be effective. This entails understanding the communication players, including communicators/message senders (e.g., the organization, the leader, or employees) and internal audiences/message receivers, the communication process (e.g., communication strategies, tactics, channels; how meanings are encoded/decoded, how messages are transmitted, and the feedback loop) and the context of internal communication (e.g., culture, climate, structure, leadership, etc.) (Keyton, 2011). Equally, if not more importantly, as a strategic public relations function, effective internal communication requires understanding of how organization and management work and can clearly see how internal communication fits in organizational strategy and contribute to the attainment of organizational goals and organizational effectiveness.

Evolving Roles and Functions of Internal Communication

What can internal communication do? Functions of internal communication pertain to various roles that internal communication serves in the organization. A significant amount of research has discussed the functions of internal communication and resulting outcomes. Consolidating these perspectives, the evolving roles, and functions of internal communication can be categorized as the following:

Inform. Traditionally perceived as a function of information exchange, a fundamental role of internal communication is to keep employees informed and updated regarding their job roles, the organization, market, environment, and each other (Berger, 2008; Jiménez-Castillo, 2016; Men & Bowen, 2017). This serves as the basis of operations coordination and a fully functioning organization. Also, employees are the backbone of the organizational production and innovation. They need to be *aligned* with the organization's strategies, decisions, mission, vision, purpose, and long-term goals so that they can make meaningful contribution (Hume & Leonard, 2014). Keeping employees informed is the first step toward aligning employees with the organization's strategic intent and implementing goals and strategies.

Listen. Communication should not be a one-way street. As a strategic management function, internal communication involves listening to gather employee feedback, views, perspectives, and ideas. Symmetrical internal communication which highlights listening, feedback, reciprocity, and an employee-centered approach has been recognized as an important characteristic for excellent public relations (Grunig, 1992). Hume and Leonard (2014) emphasize the importance of incorporating the views of internal stakeholders in organizational strategy development. Active listening constitutes two-way communication, promotes dialogue where meanings can be co-created and mutual understanding can be achieved and also breeds innovation as employee voices and constructive feedback can serve as the source of innovative ideas and intrapreneurship (Park et al., 2014).

Connect. As indicated by the definition, building relationships is a fundamental function of internal communication. To that end, employees need to feel connected inside the organization—with the company, with the leader, and with one another. A deeper level of connection goes beyond an employer-employee exchange relationship. Rather, employee minds, hearts, and souls are bonded with the organization. Employees are committed, identified, and engaged. Such outcomes can only be achieved over time via effective and systematic internal communication incorporating various players at different levels in the organization.

Acculturate and Inspire. Internal communication helps employees make sense of the organization, including its mission, vision, values, beliefs, and purpose (Men & Bowen, 2017). By communicating, interpreting, and instilling the values and beliefs among employees, internal communication helps acculturate employees and create a shared identity inside the organization. Culture not only represents the personality and character of the organization, but also serves as the glue that binds employees. Culture is intertwined with internal communication (Grunig et al., 2002; Men & Jiang, 2016). While culture provides a context and climate for internal practice, culture is created, reinforced, preserved, and transformed via internal communication. Internal communication exerted at both organizational and leadership levels influences the way employees think and act, which is an important manifest of culture.

Motivate and Engage. An organization's internal communication, especially from the leadership communication perspective, plays an essential role in motivating employees. To motivate is to create a desire to stimulate employee efforts and performance which connects strategies to action and drives goal attainment (Timm & Peterson, 2000). Communicating an inspiring vision motivates employees (Men, 2014a; Mishra et al., 2014). Employees can also be motivated by organizations and leaders meeting intrinsic needs such as the need for autonomy, competence, and relatedness (Ryan & Deci, 2000). For instance, leadership communication of positive feedback, encouragement, appreciation, and recognition can meet employee needs for self-efficacy, which then motivates employees (Ryan & Deci, 2000). Internal communication that connects personal employee goals to a higher purpose of the organization can help employees see the meaning and impact of their work, enhancing their intrinsic motivation for the job (Mayfield & Mayfield, 2018).

Internal communication engages employees. This linkage has been empirically established in a number of studies (e.g., Mishra et al., 2014; Tkalac Verčič & Vokić, 2017). For instance, in discussing the expanded role of internal communication in driving employee engagement, Mishra et al. (2014) established that internal communication develops a bond of trust between organizations and employees, which leads to employee engagement. Likewise, Tkalac Verčič and Vokić (2017) linked multiple dimensions of internal communication satisfaction with employee feelings of vigor, absorption, and dedication in the organization, further reinforcing the role of internal communication in engagement.

Overall, the role and function of internal communication can be summarized as informational (to inform), relational (to listen, connect), motivational (to acculturate, inspire, motivate), and behavioral (to engage). Various by products can be generated in the process of internal communication such as employee trust, satisfaction, commitment, alignment, enhanced organizational reputation, and customer satisfaction (Mishra et al., 2014), which can eventually lead to financial indicators as well (Men & Bowen, 2017). Given the modern integration of communication functions and multiple touchpoints employees have with the organization online and offline, and inside and outside of the organization, an emerging role of internal communication is to create a wholistic employee experience based on cumulative interactions employees have with the organization in their journey (from on-boarding to offboarding). This requires an integrated view of internal communication practice and an emphasis on not only employee perceptions and attitudes, but more importantly on actions and behaviors. Organizations also need to think holistically about the entire employee experience in the organization rather than discrete events and recognize that employee relationships with the organization begin before they join the company and persist after they leave (Plaskoff, 2017). While human resources management is critical in crafting employee experience during the process of employment, internal communication needs to go hand in hand. As such, internal communication practitioners play the role of not only facilitators, trainers, relationship managers, motivators, but also experience designers in the organization.

State of Research in Internal Communication

Decades of internal communication research has yielded an abundance of scholarship. Research in this arena has grown exponentially, particularly after 2000 with a sharp increase in the past decade (Lee & Yue, 2020). Overall, research on internal communication can be broadly categorized as the following streams:

1. Defining internal communication and describing the practice
2. Demonstrating the value of internal communication
3. Exploring best practices/excellence in internal communication
4. Internal communication in various contexts (special topics) such as in change, crisis management, multi/cross-cultural communication context.

(1) **Defining and describing internal communication**. Pioneer public relations scholars (Grunig, 1992; Wright, 1995) highlighted internal communication as a public relations function and specialization over twenty years ago. However, research on internal communication from a public relations perspective has been lagging until the

start of the new millennium. Public relations and corporate communication scholars have since defined internal communication from the tactical channels perspective (Cornelissen, 2004), the integrated, multidisciplinary perspective (Kalla, 2005), stakeholder (Welch & Jackson, 2007), strategic management/alignment (Hume & Leonard, 2014), and relationship perspectives (Jiménez-Castillo, 2016; Men & Bowen, 2017). Efforts have also been made to position the field, describe the functions and practice, and explicate the differences between internal communication and its sister fields such as organizational communication, business communication, or management communication (Kalla, 2005; Men & Bowen, 2017; Tkalac Verčič et al., 2012; Welch & Jackson, 2007).

(2) **Demonstrating the value of internal communication**. An important body of work in the past ten years pertains to demonstrating the value of internal communication. Research has evidenced the positive impact of internal communication on a number of positive employee outcomes, such as employee-organizational relationships (e.g., Kim & Rhee, 2011; Lee & Kim, 2017; Men, 2014a), employee trust (e.g., Men, Yue, et al., 2020), organizational reputation (e.g., Dortok, 2006; Men, 2014b), employee engagement (Kang & Sung, 2017; Mishra et al., 2014; Tkalac Verčič & Vokić, 2017), organizational identification (e.g., Yue et al., 2020), employee advocacy (Men, 2014a; Thelen, 2019; Walden & Westerman, 2018), employee communication behavior (Kim & Rhee, 2011), employee voice behavior (Ruck et al., 2017), organizational citizenship behavior (Men & Yue, 2019), work-life enrichment (Jiang & Men, 2017), and employee life satisfaction (Coric et al., 2020). Beyond these outcomes at cognitive, attitudinal, and behavioral levels, internal communication has also been linked to financial indicators, such as employee retention (Kang & Sung, 2017), innovative performance (Jiménez-Castillo, 2016), and intrapreneurship (Park et al., 2014). Recognizing the multiple levels of impact of internal communication on organizational effectiveness, scholars have also devoted effort to providing guidance on measuring the effectiveness of internal communication, which incorporates output, outtake, and outcome measures and is tied to business objectives and organizational bottom lines (e.g., Meng & Berger, 2012; O'Neil et al., 2018; Ruck & Welch, 2012).

(3) **Exploring best practices/excellence in internal communication**. Another important stream of research focuses on the "know-how" of internal communication; that is, how can internal communication be managed/practiced to contribute to organizational effectiveness. Overall,

research has explored internal communication strategies, channels, and other organizational contextual factors that foster excellence in internal communication. For instance, symmetrical (e.g., Kang & Sung, 2017; Kim & Rhee, 2011; Men, 2014a; Men & Stacks, 2014) and transparent communication (e.g., Jiang & Men, 2017; Men, 2014b; Yue et al., 2020) have been consistently demonstrated as excellence characteristics for internal communication that contribute to numerous positive employee outcomes. Authentic, empathetic, responsive, and assertive communications, especially from the leadership perspective (Jiang & Men, 2017; Mayfield & Mayfield, 2018; Men, 2015) have been shown to affect positive employee outcomes such as motivation, engagement, and relational outcomes. A bulk of works have also examined the optimization of communication channels in achieving communication effectiveness. Face-to-face communication (Mishra et al., 2014) and internal social media (e.g., Ewing et al., 2019; Madsen, 2016) have especially achieved enormous scholarly attention and demonstrated the efficacy in engaging employees and fostering positive employee relationships. Scholars have also explored sundry organizational contextual factors that contribute to internal communication effectiveness. Among these factors, organizational culture, and leadership have been most prominently discussed. For instance, participative, innovative, and supportive organizational cultures and positive emotional cultures of joy, companionate love, pride, and gratitude have been tied to excellent internal communication (Grunig et al., 2002; Jiang & Men, 2017; Yue et al., 2020). Leadership factors, including CEO leadership communication style, strategies, channels, and credibility (Men, 2015; Men, Yue, et al., 2020), and supervisory leadership styles, including transformational, authentic, ethical, and servant leadership behaviors have been demonstrated as important organizational antecedents that affect the organization's internal communication practice and effectiveness (e.g., Jiang & Men, 2017; Men, 2014a, 2014b; Men & Stacks, 2014; Thelen, 2020).

(4) **Internal communication in various contexts**. A growing amount of research has examined internal communication issues in various contexts, such as issue or crisis management, change management, multi/cross-cultural communication, corporate social responsibility (CSR) communication, and so forth. For instance, public relations scholars have explored the role of internal communication in different stages of crisis management (Frandsen & Johansen, 2011) and how effective internal crisis communication strategies contribute to positive

employee relational and behavioral outcomes (Kim, 2018; Mazzei & Ravazzani, 2015). Change communication, despite being long discussed in the management literature, has recently caught the attention of public relations scholars. Research has revealed the functions of internal communication/public relations during change (Elving, 2005; Luo & Jiang, 2014) and the impact of internal communication climates, public relations strategies, channels (Men, O'Neil, et al., 2020; Neill et al., 2019), and employee-organization relationships (Men, Yue, et al., 2020) on employee change reactions. In comparison, research on internal communication in the global/cross-cultural or multi-cultural context has been limited. Most studies that incorporated a global or international perspective examined some aspects of internal communication in a different country or cultural context (e.g., Chong, 2007; Mazzei & Ravazzani, 2015). An important work that filled the gap of global and cross-cultural internal communication, by Tkalac Verčič (2019), provided concrete suggestions for multi-cultural organizations to effectively communicate with their global employee base. However, the lack of empirical research on internal communication in the cross-cultural and multi-cultural contexts still warrants opportunity for future research.

The current internal communication scholarship seems to be dominated by the management paradigm. To advance research in this arena, scholars could incorporate other theoretical approaches such as the critical or rhetoric perspective (Lemon & Palenchar, 2018; Pompper, 2012) to better understand the internal discourse and dialogue, address employee needs and experiences, and explore other important but under-researched issues such as gender, diversity, activism, and power in internal communication. Despite being a multidisciplinary area of study where theories from mass communication, human resources, management, and social psychology hold explanatory power, internal communication as a core public relations function and sub-discipline warrants the establishment of a clearer scholarly identity to advance theory development.

Current Trends and Issues in Internal Communication

Multiple trends have reshaped the internal communication landscape and practice today. First and foremost, with social, economic, and technological transformations happening at an unprecedented pace, companies and their leaders are challenged to harness disruption in a rapidly changing environment. Workplace dynamics and culture today have shifted with the dominance of millennials and the entry of Gen Z into the workplace (Men & Bowen, 2017). Today employees demand high levels of transparency and authenticity from their organization and leaders. We have seen more and more employees speak or walk out for or against their employers on controversial social issues or push their companies and leaders to take a political stance (Wingard, 2020). Employee activism is on the rise and changing the workplace. With declining trust in public institutions globally (as shown in Edelman's Trust Barometer study), companies are under pressure to be an important force driving positive social change. Communicating purpose and social conscience and aligning values and mission with business goals has become an important challenge for organizations.

Technological advancements have blurred the line between internal and external. Web 2.0, social media, and emerging technologies such as artificial intelligence, virtual reality and augmented reality, big data, blockchain, etc., have brought new opportunities and challenges for internal communication and employee engagement. Additionally, the workforce has become more diverse and globalized. Many leaders face increasing challenges in leading global teams comprised of workers from different cultural backgrounds or face scrutiny or even backlash when implementing the same internal messages to culturally diverse internal audiences.

While some of the above-mentioned issues are emergent, others are long-standing. Regardless, the evolving environment, new trends, issues, and audiences are calling for updated internal communication theories, models, research, and practices. Internal communication research has long lagged behind practice until the recent decade (Lee & Yue, 2020; Tkalac Verčič et al., 2012). While scholarship on internal communication especially from a public relations perspective has grown significantly, review work that integrates the accumulated knowledge and research has been lacking. Men and Bowen's (2017) book lays a fine foundation for theorizing internal public relations. The scope and width of book, however, could be extended to cover the emerging internal communication issues that come with current trends. An abundance of recent research in this arena published in the past five years may also be integrated. In that effort, this book assembles a group of top-notch scholars and thought leaders in internal communication from across the globe to provide a comprehensive review of the evolving internal communication research and practice addressing current trends and emerging issues. Specifically, this edited volume will tackle the following sets of questions:

- What are organizational leaders' internal communication roles? What is the relationship between leadership and communication? What communication channels can leaders utilize to communicate, connect, and engage with stakeholders? How should CEOs lead and communicate in turbulent times such as during a change or crisis (e.g., COVID-19)? *[Chapter* 2: *Leaders as Communication Agents].*
- How can organizations effectively segment internal publics? What are the implications for internal issue management? How can the situational theory of problem-solving inform this process? *[Chapter* 3: *Internal Public Segmentation for Effective Internal Issue Management].*
- How can emerging technologies (e.g., internal social media, AI) be integrated into internal communication efforts? What are some potential benefits, challenges, and nuances in adopting internal social media? How can organizational leaders adapt their management philosophy and managerial practices to the new communicative environment enabled by new technologies? *[Chapter* 4: *Internal Social Media, Emerging Technologies, and Internal Communication].*
- What is employee advocacy? Why is employee advocacy important for organizations from a public relations perspective? How does internal communication drive employee advocacy? *[Chapter* 5: *Employee Advocates: Unlocking Their Power Through Internal Communication].*
- How do organizations promote dialogue in the workplace through "informed employee voice?" What is the relationship between listening, voice, and dialogue? How are these concepts related to internal communication? *[Chapter* 6: *Employee Voice and Internal Listening: Towards Dialogue in the Workplace].*
- What is employee activism? What are the roles of internal communication in the rise of employee activism? How should organizations resolve conflicts and manage relationships with employee activists? *[Chapter* 7: *Employee Activism and Internal Communication].*
- How does internal communication contribute to a purposeful organization? How can organizations involve employees in corporate social responsibility (CSR) communication efforts, and why does it

matter? How to develop purpose-aligned internal CSR communication? *[Chapter* 8: *Beyond Internal Corporate Social Responsibility Communication (ICSRC): Creating a Purposeful Organization].*

- How can strategic communicators and organizational leaders hinder and promote various aspects of employee wellbeing? How could internal communication affect employee wellbeing? *[Chapter* 9: *Enhancing Employee Well-being Through Internal Communication].*
- How does internal communication contribute to organizational crisis prevention and management? What is the role of internal communication in the three dynamic stages of a crisis: pre-crisis, the acute phase, and post-crisis organizational recovery and renewal? How are existing crisis communication theories applied to the internal context? *[Chapter* 10: *Internal Crisis Communication].*
- How does internal communication serve to manage organizational change and disruption? When, how, and what should be communicated to employees regarding organizational change? What are the underlying mechanisms of effective change communication? *[Chapter* 11: *Strategic Change Communication].*
- How can organizations measure internal communication effectiveness? What should be measured and evaluated in internal communication? What are the new ways of measuring and evaluating internal communication? *[Chapter* 12: *Measurement and Evaluation Internal Communication].*
- How does culture shape global internal communication? What effect does technology have on global internal communication? What are the necessary competencies for intercultural or multi-cultural communication? What are the most important trends which will be affecting the future of internal communication in a cross-cultural and global context? *[Chapter* 13: *Internal Communication in a Cross-Cultural and Global Context].*

This book is grounded in solid scientific research and informed by evolving theories and practice in internal communication. Each chapter includes a practitioner's perspective at the end contributed by an industry leader in internal communication, being a professional interview or a mini-case study. Given its depth, currency, and integration of theory and best practices, the book will provide a comprehensive source for internal communication researchers and practitioners.

References

Berger, B. (2008). *Employee/organizational communications*. Institute for Public Relations. Retrieved from http://www.instituteforpr.org/topics/employee-organizationalcommunications/.

Chong, M. (2007). The role of internal communication and training in infusing corporate values and delivering brand promise: Singapore Airlines' experience. *Corporate Reputation Review, 10*, 201–212.

Coric, D. S., Vokic, N. P., & Tkalac Verčič, A. (2020). Does good internal communication enhance life satisfaction? *Journal of Communication Management, 24*(4), 363–376. https://doi.org/10.1108/JCOM-11-2019-0146.

Cornelissen, J. (2004). *Corporate communications theory and practice*. Sage.

Deetz, S. A. (2001). Conceptual foundations. In F. M. Jablin & L. L. Putnam (Eds.), *The new handbook of organizational communication: Advances in theory, research, and methods* (pp. 3–46). Sage.

Dortok, A. (2006). A managerial look at the interaction between internal communication and corporate reputation. *Corporate Reputation Review, 8*, 322–338.

Elving, W. (2005). The role of communication in organisational change. *Corporate Communications: An International Journal, 10*, 129–138.

Ewing, M., Men, L. R., & O'Neil, J. (2019). Using social media to engage employees: Insights from internal communication managers. *International Journal of Strategic Communication, 13*, 110–132. https://doi.org/10.1080/1553118X.2019.1575830.

Frandsen, F., & Johansen, W. (2011). The study of internal crisis communication: Towards an integrative framework. *Corporate Communications: An International Journal, 16*, 347–361.

Grunig, J. E. (1992). Symmetrical systems of internal communication. In J. E. Grunig (Ed.), *Excellence in public relations and communication management* (pp. 531–576). Erlbaum.

Grunig, L. A., Grunig, J. E., & Dozier, D. M. (2002). *Excellent public relations and effective organizations*. Lawrence Erlbaum.

Hume, J., & Leonard, A. (2014). Exploring the strategic potential of internal communication in international non-governmental organisations. *Public Relations Review, 40*, 294–304. https://doi.org/10.1016/j.pubrev.2013.10.011.

Jiang, H., & Men, L. R. (2017). Creating an engaged workforce: The impact of authentic leadership, transparent communication, and work-life enrichment. *Communication Research, 44*(2), 225–243. https://doi.org/10.1177/0093650215613137.

Jiménez-Castillo, D. (2016). Beyond mere information transfer: The importance of a relational approach to market-related internal communication. *Journal of Public Relations Research, 28*(5–6), 268–281. https://doi.org/10.1080/1062726X.2016.1258564.

Kalla, H. K. (2005). Integrated internal communications: A multidisciplinary perspective. *Corporate Communications: An International Journal, 10*, 302–314. https://doi.org/10.1108/13563280510630106.

Kang, M., & Sung, M. (2017). How symmetrical employee communication leads to employee engagement and positive employee communication behaviors: The mediation of employee-organization relationships. *Journal of Communication Management, 21*, 82–102.

Kelly, J. (2020, May 6). Airbnb lays off 25% of its employees: CEO Brian Chesky gives a master class in empathy and compassion. *Forbes*. Retrieved from https://www.forbes.com/sites/jackkelly/2020/05/06/airbnb-lays-off-25-of-its-employees-ceo-brian-chesky-gives-a-master-class-in-empathy-and-compassion/#5ddf0357ee30.

Keyton, J. (2011). *Communication and organizational culture: A key to understanding work experience*. Sage.

Kim, J.-N., & Rhee, Y. (2011). Strategic thinking about employee communication behaviour (ECB) in public relations: Testing the models of megaphoning and scouting effects in Korea. *Journal of Public Relations Research, 23*, 243–268.

Kim, Y. (2018). Communication behaviors for sensemaking and sensegiving in crisis situations: Strategic management approach for effective internal crisis communication. *Journal of Communication Management, 22*, 451–475.

Kuhn, T., Ashcraft, K. A., & Cooren, F. (2019). Introductory essay: What work can organizational communication do?. *Management Communication Quarterly, 33*(1), 101–111.

Lee, Y., & Kim, J. N. (2017). Authentic enterprise, organization-employee relationship, and employee-generated managerial assets. *Journal of Communication Management, 21*, 236–253. https://doi.org/10.1108/JCOM-02-2017-0011.

Lee, Y., & Yue, C. A. (2020). Status of internal communication research in public relations: An analysis of published articles in nine scholarly journals from 1970 to 2019. *Public Relations Review, 46*(3), 101906. https://doi.org/10.1016/j.pubrev.2020.101906.

Lemon, L. L., & Palenchar, M. J. (2018). Public relations and zones of engagement: Employees' lived experiences and the fundamental nature of employee engagement. *Public Relations Review, 44*, 142–155.

Luo, Y., & Jiang, H. (2014). Effective public relations leadership in organizational change: A study of multinationals in Mainland China. *Journal of Public Relations Research, 26*, 134–160. https://doi.org/10.1080/1062726X.2013.864241.

Madsen, V. T. (2016). Constructing organizational identity on internal social media: A case study of coworker communication in Jyske Bank. *International Journal of Business Communication, 53*, 200–223.

Mayfield, J., & Mayfield, M. (2018). *Motivating language theory: Effective leader talk in the workplace*. Palgrave Macmillan. https://doi.org/10.1007/978-3-319-66930-4.

Mazzei, A., & Ravazzani, S. (2015). Internal crisis communication strategies to protect trust relationships: A study of Italian companies. *International Journal of Business Communication, 52*, 319–337.

Men, L. R. (2014a). Why leadership matters to internal communication: Linking transformational leadership, symmetrical communication, and employee outcomes. *Journal of Public Relations Research, 26*(3), 256–279.

Men, L. R. (2014b). Internal reputation management: Effects of authentic leadership and transparent communication. *Corporate Reputation Review, 17*, 254–272.

Men, L. R. (2015). The internal communication role of the Chief Executive Officer: Communication channels, style, and effectiveness. *Public Relations Review, 41*(4), 461–471.

Men, L. R., & Bowen, S. (2017). *Excellence in internal communication management*. Business Expert Press.

Men, L. R., & Jiang, H. (2016). Toward an integrated model of internal relationship management: Understanding the interplay between authentic leadership, organizational culture, and symmetrical communication. *International Journal of Strategic Communication, 10*(5), 462–479. https://doi.org/10.1080/1553118X.2016.1226172.

Men, L. R., Neill, M. S., & Yue, C. A. (2020). Examining the effects of symmetrical internal communication and employee engagement on organizational change outcomes. *Public Relations Journal, 13*(4), 1–19.

Men, L. R., O'Neil, J., & Ewing, M. (2020). Examining the effects of internal social media on employee engagement. *Public Relations Review, 46*(2), 101880. https://doi.org/10.1016/j.pubrev.2020.101880.

Men, L. R., & Stacks, D. W. (2014). The effects of authentic leadership on strategic internal communication and employee-organization relationships. *Journal of Public Relations Research, 26*, 301–324.

Men, L. R., & Yue, A. C. (2019). Creating a positive emotional culture: Effects of strategic internal communication and its impact on employee supportive behaviors. *Public Relations Review, 45*(3), 101764. https://doi.org/10.1016/j.pubrev.2019.03.001.

Men, L. R., Yue, C. A., & Liu, Y. (2020). "Vision, passion, and care": The impact of charismatic executive leadership communication on employee trust and support for organizational change. *Public Relations Review, 46*(3), 101927. https://doi.org/10.1016/j.pubrev.2020.101927.

Meng, J., & Berger, B. (2012). Measuring return on investment (ROI) of organizations' internal communication efforts. *Journal of Communication Management, 16*, 332–354.

Mishra, K., Boyton, L., & Mishra, A. (2014). Driving employee engagement: The expanded role of internal communications. *International Journal of Business Communication, 51*, 183–202.

Neill, M., Men, L. R., & Yue, C. A. (2019). Examining the impact of communication climate on organizational change outcomes: The mediating role of organizational identification. *Corporate Communication: An International Journal, 45*(3), 101779. https://doi.org/10.1108/CCIJ-06-2019-0063.

O'Neil, J., Ewing, M., Smith, S., & Williams, S. (2018). A delphi study to identify standards for internal communication. *Public Relations Journal, 11*(3), 1–16. https://prjournal.instituteforpr.org/wp-content/uploads/1.-A-Delphi-Study-to-Identify-Standards-for-IC-1-1.pdf.

Park, S. H., Kim, J.-N., & Krishna, A. (2014). Bottom-up building of an innovative organization: Motivating employee intrapreneurship and scouting and their strategic value. *Management Communication Quarterly, 28*, 531–560.

Plaskoff, J. (2017). Employee experience: The new human resource management approach. *Strategic HR Review, 16*, 136–141.

Pompper, D. (2012). On social capital and diversity in a feminized industry: Further developing a theory of internal public relations. *Journal of Public Relations Research, 24*, 86–103. https://doi.org/10.1080/1062726X.2012.626137.

Ruck, K., & Welch, M. (2012). Valuing internal communication; management and employee perspectives. *Public Relations Review, 38*, 294–302.

Ruch, K., Welch, M., & Menara, B. (2017). Employee voice: An antecedent to organisational engagement? *Public Relations Review, 43*, 904–914.

Ryan, R. M., & Deci, E. L. (2000). Self-determination theory and the facilitation of intrinsic motivation, social development, and wellbeing. *American Psychologist, 55*, 68–78.

Timm, P., & Peterson, B. (2000). *People at work: Human behavior in organizations* (5th ed.). South-Western College Publishing.

Thelen, P. D. (2019). Supervisor humor styles and employee advocacy: A serial mediation model. *Public Relations Review, 45*(2), 307–318. https://doi.org/10.1016/j.pubrev.2019.02.007.

Thelen, P. D. (2020). *Nurturing employee advocacy: The determining role of internal communication*. Unpublished dissertation. Gainesville, FL.

Tkalac Verčič, A. (2019). Internal communication with a global perspective. In K. Shriramesh & D. Verčič (Eds.), *The global public relations handbook theory, research, and practice*. Routledge.

Tkalac Verčič, A., & Špoljarić, A. (2020). Managing internal communication: How the choice of channels affects internal communication satisfaction. *Public Relations Review, 46*(3), 101926. https://doi.org/10.1016/j.pubrev.2020.101926.

Tkalac Verčič, A., Verčič, D., & Sriramesh, K. (2012). Internal communication: Definition, parameters, and the future. *Public Relations Review, 38*, 223–230. https://doi.org/10.1016/j.pubrev.2011.12.019.

Tkalac Verčič, A., & Vokić, N. P. (2017). Engaging employees through internal communication. *Public Relations Review, 43*, 885–893.

Walden, J., & Westerman, C. Y. K. (2018). Strengthening the tie: Creating exchange relationships that encourage employee advocacy as an organizational citizenship behavior. *Management Communication Quarterly, 32*, 593–611.

Welch, M. (2012). Appropriateness and acceptability: Employee perspectives of internal communication. *Public Relations Review, 38*, 246–254. https://doi.org/10.1016/j.pubrev.2011.12.017.

Welch, M., & Jackson, P. R. (2007). Rethinking internal communication: A stakeholder approach. *Corporate Communications: An International Journal, 12*, 177–198. https://doi.org/10.1108/13563280710744847.

Whitworth, B. (2011). Internal communication. In T. Gillis (Ed.), *The IABC handbook of organizational communication* (2nd ed., pp. 195–206). Jossey-Bass.

Wingard, J. (2020, January 10). Employee activism is the new normal: So why is Amazon leadership freaking out? *Forbes*. Retrieved from https://www.forbes.com/sites/jasonwingard/2020/01/10/employee-activism-is-the-new-normal-so-why-is-amazon-leadership-freaking-out/#3110658827f1.

Wright, D. K. (1995). The role of corporate public relations executives in the future of employee communications. *Public Relations Review, 21*, 181–198.

Yue, A., Men, L. R., & Ferguson, M. (2020). Examining the effects of internal communication and emotional culture on employees' organizational identification. *International Journal of Business Communication, 58*(2), 169–195. https://doi.org/10.1177/2329488420914066.

CHAPTER 2

Leaders as Communication Agents

Cen April Yue, Linjuan Rita Men, and Bruce K. Berger

Leadership and Communication

In the past century, our understanding of leadership has evolved from the leader trait perspective and behavioral approaches to defining leadership in terms of influence, interactions, and relationships (Lord et al., 2017). For instance, Van Vugt et al. (2008) defined leadership in terms of "influencing individuals to contribute to group goals" and "coordinating the pursuit of those goals" (pp. 182–183). Similarly, Yukl (2010) believed leadership is "the process of influencing others to understand and agree

C. A. Yue (✉)
University of Connecticut, Stamford, CT, USA

L. R. Men
University of Florida, Gainesville, FL, USA
e-mail: rlmen@jou.ufl.edu

B. K. Berger
University of Alabama, Tuscaloosa, AL, USA
e-mail: berger@apr.ua.edu

L. R. Men and A. Tkalac Verčič (eds.), *Current Trends and Issues in Internal Communication*, New Perspectives in Organizational Communication, https://doi.org/10.1007/978-3-030-78213-9_2

about what needs to be done and how to do it, and the process of facilitating individual and collective efforts to accomplish shared objectives" (p. 8).

Leaders exert influence on the effectiveness of an organization or group through various activities. Some activities are more abstract and strategic, such as choosing the right goals and objectives, designing structures and programs, and cultivating shared values and culture. Some are more direct and concrete, including mentoring and motivating followers, imparting knowledge and skills, and coordinating work activities (Yukl, 2010).

Leadership and communication are inextricably linked. Many researchers suggest a communicative lens to studying leadership; they view leadership as a language game and a special form of human communication. For instance, Johnson and Hackman (2018) offered a communication-based definition of leadership as "human (symbolic) communication that modifies the attitudes and behaviors of others in order to meet shared group goals and needs" (2018, p. 12). Similarly, De Vries et al. (2010, p. 368) defined a leader's communication style as "a distinctive set of interpersonal communicative behaviors geared toward the optimization of hierarchical relationships in order to reach certain group or individual goals." The communicative constitution of organization perspective, spearheaded by organizational communication scholars, regards communication as the central, fundamental element that constitutes and constructs leadership (Fairhurst & Connaughton, 2014).

Common in these conceptualizations is the belief effective leadership requires skillful use of communications, storytelling, active listening, emotional intelligence, and strategic self-reflection. Excellent communication pertains to how leaders influence others, build trust, strengthen relationships, enrich workplace culture, and forge employee alignment and engagement to achieve a shared vision. Importantly, understanding leadership from a communication standpoint does not negate the importance of other widely acknowledged components of leadership such as abstract reasoning, strategic and tactical knowledge, and management skills. Rather, communication is a valuable resource that complements leadership repertoire.

Despite its importance and relevance, research into the communication aspects of leadership has been sparse (De Vries et al., 2010). As Mayfield and Mayfield (2017, p. 6) pinpointed, communication is "the elephant in the room of leadership" as most research collapses assessment of leader communication into broader leadership styles, such as charismatic-transformational leadership (van Knippenberg & Stam, 2014). However, there are several benefits of distinguishing leadership communication from leadership styles (e.g., transformational, ethical, authentic leaderships).

To start, measures of leadership styles are typically too parsimonious to account for the specific communication acts that occur between leaders and followers. By constructing leadership in a higher-level, gestalt manner, researchers overlooked the conceptual richness of communication behaviors and their predictive power on outcomes (De Vries et al., 2010). From a practical standpoint, a dive into precise communication strategies provides clear guidance for leaders and communication managers regarding which communication behaviors likely elicit positive outcomes, so crucial to developing actionable, concrete behavioral interventions (Van Quaquebeke & Felps, 2018). In what follows, we break down leadership communication into executive and supervisory levels and discuss their respective functions.

Leaders as Communicators

Executive Leadership Communication

Executive leaders are senior managers of an organization, including CEOs, heads of business units, and top management team members. Internally, executive leaders, in particular CEOs and founders, define an organization's DNA and shape culture, character, and value of the organization. They are also the representatives, spokespersons, and faces of their organizations to external constituencies (Men & Bowen, 2017; Park & Berger, 2004).

A key internal function of executive communication is to express the organizational vision to followers and align followers' personal goals with the vision. Vision communication is "the act of motivating followers by communicating images of the future of the collective" (Stam et al., 2014, p. 1172). Leaders do so by creating stories, legends, and anecdotes of their organizations and consistently publicizing and interpreting them to followers (Men & Bowen, 2017). Strategic vision communication attracts followers and improves leadership evaluations, follower attitudes, and performance (Stam et al., 2014). Senior leaders' vision communication has proven effective in inducing followers' support especially during organizational change (e.g., Men, Yue, et al., 2020).

The role of senior leaders expanded rapidly in recent years. Public relations professionals used the term "chief engagement officer" to highlight CEOs' communication and engagement responsibility (Edelman, 2014). Research has explored how senior leaders can leverage personalized and interactive communication to build relationships with internal and external stakeholders. For instance, CEOs with a professional online disclosure strategy (i.e., posting about corporate issues) are likely to increase positive perceptions of the organization from online audiences (Yue, Chung, et al., 2020). Internally, when communicating with compassion, sincerity, and warmth, CEOs can cultivate good employee-organization relationships and build internal reputation (Men, 2015). Senior leaders also can influence internal communication by installing systems and programs, and fostering a positive, participative culture to facilitate two-way, transparent communication.

Supervisory Leadership Communication

Supervisors are described as "the linchpin of employees" and "the surest, most direct path" to followers' support and loyalty (Therkelsen & Fiebich, 2003, p. 120). Supervisor communication is one of the most salient elements of communication for organizational members because it serves multiple functions in daily interactions with subordinates. As information providers, supervisors keep members informed about jobs and the workplace (e.g., job instructions, policies, and rules). Many employees rated information provided by supervisors as more accurate, timely, and useful than by senior management during organizational change (Allen et al., 2007). Employees depend on immediate supervisors for instrumental support, including clarifying tasks and improving their skills and efficacy. They also go to supervisors to negotiate matters related to workplace flexibility (e.g., work schedule, location, job duties, task autonomy). Therefore, supervisors should solicit questions and suggestions, offer timely feedback on subordinates' performance, and communicate openly and sensitively (Myers, 2015).

Supervisors' communication styles and effectiveness have received increasing scholarly attention in recent decades (Myers, 2015). Research has examined the positive impact of supervisor communication on employee and organizational outcomes from various angles, including communication styles, content, quality, and quantity (Jian & Dalisay, 2017). For example, Bakar and Connaughton (2010) found that supervisory communication, characterized by upward openness, positive relationship messages, and job-relevant information, engendered followers' organizational commitment (OC). Conversation quality, defined by "efficiency, coordination, and accuracy in meaning interpretation and information transfer in the process of task accomplishment," also fostered followers' OC (Jian & Dalisay, 2017). Additionally, supervisors' use of motivating language cultivated a positive organizational emotional culture and facilitated employees' organizational identification (Yue, Men, et al., 2020). Other positive outcomes, such as supervisor-subordinate relationship quality, workgroup relationship, job satisfaction, trust, loyalty, engagement, and advocacy behaviors were positively related to effective supervisory leadership communication (Men & Yue, 2019; Myers, 2015).

Leadership Communication: An Overview of Theoretical Frameworks

In this chapter, we focus on leaders' communication styles rather than leadership styles, though we acknowledge the influence of leadership styles on organizational communication climate. Scholars have empirically supported that transformational (e.g., Men, 2014a) and authentic leadership (e.g., Jiang & Men, 2017) helped foster a symmetrical internal communication system and transparent communication climate, featured by trust, openness, feedback, negotiation, accountability, and employee empowerment. Leaders with these styles are likely more committed to creating systems and programs to facilitate an open, inclusive communication culture. The culture may also form via a cascading mechanism, i.e., senior leaders' attributes and working styles—including their communication styles—get transmitted down the organizational hierarchy. We offer three theoretical approaches to studying leadership communication.

Socio-Communicative Style

Socio-communicative style (SCS) refers to the skills individuals use to initiate, adapt, and respond to interpersonal communication (Thomas et al., 1994). The two primary dimensions of SCS are assertiveness and responsiveness. *Assertive* communicators are dominant, independent, forceful, competitive, and willing to take a stand. *Responsive* communicators are warm, friendly, tender, compassionate, and sensitive to others' needs. Responsive communicators also place greater emphasis on maintaining "liking" in a relationship, while assertive communicators focus on the task dimension of a relationship (Richmond, 2002). However, assertiveness should not be confused with aggressiveness. Unlike aggressive communicators who make demands, assertive communicators make requests without hurting others' chances to succeed (Richmond, 2002).

Scholars have recently integrated SCS in examining leadership communication. Men (2015) found CEOs with responsive communication style (vs. assertive style) were perceived to be more effective communicators, though both communication styles fostered quality employee-organizational relationships. Similarly, CEOs who applied personal messages and a down-to-earth tone (i.e., responsive communication) on social media were more likely to cultivate meaningful interactions and relationships with the online publics (Tsai & Men, 2017). Most recently, researchers found positive connections between responsive communication employed by supervisors, the cultivation of a positive emotional culture, and employees' extra-role behaviors (Men & Yue, 2019).

Motivating Language Theory

Motivating language theory (MLT) is a linguistic framework primarily applied in leadership communication context. This theory, known as "a systematic, research-tested model that covers all forms of leader-to-follower speech," places communication in the center of leadership behavior (Mayfield & Mayfield, 2018, p. 2). According to MLT, strategic leader speech is comprised of three categories—direction-giving, meaning-making, and empathetic language—and is most effective when all three are used. *Direction-giving* language contains articulating task parameters, role expectations, reward contingencies, performance feedback, and emphasizes transparency and uncertainty reduction. *Meaning-making* language concerns successfully translating and transmitting organizational mission, value, and purpose to followers. By telling organizational stories and using metaphors, leaders align followers' individual pursuits with higher organizational purpose and help followers understand how their work contributes to the big picture. *Empathetic* language refers to leaders using empathy, compassion, and care to connect with followers emotionally. Empathetic language is not limited to work-related tasks, but can also be applied in personal life events. For instance, leaders can show their authentic, human side by congratulating followers on achieving personal milestones or expressing genuine, heartfelt concerns for their setbacks.

Motivating language has been consistently linked to positive employee outcomes such as job satisfaction, organizational identification, work engagement, job performance, and creativity and innovation (Mayfield & Mayfield, 2018). Leader motivating language also is instrumental in creating a positive communication culture (Mayfield & Mayfield, 2017) and a positive organizational emotional culture replete with joy, pride, gratitude, and companionate love (Yue, Men, et al., 2020).

Leadership Listening

Leaders who have their followers' best interests at heart are active listeners. As Lacey eloquently noted, "without a listener, speech is nothing but noise in the ether" (2013, p. 166). Management scholars have studied listening in the context of interpersonal, dyadic interactions between leaders and followers. Rogers (1959) referred to active listening as an accepting and non-judgmental way of perceiving and attending to an individual. Lloyd et al. (2017) defined listening quality as "the individual's perception of being attended to, accepted, and appreciated" (p. 433). Van Quaquebeke and Felps (2018) incorporated verbal and non-verbal signals in describing attentive listening in interpersonal communication. Specifically, leaders demonstrate attentive listening by adopting "adequate eye contact, appropriate facial expressions…, head movements that convey understanding…, occasional verbal reassurances that encourage the speaker to continue…, and showing that the content resonates…" (p. 5). In contrast, poor listening entails leaders gazing off, interrupting responses, or checking phones. Research examining supervisor listening behavior has identified a positive link between supervisor listening and perceived leader-follower relationship quality, follower job satisfaction, and organizational citizenship behaviors. It also decreased follower turnover intention and emotional exhaustion (Lloyd et al., 2017).

Macnamara (2016) lamented that "listening is mostly referred to in passing with no examination of what listening entails at an organization-public level" (p. 152). Often, listening is present, yet implicit, in the conceptualization of various organization-public communication strategies. For instance, researchers define a two-way communication model in public relations as entailing active organizational *listening*, mutual understanding, and a balance of power through negotiation between organizations and publics. However, listening has been too little explored in public relations and internal communication research.

Public relations scholarship has traditionally explored listening as an organizational rather than leadership behavior. For instance, the two-way symmetrical communication model highlights the importance of organizational listening in building mutual understanding and quality relationships with strategic publics (Grunig et al., 2002). Dialogue also requires organizations to demonstrate the capacity to "*listen* without anticipating, interfering, competing, refuting, or warping meanings into preconceived interpretations" (Kent & Taylor, 2002, p. 27). However, organizational listening cannot be achieved without the support of leadership. Leaders can enhance organizational listening by serving as a good role model and actively managing listening. To elaborate, leaders who demonstrate exceptional listening skills are likely to cultivate a listening culture in their organizations. Understanding the importance of listening, leaders can create tools, systems, and policies to enable and encourage large-scale listening on the organizational level. We invite future research to explore the mechanisms through which leadership listening may impact organizational listening.

Leadership Communication Channels and Effectiveness

Organizational leaders today have numerous communication channels within the organization and externally, including traditional face-to-face interactions, print, electronic media, and digital channels. Leaders' choices of communication channels depend on multiple factors—the organization's size, culture, communication content, purpose, cost, reach, channel richness, and employees' preferences (Men & Bowen, 2017; Tkalac Verčič & Špoljarić, 2020).

Traditional Communication Channels

Traditional communication channels include face-to-face interactions (e.g., town halls, small group meetings, one-on-one meetings, management by walking around, and after-work informal meetings), print publications (e.g., newsletters, memos), phone calls, and voice mails. According to media richness theory, which centers on matching the richness of a medium to the equivocality of a task, print publications are lean media best used for one-way, routine messages in the workplace. Phone calls and e-mails fall in the middle of the media richness continuum (Lengel & Daft, 1988).

Face-to-face communication is the richest medium for conveying complex, nonroutine messages and facilitating immediate feedback. Face-to-face communications from supervisors are immensely valued. In comparison with social media, employees were more satisfied with one-on-one or team meetings with supervisors (Tkalac Verčič & Špoljarić, 2020). Similarly, Men (2014b) found supervisors most often used face-to-face communications with followers, which engendered followers' satisfaction with organizations and perceived symmetrical internal communication. In addition, there is a high demand among employees for some degree of face time with senior leaders (Roy, 2018). Thus, senior leaders should consider creating more opportunities for interpersonal interactions, such as "lunch and learn" programs, daily executive rounding, and an open-door policy. For instance, Credit Karma founder and CEO Kenneth Lin invites anyone to come by his office and share their thoughts about the company, whenever he is in office and available. These interpersonal interactions put a human face on a leader's title and help build trust, understanding, and a sense of a shared goal. However, depending on company size and location, employees' face-to-face time with senior management, particularly with the CEO, may be limited. In this case, digital and electronic forms of communication should come into play.

New Digital Channels

New digital channels, such as intranets, instant messengers, social networking sites, and videoconferencing systems, are at the forefront of leadership communication with diverse stakeholders. The two-way, interactive feature of digital media amplifies stakeholder voices and provides leaders convenient venues for listening and responding. Rich features (e.g., online chat functions, embedded audio or video, webcams, liking, commenting, and sharing features) of digital channels mimic the communal and relational aspect of offline face-to-face communication (Tsai & Men, 2017). Consequently, digital channels flatten the traditional hierarchical structure of internal communication and narrow the psychological distance between leaders and stakeholders (Men, 2014b; Yue, Chung, et al., 2020).

Furthermore, leaders with a strong internal digital presence were found to facilitate employees' upward communications, relationship outcomes, and work engagement (Tsai & Men, 2017). Today, stakeholders demand greater access to the opinions and insights of corporate leadership in open communications. Executive leaders' social media activities influence how external stakeholders perceive the leader and the organization (Yue, Chung, et al., 2020). Examination of U.S. CEOs' use of social presence strategies, dialogical principles, disclosure types, and message strategies on social media supported the CEO's role as the relationship builder and engagement officer (e.g., Men et al., 2018; Yue et al., 2019; Yue, Chung, et al., 2020).

More recently, prominent CEOs from the U.S. have spoken out on thorny social and political issues online and offline. Business leaders like Tim Cook of Apple and Marc Benioff of Salesforce agree that CEOs today need to stand up for everybody, not just shareholders, but also employees, customers, partners, the community, and the environment. Despite ongoing debates on the impact of CEO activism on business and society, one thing is certain: In the social media age, "silence is more conspicuous—and more consequential" (Chatterji & Toffel, 2018, p. 81). Therefore, it has become essential for public relations and communication officers to help senior leaders decide what, when, and how to weigh in on controversial topics and measure progress and outcomes on various communication platforms.

Leadership Communication in Turbulent Times

One of the many challenges leaders must cope with in today's increasingly VUCA (volatility, uncertainty, complexity and ambiguity) world is regarding how to lead through changes (e.g., merger & acquisition, layoffs, culture change, leadership change, etc.) and crises (e.g., natural disaster, product recall, financial scandal, etc.). Leadership communication, if done properly, can help facilitate organizational change and maintain stakeholder relationships during crisis times, which contribute to organizational resilience and effectiveness.

Leadership Communication in Organizational Change

There's no doubt leadership communication is a key determinant of successful change management. Aiken and Keller (2007) discussed four roles of CEOs leading through transformation: (1) making the transformation meaningful, (2) role-modeling, (3) building committed teams, and (4) pursuing impact while being accountable, all of which can't be achieved without effective leadership communication. For instance, to make transformation meaningful, leaders, especially CEOs, should clearly define the vision of the change and explain why change is happening and where the organization is heading. Such clarity can reduce employees' uncertainty and resistance, and facilitate change implementation (Men & Bowen, 2017).

In fact, leaders' visionary communication during change has been recognized as a key vehicle in motivating employees toward change (Venus et al., 2019). Recently, Men, Yue, et al. (2020) identified three communicative behaviors of charismatic leaders that contribute to employees' support for change: envisioning, energizing, and enabling. *Envisioning* refers to executive leaders' communication about the vision of change. *Energizing* refers to executive leaders channeling personal passion, energy, and confidence about the change initiative. *Enabling* refers to executive leaders' communication of care, support, empathy, and showing an understanding of employees' feelings and concerns during change.

Leadership Communication in Crisis Times

Crises can pose immense challenges for leadership communication as employees are often faced with increased uncertainties, stress, and negative emotions. Communication has been recognized as one of the two most critical leadership competencies required to successfully handle crises, along with decision-making under pressure (Wooten & James, 2008). Jamal and Abu Bakar (2017) showed that charismatic leadership communication during a crisis can effectively mitigate the crisis impact and strengthen organizational reputation. Increased research on crisis leadership has revealed a preference for certain leadership styles during crisis times, which provides implications for leadership communication. In particular, transformational leadership is preferred as such leaders demonstrate care for the welfare of followers and provide inspiration by connecting employees' roles to a higher organizational purpose, needed more in turbulent times. However, research has also shown that as threats become overwhelming, such as during times of catastrophic crises, employees expect leaders to centralize authority and take actions; more power and less open consultation become more acceptable than during normal times (Haddon et al., 2014).

More recently, literature related to the COVID-19 pandemic has discussed best practices of leadership communication during crisis times. Corroborating such literature, Men, Heffron, and colleagues (2020) proposed the TAEO leadership communication framework (transparency, authenticity, empathy, and optimism) and empirically demonstrated the strong positive impacts of CEOs' TAEO communication in reducing employees' uncertainty, enhancing their psychological wellbeing, and building their trust during the pandemic. In particular, leaders' *transparent* communication involves openly and proactively sharing relevant information to stakeholders in a timely and digestible manner and being honest and upfront about the impact of the crisis. Transparency also emphasizes listening to employees' needs and understanding what transparency really means for each stakeholder group. *Authentic* leadership communication refers to leaders being truthful to their characters, values, and beliefs, being genuine, real, and personable in their communication, and being cognizant of their self-limitations in handling the situation. *Empathetic* leadership communication is characterized by a people-first mindset and leading with humanity. It involves leaders' perspective-taking and communicating understanding, compassion, care, support, encouragement, sympathy, and gratitude. Leadership *optimistic* communication stresses positivity, calmness, faith, hope, and confidence which fosters stakeholders' positive thinking. It is strategic, inspirational, and motivating aimed to cultivate employees' confidence and resilience.

Leadership Self-Reflection

The practice of self-reflection (SR) provides a rich opportunity for improving leadership communications—if we but seize it. Self-reflection is the primary way we examine ourselves and how others see us to increase self-awareness, a crucial quality for leaders. Greek philosophers believed self-knowledge was the highest form of knowledge. American educational pioneer John Dewey claimed we do not learn *from* experience but rather from *reflecting on* that experience. The value of SR for leaders is documented in studies in many fields but is largely absent in public relations research and education (Mules, 2018). However, a recent study of SR among public relations leaders underscored its crucial role in improving employee communications, team building, decision-making, and overall performance (Berger & Erzikova, 2019).

The Strategic Self-Reflection Process

Self-reflection (SR) is deliberate, conscious introspection to better understand our thoughts, experiences, and emotions—to become aware of them, learn from them, and increase self-awareness. Many public relations leaders say they practice SR, though frequency and approaches vary (Berger & Erzikova, 2019). Some use a *me-reflection* approach, focusing almost totally on the self. Others use a more holistic *we-reflection* approach, considering others' perceptions and feelings, too, or sometimes even including others in the process. The most common approaches include: (1) daily self-talks, (2) inspired writings or journaling, and (3) seeking feedback from team members, colleagues, or others.

The two biggest barriers to meaningful SR are (1) the ego problem, which may inhibit honest self-evaluation, or lead to excessive self-criticism and (2) real, or perceived time pressures. Drawing upon their research, Berger and Erzikova (2019) developed a six-step, strategic process for SR. This includes: deliberately *making time for SR each day*, no matter how busy; *creating the right mindset*, by adjusting mental focus; *being self-honest* and not letting ego overpower self-assessment; *formulating*, *calendaring*, and then *carrying out* relevant actions; and *writing things down* to evaluate action outcomes.

Crucial Benefits of Self-Reflection for Leaders

Studies in communication, education, and psychology over the past 40 years documented a handful of crucial benefits for leaders at all levels. Self-reflection can be a transformative experience through which we examine who we are and our values, question our assumptions, and come to an altered awareness and sense of identity. Making SR a crucial part of work *and* personal life may yield substantial benefits.

SR can improve leadership communications and growth by "gaining wisdom from an experience" (Kail, 2012). It boosts emotional intelligence by helping us recognize and understand our emotions, listen better, and be more empathetic (Goleman, 1995). SR also enriches critical-thinking and decision-making (Miller, 2012), and builds stronger relationships with team members, as well as more engaged and productive work teams (Eurich, 2017).

SR seems implicit in the three theoretical approaches noted earlier, especially *motivating language theory* and *leadership listening*. In addition, the potential benefits of SR could empower those in the profession and the classroom: the opportunity for advancement of leadership communications is huge. Yet, while many leaders say they are active and honest self-reflectors, research findings challenge such claims. Eurich's (2017) extensive research with thousands of leaders across professions indicated that only 10–15% of leaders are highly self-aware; most strongly overvalue their own skills and performance.

Conclusion

Leadership and communication are inherently linked. This chapter discussed three theoretical frameworks—i.e., sociocommunicative style, motivating language theory, and leadership listening—that should provide insight into future research in leadership communication. Furthermore, we examined leadership communication from both executive and supervisory levels and reviewed their respective functions in organizations. Understanding the increasingly versatile communication channels that leaders can leverage to reach internal and external stakeholders, we reviewed both traditional and new digital channels, and pointed out the advantages of a strong digital presence for organizational leaders. As the impact of COVID-19 intensifies globally, how to lead organizations through disruption and adapt to complex realities has never been more important for leaders. This chapter concluded with a call for leaders' self-reflection, which can be used to improve leadership communication and growth.

A Mini-Case Study: Transparency in a Crisis

Kylie McQuain, Internal Communication Director, Airbnb

One of the key tenets of internal communication at Airbnb is transparency. When you're a business built on the premise of trust, being open and honest with your employees is table stakes. Whether it's an email or an all-hands meeting, we start with why, we provide context for the decisions we make, and we communicate in a conversational and human way.

Our commitment to transparency has never been more important than when the world and our business faced a global pandemic. Within a matter of weeks, our entire company began working remotely, our industry (travel) came to a standstill, and our business began to struggle. It would be natural for most leaders to hunker down behind closed doors during a time like this. We took a much different approach.

Our CEO increased the frequency of his company-wide Q&As from twice a month to weekly. Each Thursday, he addressed employees honestly about the business, shared the Executive Team's plans for recovery, and openly acknowledged that we would have to make difficult decisions to reduce costs. He told the company that nothing was off the table. Employees submitted and upvoted questions, and we didn't shy away from any of them: Will there be layoffs? Should we expect pay cuts? What about our plans to go public? We worked hard every week to be as transparent as possible about the situation we were in.

In a time of such uncertainty, you might expect the culture to suffer or trust in leaders to plummet. In our case, just the opposite happened. Our CEO received hundreds of e-mails from employees expressing gratitude for his openness and authenticity during such a difficult time. Employees said the weekly Q&As were the highlight of their week and that watching alongside their teammates helped them feel like we were all in this together. An engineer even built a tool where employees could choose a seat in a virtual audience and "sit together" as teams and react to the meetings with emojis and comments. In a time when employees felt isolated, these Thursday meetings brought the company together in a way we never anticipated.

The goodwill we built was put to the ultimate test in early May 2020 when we announced we had to let go around 25% of the company. Our founders and Executive Team worked hard to do it compassionately and respectfully. Employees received generous severance packages, and we helped people impacted find new jobs. Instead of retreating in this painful moment, our CEO once again leaned in. Just two days after the layoffs were announced, he showed back up in front of our team—1900 of whom had just learned they were losing their jobs—and hosted his weekly Q&A. The questions weren't easy to answer, but he was honest and open. In a time of crisis, being transparent is one of the most important things you can do.

References

Aiken, C. B., & Keller, S. P. (2007, February). *The CEO's role in leading transformation*. Mckinsey & Company. Retrieved from https://www.mckinsey.com/businessfunctions/organization/our-insights/the-ceos-role-in-leading-transformation.

Allen, J., Jimmieson, N. L., Bordia, P., & Irmer, B. E. (2007). Uncertainty during organizational change: Managing perceptions through communication. *Journal of Change Management, 7*(2), 187–210. https://doi.org/10.1080/14697010701563379.

Bakar, H. A., & Connaughton, S. L. (2010). Relationships between supervisory communication and commitment to workgroup: A multilevel analysis approach. *International Journal of Strategic Communication, 4*(1), 39–57. https://doi.org/10.1080/15531180903415939.

Berger, B. K., & Erzikova, E. (2019). Self-reflection in public relations leaders: A study of its practice and value in Russia and North America. *Public Relations Journal, 13*(1). Advance online publication. https://prjournal.instituteforpr.org/wp-content/uploads/Self-Reflection-Berger.pdf.

Chatterji, A., & Toffel, M. (2018). The new CEO activists. *Harvard Business Review, 96*(1), 78–89.

De Vries, R. E., Bakker-Pieper, A., & Oostenveld, W. (2010). Leadership = communication? The relations of leaders' communication styles with leadership styles, knowledge sharing and leadership outcomes. *Journal of Business and Psychology, 25*(3), 367–380.

Edelman. (2014). *2014 Edelman trust barometer*. https://www.scribd.com/document/200429962/2014-Edelman-Trust-Barometer.

Eurich, T. (2017). *Insight*. Crown Business.

Fairhurst, G. T., & Connaughton, S. L. (2014). Leadership: A communicative perspective. *Leadership, 10*(1), 7–35. https://doi.org/10.1177/1742715013509396.

Goleman, D. (1995). *Emotional intelligence*. Bantam Books.

Grunig, L. A., Grunig, J. E., & Dozier, D. M. (2002). *Excellent public relations and effective organizations: A study of communication management in three countries*. Lawrence Erlbaum Associates.

Haddon, A., Loughlin, C., & McNally, C. (2014). Leadership in a time of financial crisis: What do we want from our leaders? *Leadership & Organization Development Journal, 36*(5), 612–627.

Jamal, J., & Abu Bakar, H. (2017). The mediating role of charismatic leadership communication in a crisis: A Malaysian example. *International Journal of Business Communication, 54*(4), 369–393.

Jian, G., & Dalisay, F. (2017). Conversation at work: The effects of leader-member conversational quality. *Communication Research, 44*(2), 177–197. https://doi.org/10.1177/0093650214565924.

Jiang, H., & Men, R. L. (2017). Creating an engaged workforce: The impact of authentic leadership, transparent organizational communication, and work-life enrichment. *Communication Research, 44*(2), 225–243. https://doi.org/10.1177/0093650215613137.

Johnson, C. E., & Hackman, M. Z. (2018). *Leadership: A communication perspective* (7th ed.). Waveland.

Kail, E. (2012, March 9). Leadership character: The role of reflection. *Washington Post*. Retrieved from https://www.washingtonpost.com.

Kent, M. L., & Taylor, M. (2002). Toward a dialogic theory of public relations. *Public Relations Review, 28*(1), 21–37. https://doi.org/10.1016/S0363-8111(02)00108-X.

Lacey, K. (2013). *Listening publics: The politics and experience of listening in the media age*. Wiley Blackwell/Polity.

Lengel, R. H., & Daft, R. L. (1988). The selection of communication media as an executive skill. *Academy of Management Perspectives, 2*(3), 225–232. https://doi.org/10.5465/ame.1988.4277259.

Lloyd, K. J., Boer, D., & Voelpel, S. C. (2017). From listening to leading: Toward an understanding of supervisor listening within the framework of leader-member exchange theory. *International Journal of Business Communication, 54*(4), 431–451. https://doi.org/10.1177/2329488415572778.

Lord, R. G., Day, D. V., Zaccaro, S. J., Avolio, B. J., & Eagly, A. H. (2017). Leadership in applied psychology: Three waves of theory and research. *Journal of Applied Psychology, 102*(3), 434–451. https://doi.org/10.1037/apl0000089.

Macnamara, J. (2016). Organizational listening: Addressing a major gap in public relations theory and practice. *Journal of Public Relations Research, 28*(3–4), 146–169. https://doi.org/10.1080/1062726X.2016.1228064.

Mayfield, J., & Mayfield, M. (2018). *Motivating language theory: Effective leader talk in the workplace*. Palgrave Macmillan. https://doi.org/10.1007/978-3-319-66930-4.

Mayfield, M., & Mayfield, J. (2017). Leader talk and the creative spark: A research note on how leader motivating language use influences follower creative environment perceptions. *International Journal of Business Communication, 54*(2), 210–225. https://doi.org/10.1177/2329488416687057.

Men, L. R. (2014a). Why leadership matters to internal communication: Linking transformational leadership, symmetrical communication, and employee outcomes. *Journal of Public Relations Research, 26*(3), 256–279. https://doi.org/10.1080/1062726X.2014.908719.

Men, L. R. (2014b). Strategic internal communication: Transformational leadership, communication channels, and employee satisfaction. *Management Communication Quarterly, 28*(2), 264–284. https://doi.org/10.1177/0893318914524536.

Men, L. R. (2015). The internal communication role of the chief executive officer: Communication channels, style, and effectiveness. *Public Relations Review, 41*(4), 461–471. https://doi.org/10.1016/j.pubrev.2015.06.021.

Men, L. R., & Bowen, S. A. (2017). *Excellence in internal relations management*. Business Expert Press.

Men, L. R., Heffron, E., Bajalia, A., & Qin, S. (2020). *Exploring the impact of strategic CEO communication on employee trust during the COVID-19 pandemic: Introducing the TAEO Framework*. Unpublished manuscript.

Men, L. R., Tsai, W. S., Chen, Z. F., & Ji, Y. G. (2018). Social presence and digital dialogic communication: Engagement lessons from top social CEOs. *Journal of Public Relations Research, 30*(3), 83–99. https://doi.org/10.1080/1062726X.2018.1498341.

Men, L. R., & Yue, C. A. (2019). Creating a positive emotional culture: Effect of strategic internal communication and its impact on employee supportive behaviors. *Public Relations Review, 45*(3), 101764. https://doi.org/10.1016/j.pubrev.2019.03.001.

Men, L. R., Yue, C. A., & Liu, Y. (2020). "Vision, passion, and care": The impact of charismatic executive leadership communication on employee trust and support for organizational change. *Public Relations Review, 46*(3), 101927. https://doi.org/10.1016/j.pubrev.2020.101927.

Miller, P. (2012). Self-reflection: The key to effective leadership. *Today's Manager*, December 2011–January 2012. https://works.bepress.com/peter_miller/133/.

Mules, P. (2018). Reflections on the absence of formal reflection in public relations education and practice. *Public Relations Review, 44*, 174–179.

Myers, K. K. (2015). Supervisor-subordinate communication. In C. Berger & M. Roloff (Eds.), *International encyclopedia of interpersonal communication* (pp. 1–10). Wiley-Blackwell.

Park, D. J., & Berger, B. K. (2004). The presentation of CEOs in the press, 1990–2000: Increasing salience, positive valence, and a focus on competency and personal dimensions of image. *Journal of Public Relations Research, 16*(1), 93–125. https://doi.org/10.1207/s1532754xjprr1601_4.

Richmond, V. P. (2002). Socio-communicative style and orientation in instruction. In J. L. Chesebro & J. C. McCroskey (Eds.), *Communication for Teachers* (pp. 104–115). Allyn & Bacon.

Rogers, C. R. (1959). A theory of therapy, personality and interpersonal relationships as developed in the client-centered framework. In S. Koch (Ed.), *Psychology: A study of a science. Formulations of the person and the social context* (pp. 184–256). McGraw-Hill.

Roy, T. (2018). *How HR can bring employees and the CEO together in three steps*. Retrieved from https://www.hrtechnologist.com/articles/culture/how-hr-can-bring-employees-and-the-ceo-together-in-three-steps/.

Stam, D., Lord, R. G., Knippenberg, D. V., & Wisse, B. (2014). An image of who we might become: Vision communication, possible selves, and vision pursuit. *Organization Science, 25*(4), 1172–1194. https://doi.org/10.1287/orsc.2013.0891.

Therkelsen, D. J., & Fiebich, C. L. (2003). The supervisor: The linchpin of employee relations. *Journal of Communication Management, 8*(2), 120–129. https://doi.org/10.1108/13632540410807592.

Thomas, C. E., Richmond, V. P., & McCroskey, J. C. (1994). The association between immediacy and socio-communicative style. *Communication Research Reports, 11*, 107–115.

Tkalac Verčič, A., & Špoljarić, A. (2020). Managing internal communication: How the choice of channels affects internal communication satisfaction. *Public Relations Review, 46*(3), 101926. Advance online publication. https://doi.org/10.1016/j.pubrev.2020.101926.

Tsai, W. H. S., & Men, L. R. (2017). Social CEOs: The effects of CEOs' communication styles and parasocial interaction on social networking sites. *New Media & Society, 19*(11), 1848–1867. https://doi.org/10.1177/1461444816643922.

van Knippenberg, D., & Stam, D. (2014). Visionary leadership. In D. V. Day (Ed.), *Oxford handbook of leadership and organizations* (pp. 241–259). Oxford University Press.

Van Quaquebeke, N., & Felps, W. (2018). Respectful inquiry: A motivational account of leading through asking questions and listening. *Academy*

of Management Review, 43(1), 5–27. https://doi.org/10.5465/amr.2014.0537.
Van Vugt, M., Hogan, R., & Kaiser, R. B. (2008). Leadership, followership, and evolution: Some lessons from the past. *American Psychologist, 63*(3), 182–196. https://doi.org/10.1037/0003-066X.63.3.182.
Venus, M., Stam, D., & van Knippenberg, D. (2019). Visions of change as visions of continuity. *Academy of Management Journal, 62*(3), 667–690. https://doi.org/10.5465/amj.2015.1196.
Wajcman, J., & Rose, E. (2011). Constant connectivity: Rethinking interruptions at work. *Organization Studies, 32*(7), 941–961. https://doi.org/10.1177/0170840611410829.
Wooten, L. P., & James, E. H. (2008). Linking crisis management and leadership competencies: The role of human resource development. *Advances in Developing Human Resources, 10*(3), 352–379.
Yue, C. A., Chung, Y. J., Kelleher, T., Bradshaw, A. S., & Ferguson, M. A. (2020). How CEO social media disclosure and gender affect perceived CEO attributes, relationship investment, and engagement intention. *Journalism & Mass Communication Quarterly*. Advance online publication. https://doi.org/10.1177/1077699020943521.
Yue, C. A., Men, L. R., & Ferguson, M. A. (2020). Examining the effects of internal communication and emotional culture on employees' organizational identification. *International Journal of Business Communication, 58*(2), 169–195. Advance online publication. https://doi.org/10.1177/2329488420914066.
Yue, C. A., Thelen, P., Robinson, K., & Men, L. R. (2019). CEO leadership communication on Twitter: Comparison between Startup and Fortune 500 CEOs. *Corporate Communications: An International Journal, 24*(3), 532–552. https://doi.org/10.1108/CCIJ-03-2019-0031.
Yukl, G. (2010). *Leadership in organizations* (7th ed.). Prentice Hall.

CHAPTER 3

Internal Public Segmentation for Effective Internal Issue Management

Yeunjae Lee and Jarim Kim

Effectively segmenting internal publics based on certain characteristics and common interests is key to improving targeted employee communication (Men & Bowen, 2017). Internal public segmentation is especially valuable in identifying and analyzing internal publics and understanding their perceptions and behaviors for organizations facing issues or crises (Lee, 2019). Strategically selecting identifiable, accessible, and actionable segmentation tools is thus critical for public relations and internal communication practitioners. This chapter focuses on using the internal public segmentation method as a tool for understanding internal publics' perceptions and behaviors in relation to organizational issues. It explains

Y. Lee (✉)
University of Miami, Coral Gables, FL, USA
e-mail: yxl992@miami.edu

J. Kim
Yonsei University, Seoul, South Korea
e-mail: jarimkim@yonsei.ac.kr

L. R. Men and A. Tkalac Verčič (eds.), *Current Trends and Issues in Internal Communication*, New Perspectives in Organizational Communication, https://doi.org/10.1007/978-3-030-78213-9_3

how public relations theory (e.g., the situational theory of problem-solving: Kim & Grunig, 2011) can be applied in the internal issue context and how the segmentation method can be utilized to effectively manage internal issues. It also includes two empirical studies—one of a "high-responsibility" issue, the other of a "low-responsibility" issue—to compare and analyze internal publics' situational perceptions and behaviors.

Internal Publics

In public relations, "publics" are defined as groups of people who face problems, are divided regarding the solutions, and organize to discuss them (Grunig, 2003). "Publics" are often differentiated from "stakeholders," a term that refers to individuals or groups who affect or are affected by organizations' decisions, policies, and communication practices. In other words, stakeholders can encompass broader groups of people with similar stakes in organizations including employees, customers, and community members, while publics arise independently when they recognize problems around organizations (Grunig & Repper, 1992). Therefore, several different kinds of public (e.g., active, passive publics) can be found within each stakeholder category.

This definition of publics provides important insights for defining internal publics. As members of interdependent groups who are mostly involved in organizational issues, problems, or events, employees are often considered organizations' primary stakeholders (Broom & Sha, 2013). Internal publics—the key stakeholders in effective public relations practices—are thus defined as internal members at all levels of an organization ranging from frontline workers, line managers, and middle-level management to senior management and executives (Men & Bowen, 2017). However, when facing organizational issues, not all employees cognitively engage or respond similarly. Indeed, their responses to different types of organizational issues may vary, depending on their experiences at work, individual values, attitudes toward the issues in question, and relationships with their organizations. In other words, although internal members can be important stakeholders who are directly involved in organizational issues, they are not necessarily "publics" who share common problems and address issues through individual or collective behaviors. Therefore, from a public relations perspective, *internal publics* can be defined as groups of members within organizations who recognize given organizational issues as problematic and take action to solve them.

Public Segmentation

Public segmentation, defined as "divid[ing] a population, market, or audience into groups whose members are more like each other than members of other segments" (Grunig & Repper, 1992, p. 129), is an important tool in public relations. Different public segments have different beliefs and attitudes toward organizations. To effectively communicate with each public segment, therefore, organizations need to employ different strategies with messages tailored to the target publics (Berkowitz & Turnmire, 1994; Kim & Grunig, 2011). Segmenting publics allows organizations to strategically and effectively manage issues and relationships with different publics. Specifically, it makes communicating with various publics more cost-efficient and facilitates the attainment of goals such as gaining publics' support or fostering stronger relationships with publics (Kim et al., 2008).

Internal Public Segmentation

Like external publics, internal publics vary depending on socio-demographic, psychographic, cultural, or behavioral characteristics (Grunig, 1989). Segmenting employees helps organizations understand working environments, their relationships with their employees, communication flows, and the information needs of given groups, which facilitates more effective communication with said groups about their problems and interests. The multigenerational and diverse nature of contemporary workforces and accelerating digitization are making the current business environment increasingly complicated (Men & Bowen, 2017). Effectively analyzing employees is, therefore, crucial to achieving targeted communication and tailoring messages to meet their communication needs.

More importantly, as noted above, the members of internal publics respond differently to organizational communication messages about issues depending on their characteristics. In particular, some contend that active publics, who have high levels of situational motivation to solve problematic situations, are more likely to actively communicate with organizations than non-active publics (Kim & Grunig, 2011). These active publics can thus serve as both assets and threats to organizations during periods when issues arise. Similarly, when internal publics become active by reacting either positively or negatively to organizations' behaviors, organizations must actively communicate with these publics to effectively deal with the voices from inside. These active publics typically make issues out of the consequences of organizational decisions (Grunig, 1989). Thus, organizations that fail to effectively identify and communicate with these publics will face issues or crises that will require greater effort and resources to resolve. More strategic communication targeted to each segment of internal publics will better satisfy their communication needs, thereby enhancing the effectiveness of issue/crisis communication efforts.

Different Approaches to Identify and Segment Internal Publics

The idea of segmenting employees (or internal publics) is not new in the literature. Scholars from various disciplines including marketing, human resources (HR) management, and public relations have developed a diverse segmentation method (e.g., Boudreau & Ramstad, 2005; Moroko & Uncles, 2009; Waite, 2007). These studies, however, include a somewhat disorganized list of segmentation tools (Grunig, 1989). In general, there are several ways to segment employees based on certain characteristics such as demographic factors, psychographic factors, and behavioral factors.

First, employees in organizations can be segmented based on observed variables (i.e., demographic/geographic factors) such as age, gender, race/ethnicity, income, education level, physical location, organizational tenure, position, and job classification. During the organizational issue stage, employees in different segments may perceive the issue itself differently depending on the issue's nature. For example, for workplace discrimination issues, minority employees (e.g., women, African Americans, and LGBT employees) may have different needs and expectations for their companies than majority group employees. Employees' positions at work also play an important role in how they respond to organizational issues. High-level employees (e.g., managers) are more likely to speak up during issue periods to solve the issues and defend the company externally (Lee, 2017). Younger and new employees may also have higher levels of uncertainty and job ambiguity than older and experienced employees when organizational issues arise, and these characteristics require different communication approaches from organizations.

In addition to the objective variables observed by secondary sources (i.e., demographics), the use of inferred variables, which include individuals' perceptions, attitudes, and cognitions, can make segmentation more effective. Accordingly, psychographic factors can serve as important bases for employee segmentation. Such factors include individual employees' values, attitudes, political views, social needs, interests, personalities, lifestyles, work styles, career focus and preferences, and desired career benefits (Men & Bowen, 2017). During periods in which organizational issues arise, individual employees' personal beliefs and values may affect how they respond to organizations' decisions to deal with the issues. For example, employees who value economic as opposed to ethical managerial approaches to solving organizational issues may require different approaches and messages from organizations. Likewise, employees' who prioritize economic rewards over work-life balance or job stability may have different information needs during such periods.

Lastly, behavioral variables such as employees' media consumption habits, involvement and engagement levels, organizational citizenship behaviors, and adoption of new changes or initiatives can also be important criteria for internal public segmentation (Men & Bowen, 2017). Public relations scholars have paid particular attention to individuals' communication behaviors (i.e., information seeking). Grunig (1989) developed a nested segmentation model, composed of the following seven layers of segmentation concepts: individual communication behaviors in the core nest; publics; communities; inferred variables such as psychographics, lifestyles, subcultures, or social relationships; geo-demographics; socio-demographics; and the mass audience in the most outer nest. The more a segmentation tool is located in the inner nest, the more specific, powerful, and precise its predictions (Grunig, 1989; Grunig & Repper, 1992). Several scholars (Grunig, 1997; Hallahan, 2000; Kim et al., 2008) have thus developed useful segmentation models that utilize individuals' communication behaviors. One representative theory in this vein is the situational theory of problem-solving (STOPS).

Segmenting Internal Publics Using the Situational Theory

The situational theory of publics (STP), first developed by J. E. Grunig (1968), is one of the most useful frameworks in public relations scholarship to understand why and how the publics become motivated to engage in communicative behaviors (Aldoory & Sha, 2006). Formed by Dewey's

(1927) conceptualization of the public—which arises when people face and recognize similar problems and organize to resolve the problem—the situational theory of publics (STP; Grunig, 2003) focuses on publics' perceptual and cognitive variables (i.e., problem recognition, involvement recognition, and constraint recognition).

Specifically, *problem recognition* refers to "one's perception that something is missing and that there is no immediately applicable solution to it" (Kim & Grunig, 2011, p. 128). People enter problematic situations when they recognize a problem but fail to resolve it immediately (Grunig, 1997). *Involvement recognition* is defined as "the extent to which people connect themselves with a situation" (Grunig, 1997, p. 10). Lastly, *constraint recognition* refers to the extent to which "people perceive that there are obstacles in a situation that limit their ability to do anything about the situation" (Grunig, 1997, p. 10); such perceived obstacles discourage publics' communication behaviors, even when publics' problem recognition and involvement are high. The STP (Grunig, 2003) also explains how the three independent variables predict communication behaviors, which can be either active or passive. Grunig (1989) argued that active communicative behavior involves effortful information seeking regarding an issue under consideration, whereas passive communicative behavior involves passive processing of information that is given to them (Hamilton, 1992).

This theory allows for public segmentation based on these publics' perceptions of given issues. Grunig and Hunt (1984) identified four public types (i.e., non-public, latent public, aware public, and active public) based on their perceptions of given issues. *Non-publics* include those who do not recognize any problems or the relevance of any problems. *Latent publics* comprise those who engage in an issue, but do not recognize given problematic situations. Latent publics are often the targets of communication campaigns that attempt to increase their problem recognition levels and convert them into active publics. Once members of such a public detect problems, they become an aware public. *Aware publics* needs organizational communication efforts; otherwise, they are likely to become active publics. Finally, active publics include those who face problematic situations, perceive-related issues as highly relevant, and recognize few constraints. *Active publics* are likely to organize and act together to resolve their problems, potentially decreasing organizational effectiveness since managing active publics requires organizational resources.

The situational theory of problem-solving (STOPS; Kim & Grunig, 2011), which extended the STP, identifies three types of individual communicative behaviors as dependent variables: information acquisition, information selection, and information transmission (Kim & Grunig, 2011). Information acquisition refers to individuals' planned scanning of the environment for messages about a given topic (i.e., information seeking) and unplanned discovery of messages followed by the continued processing of said messages (i.e., information attending). Information selection includes the extent to which individuals both fend of certain information by judging its value and relevance for given problems (i.e., information forefending) and accept information related to said problems (i.e., information permitting). Information transmission refers to individuals' proactive and planned information-giving behaviors (i.e., information forwarding) and reactive and passive information sharing about given problems (i.e., information sharing). The situational theorists (Grunig, 1997; Kim & Grunig, 2011) suggested that when individuals have high levels of problem recognition and involvement recognition, and low levels of constraint recognition, they are more likely to actively engage in communication behaviors (i.e., information acquisition, selection, transmission).

While the STOPS has been applied in various contexts (e.g., political communication, health communication (Kim & Krishna, 2014), recent internal communication studies have begun to use it as a key theoretical framework. Using the dependent variables of STOPS, Kim and Rhee (2011) developed the concept of *positive megaphoning*, which refers to positive external communicative behaviors on the parts of employees—specifically, organization-related information sharing and forwarding to people in their personal network (e.g., family, friends). As a core outcome of organizations' communication practices, previous studies have highlighted the importance of employees' positive megaphoning in issue/crisis management contexts as a managerial asset for organizations (Lee, 2019; Mazzei et al., 2012).

Applying the STOPS to segment internal publics is expected to provide insight into what types of internal publics exist and who are more or less likely to become active publics when issues arise. Organizations are not free from the various issues that can arise internally, including protests, product crises, or labor union strikes. Effective segmentation of employees based on their issue-specific perceptions can enable public relations practitioners to tailor communication strategies to satisfy the needs of different segments and effectively and efficiently communicate with key "active" internal publics.

Application of STOPS in Issue Management Communication

This chapter presents two examples of public segmentation using two organization-related issues. The first example involves an issue in which the organization has a high level of crisis responsibility (i.e., gender discrimination at work) (Study 1) and the second involves an issue in which the organization has a low level of crisis responsibility (i.e., rumor) (Study 2).

Study 1

We conducted an online survey with 150 full-time employees in the U.S. across industry sectors. In the survey, participants were given a hypothetical crisis situation involving gender discrimination at work. They were asked to imagine a situation where the company they currently worked for was sued in federal court for engaging in discriminatory practices against women in the workplace. Participants were also provided with more detailed information. Specifically, they were told that Lauren, one of their female colleagues, filed a lawsuit against the company for discriminating against female employees, as she was deprived of a senior-level promotion because of her gender. As information regarding unfair treatment in the company spread rapidly on Facebook and Twitter, it prompted a deluge of public criticism. After exposing them to this experimental material, we measured participants' issue-specific perceptions (i.e., problem, involvement, and constraint recognition) and communicative actions (i.e., information acquisition, transmission, positive megaphoning). We adopted items from previous studies that used the STOPS (e.g., Kim & Grunig, 2011; Kim & Rhee, 2011) and adjusted them to fit this study's context. Sample items include "I think this is an important corporate crisis for my company," "I believe employees in my company need to pay more attention to this crisis." for *problem recognition*, "I feel I can make a difference with regard to this crisis," "If I want, I can make my opinions and ideas about this crisis matter to those who are addressing it in my company." for *constraint recognition*, and "This crisis affects me substantially," "I am closely connected with this crisis" for *involvement recognition*. Samples items of *information acquisition* include "I would ask managers/supervisors for more explanations of this crisis," "I would proactively search for more relevant information about this crisis." For *information transmission*, items such as "I would participate in a discussion to understand the consequences of this crisis," "I would proactively develop and make suggestions for this crisis to my company." Finally, items such as "I would advocate for my company's position regarding this crisis actively to people around me (e.g., friends, family)," "I would be proactive and aggressive in defending my company during the crisis" were used for *positive megaphoning*.

For public segmentation, we used a summation method (Kim, 2011)—a simple way of segmenting publics (i.e., non-publics, aware/latent publics, and active publics) by adding the scores of individuals' perceptual variables (e.g., problem, involvement, and constraint recognition) about an issue (Kim & Ni, 2013; Kim et al., 2008). Specifically, we recoded the items measuring problem recognition, constraint recognition, and involvement recognition into two scales, 0 (= low) and 1 (= high) after taking the midpoint of the survey scale. The points ranged from 0 to 3, with three variables used. We categorized participants with scores of 3 as "active" publics, those with scores from 1 to 2 as "aware/latent" publics, and those with scores of 0 as "non-publics." Then, to compare the communicative behaviors of each segmented group, we conducted a series of analysis of variance (ANOVA).

Based on the summation method results, we segmented 39.3% of the 150 employees ($n = 59$) into active publics, 49.3% into aware/latent publics ($n = 74$), and 11.3% ($n = 17$) into non-publics. Our analysis showed significant differences among the groups in terms of their information acquisition ($F(2,147) = 37.42$, $p < 0.001$), information transmission ($F(1,247) = 29.84$, $p < 0.001$), and positive megaphoning behaviors ($F(2,147) = 17.51$, $p < 0.001$). As shown in Table 3.1, we found that active publics are more likely than either aware/latent publics or non-publics to engage in all types of communicative behaviors. We also found that aware/latent publics are more actively engaged in information acquisition and transmission than non-publics.

Table 3.1 Communicative behaviors of segmented employees regarding organizational issues: means and standard deviations

Dependent variables (DVs)	*M(SD)*		
Issue 1 *Gender discrimination*	*Non-active* *Internal publics* *(n = 17)*	*Aware/latent* *Internal publics* *(n = 74)*	*Active* *Internal publics* *(n = 59)*
Information acquisition	2.98 (0.86)	3.62 (0.78)	4.32 (0.39)
Information transmission	3.08 (0.83)	3.78 (0.69)	4.31 (0.40)
Positive megaphoning	3.14 (0.95)	3.29 (0.92)	4.06 (0.57)
Issue2 *Corporate rumor*	*Non-active* *Internal publics* *(n = 11)*	*Aware/latent* Internal publics *(n = 54)*	*Active* *Internal publics* *(n = 52)*
Information acquisition	3.34 (0.98)	3.74 (0.89)	4.25 (0.49)
Information transmission	3.37 (1.16)	3.94 (0.78)	4.25 (0.49)
Positive megaphoning	3.10 (0.93)	3.76 (0.90)	4.16 (0.55)

Study 2

In Study 2, we focused on a crisis for which the organization had a low level of responsibility. As in Study 1, we conducted an online survey with 117 full-time employees in the U.S. Participants were exposed to a hypothetical situation in which their current company had been the target of consistent negative rumors. Specifically, they were given the following information: "Your company has been a target of a false rumor (misinformation) spread by email: the company has been accused of exploiting child labor in Africa to produce its products. Vicious hate mail has been hitting inboxes for years describing how the company had used child labor and announcing consumer boycotts against your company for these practices." After exposing them to this material, we administered the same questionnaires from Study 1 to participants to measure their issue-specific perceptions and communicative behaviors. Based on their responses, we used the summation method described above to segment the participants into three groups: active publics, aware/latent publics, and non-publics.

We segmented 44.4% of the 117 employees ($n = 52$) into active publics, 46.2% ($n = 54$) into aware/latent publics, and 9.4% ($n = 11$) into non-publics. The ANOVA results revealed significant differences between these groups in terms of their information acquisition ($F(2,114) = 9.88$, $p < 0.001$), information transmission ($F(2,114) = 7.43$, $p < 0.001$), and positive megaphoning behaviors ($F(2,114) = 9.54$, $p < 0.001$). As shown in Table 3.1, we found that active publics engage in all types of communicative behaviors more than either aware/latent publics or non-publics.

Additional Analysis

The results also showed no significant differences between the participants in Studies 1 and 2 in terms of their issue-specific perceptions (i.e., problem, constraint, involvement recognition) or their communicative behaviors (i.e., information acquisition, information transmission). In other words, study participants had similar levels of situational perceptions and communicative actions for two organizational issues—gender discrimination and corporate rumor. However, we did find that the Study 2 participants, who were exposed to a crisis regarding which the organization had a low level of responsibility (i.e., rumor), more actively engaged in positive megaphoning behavior than the Study 1 participant.

Implications for Practice

Although hypothetical scenarios were used, the results of these two empirical studies highlight the theoretical and practical utility of both the situational theory of publics and the segmentation method in the context of internal issue management and communication. Supporting the main assumption of the STOPS, the results showed that active publics who are more cognitively aware of crisis situations and feel involved and less constrained when it comes to solving crises engage more actively in communication behaviors regarding crises involving both high and low levels of organizational responsibility. Those active internal publics are also more likely to engage in positive megaphoning, by advocating or sharing positive information about their companies externally. Thus, regardless of the crisis type or the attribution of responsibility, internal members who are situationally motivated in relation to a crisis are more likely to be "active" in addressing said crisis. The analysis also showed that the attribution of responsibility for an issue does not affect employees' issue-specific perceptions and communicative behaviors. This is because, unlike other types of public (e.g., consumers), employees as key internal stakeholders of organizations affect and are affected by crises to some extent, either directly or indirectly. However, employees are more likely to engage in positive megaphoning behavior when experiencing a low-responsibility issue than a high-responsibility issue. This is partially due to the fact that employees tend to protect their employer's external reputation by defending their company when it is "victimized" by an uncontrollable issue.

These two studies suggest that during crises, organizations should identify key internal publics by considering not just demographics or work-related characteristics (e.g., the positions and departments/units that are directly affected by the crisis), but also the psychological perceptions of employees. Employees who view a crisis as "problematic" and are situationally motivated should be strategically targeted because they strongly identify with the crisis and therefore may actively engage in the crisis-solving processes by cooperating with the organization. Being highly motivated to effectively and ethically solve the crisis, these active employees can be the key people who may develop practical, creative, and tailored solutions and ideas that help the organization to efficiently overcome the crisis.

Organizational leaders and practitioners of corporate communication, public relations, and human resources (HR) can use this segmentation tool for effective issue/crisis internal communication and management. Conducting formalized and regular company-wide surveys will be particularly useful by incorporating the existing measures of employees' perceptions and communicative behaviors about an issue. Formative research *before* and *during* the issue periods will help practitioners to identify employees' current perceptions and attitudes on diverse internal and external organizational issues. Evaluative research should also be conducted *after* the issue stage to assess the effectiveness of organizations' communication efforts and employees' perceptual and behavioral change.

Conclusion

This chapter examined internal public segmentation as an important tool that public relations and organizational communication scholars and practitioners can use to understand employees' responses to organizational issues. Among various approaches to segmenting employees, it suggests that the STOPS provides one useful approach for segmenting internal publics especially during the periods when issues arise; this approach helped organizations categorize publics into homogeneous groups based on their distinct perceptions, behaviors, and interests. In the context of internal publics, the STOPS can be used to reveal who is likely to become active regarding a given issue. Examining how individuals' cognitive factors (i.e., problem recognition, constraint recognition, involvement recognition) determine internal publics' levels of active engagement in internal issues helps organizations identify and reach out to groups of employees who are motivated to actively engage in issue-specific communicative behaviors. Segmenting these internal publics using the STOPS allows internal communicators to identify and predict potential internal issues or crises before they grow to the level of activism (e.g., labor union strikes, walk-outs, protests) created by active internal publics and to prevent and resolve them by proactively meeting the communication needs of each segmented public.

Professional Interview

Interviewee: Teresa Giradi is the head of internal communication at SNAM, one of the world's leading energy infrastructure operators headquartered in Italy. Her main responsibilities include planning, implementing, and directing internal communication programs.

Regarding corporates' internal issue management and employee segmentation, a professional interview was conducted in November 2020 with Teresa Giradi, who is the head of internal communication at SNAM, which is one of the main energy infrastructure companies headquartered in Italy. The interviewee's primary responsibilities include designing, implementing, and delivering internal communication programs and initiatives.

The practitioner described that the company's overarching internal communication goals can be summarized as follows: *sharing, engaging, and listening*. In specific, SNAM aims to share the information related to the company's strategy and culture to its employees effectively through a variety of communication channels (i.e., news/video, internal webinars and talks, newsletters). The company also strives to improve employees' engagement with diverse programs such as contests, volunteering programs, team building games, and holiday events and listen to employees' needs and concerns through regular surveys. The practitioner noted that these methods have been successful in increasing employees' participation in communication programs and encouraging their voices.

The practitioner pointed out the COVID-19-related issues as major issues in internal communication during the time when the interview was conducted. To effectively manage the issue, during the first phase of COVID-19, the company set up a dedicated "crisis management inter-functional team" and the department of internal communication played a huge role in it. The team was responsible for defining the company's actions, establishing communications strategies (e.g., which channels should be used, how frequently and what types of messages should be delivered, how to set up the tone of messages, etc.), and designing specific engagement activities that are aligned with the company's values with the following key initiatives: "Closeness," "Inclusion," "Caring and listening." Specifically, during the COVID-19 phase, the company adopted the "over-communication" approach to inform employees of necessary and important company decisions and policies as much as possible and as frequently as possible, using diverse online communication channels such as e-mails and corporate intranet. The company also actively conducted formative and evaluative research by launching a survey to measure employees' feelings and evaluations of the company's actions. The company received a considerable number of positive responses from employees, as they were satisfied with the company's ability to communicate and inform effectively. Employees gave compliments for the company's communication efforts and the support they received, expressing gratitude, pride, and a strong sense of belonging.

In terms of the internal segmentation method, the practitioner answered that SNAM has not used any type of public segmentation tool when communicating with employees. Rather, the company prefers an "open" approach to provide company-related information to *every* employee. This helps employees to have opportunities to learn about and selectively register for or participate in different types of corporate initiatives they are interested in. The practitioner also emphasized that the internal communication team is working closely with the external communication department to make sure that all the messages distributed externally are consistent with the messages delivered internally.

The idea of internal public segmentation for issue/crisis management is recently introduced among scholars and practitioners as one way of increasing the effectiveness of organizations' internal communication strategies. As learned from the interview, it may not be common practice to adopt and use internal public segmentation tools in real settings yet. Given its theoretical strength and practical values, however, more research and case studies with a variety of examples of internal issues seem to be necessary.

References

Aldoory, L., & Sha, B. L. (2006). Elaborations of the situational theory of publics for more effective application to public relations scholarship and practice. In E. L. Toth (Ed.), *The future of excellence in public relations and communication management*. Erlbaum.

Berkowitz, D., & Turnmire, K. (1994). Community relations and issues management: An issue orientation approach to segmenting publics. *Journal of Public Relations Research, 6*, 105–123.

Boudreau, J. W., & Ramstad, P. M. (2005). Talentship, talent segmentation, and sustainability: A new HR decision science paradigm for a new strategy definition. *Human Resource Management: Published in Cooperation with the School of Business Administration, the University of Michigan and in Alliance with the Society of Human Resources Management, 44*(2), 129–136.

Broom, G. M., & Sha, B. L. (2013). *Cutlip and Center's effective public relations* (11th int. ed.). Pearson.

Dewey, J. (1927). *The public and its problems*. Swallow.

Grunig, J. E. (1968). *Information, entrepreneurship, and economic development: A study of the decision making processes of Colombian Latifundistas.* Unpublished doctoral dissertation, University of Wisconsin.

Grunig, J. E. (1989). Publics, audiences, and market segments: Segmentation principles for campaigns. In C. Salmon (Ed.), *Information campaigns: Balancing social values and social change* (pp. 199–228). Sage.

Grunig, J. E. (1997). A situational theory of publics: Conceptual history, recent challenges and new research. In D. Moss, T. MacManus, & D. Veri (Eds.), *Public relations research: An international perspective* (pp. 3–46). International Thomson Business.

Grunig, J. E. (2003). Constructing public relations theory and practice. In B. Dervin & S. Chaffee, with L. Foreman-Wernet (Eds.), *Communication, another kind of horse race: Essays honoring Richard F. Carter* (pp. 85–115). Hampton Press.

Grunig, J. E., & Hunt, T. T. (1984). *Managing public relations*. Holt, Rinehart and Winston.

Grunig, J. E., & Repper, F. C. (1992). Strategic management, publics, and issues. In J. E. Grunig (Ed.), *Excellence in public relations and communication management* (pp. 117–157). Lawrence Erlbaum Associates.

Hallahan, K. (2000). Inactive publics: The forgotten publics in public relations. *Public Relations Review, 26*(4), 499–515.

Hamilton, P. K. (1992). Grunig's situational theory: A replication, application, and extension. *Journal of Public Relations Research, 4*, 123–149.

Kim, J. N. (2011). Public segmentation using situational theory of problem solving: Illustrating summation method and testing segmented public profiles. *Prism, 8*(2), 1–12.

Kim, J. N., & Grunig, J. E. (2011). Problem solving and communicative action: A situational theory of problem solving. *Journal of Communication, 61*(1), 120–149.

Kim, J. N., & Krishna, A. (2014). Publics and lay informatics: A review of the situational theory of problem solving. *Annals of the International Communication Association, 38*(1), 71–105.

Kim, J. N., & Ni, L. (2013). Conceptualizing publics and constructing public relations theory. In *Public relations and communication management* (126–142). Routledge.

Kim, J.-N., Ni, L., & Sha, B.-L. (2008). Breaking down the stakeholder environment: Explicating approaches to the segmentation of publics for public relations research. *Journalism & Mass Communication Quarterly, 85*, 751–768.

Kim, J. N., & Rhee, Y. (2011). Strategic thinking about employee communication behavior (ECB) in public relations: Testing the models of megaphoning and scouting effects in Korea. *Journal of Public Relations Research, 23*(3), 243–268.

Lee, Y. (2017). Exploring the impacts of relationship on employees' communicative behaviors during issue periods based on employee position. *Corporate Communications: An International Journal, 22*(4), 542–555.

Lee, Y. (2019). Crisis perceptions, relationship, and communicative behaviors of employees: Internal public segmentation approach. *Public Relations Review, 45*(4), 101832.

Mazzei, A., Kim, J. N., & Dell'Oro, C. (2012). Strategic value of employee relationships and communicative actions: Overcoming corporate crisis with quality internal communication. *International Journal of Strategic Communication, 6*(1), 31–44.

Men, R. L., & Bowen, S. A. (2017). *Excellence in internal communication management*. Business Expert Press.

Moroko, L., & Uncles, M. D. (2009). Employer branding and market segmentation. *Journal of Brand Management, 17*(3), 181–196.

Waite, A. (2007). HR's role in audience segmentation: How employee segmentation can help HR create tailored programs for its different employee groups. *Strategic HR Review, 6*(2), 16–19.

CHAPTER 4

Internal Social Media and Internal Communication

Vibeke Thøis Madsen

Introduction

Internal social media (ISM) offers a communication platform inside the organization where organizational members can share knowledge, viewpoints and connect with each other across departments, hierarchical levels, and geographical distances. ISM comes in many varieties: it can be an integrated part of the intranet, also known as a social intranet; a separate communication tool such as Yammer, Slack, or Microsoft Teams; or take the form of a closed group on social network services such as LinkedIn or Facebook. The social tools could include social networking sites, wikis, discussion forums, blogs, and instant messaging. Leonardi et al. (2013) define enterprise social media in broad terms as:

V. T. Madsen (✉)
DMJX, Danish School of Media and Journalism, Aarhus, Denmark
e-mail: vtm@dmjx.dk

L. R. Men and A. Tkalac Verčič (eds.), *Current Trends and Issues in Internal Communication*, New Perspectives in Organizational Communication, https://doi.org/10.1007/978-3-030-78213-9_4

> web-based platforms that allow workers to (1) communicate messages with specific co-workers or broadcast messages to everyone in the organization; (2) explicitly indicate or implicitly reveal particular co-workers as communication partners; (3) post, edit, and sort text and files linked to themselves or others; and (4) view the messages, connections, text, and files communicated, posted, edited and sorted by anyone else in the organization at any time of their choosing. (p. 2)

From a communication perspective it is more interesting to explore what type of communication develops on a platform, and how it evolves, than to explore the technical constitution of the platform itself. In other words, technology becomes interesting only in regard to how it influences communication. ISM exists to enable horizontal and vertical communication across different organizational sectors, making visible *people*, *communication*, and *interactions* to all organizational members (Treem et al., 2020). Madsen (2017) therefore defined ISM as "an user-friendly and visible web-based communication arena inside an organization in which employees and managers can communicate, interact, connect, and make sense of their work and organizational life" (p. 3). This chapter will first present the benefits of using ISM in internal communications, then review challenges involved. It will be argued that ISM can develop into three different types of communication arenas. Three sections will then explore different communication dynamics on ISM, explain the prerequisites for creating open and transparent communication, and illustrate how emerging technologies can interact with ISM. Finally, future research and managerial implications are discussed.

Benefits of Using ISM

ISM enable symmetrical communication (Grunig, 2009) and employee participation (Cardon & Marshall, 2015; Falkheimer & Heide, 2014; Heide, 2015). These two goals have long been hailed as an ideal toward which organizations should strive (Grunig & Hunt, 1984; Heron, 1942; Redding, 1972). Treem and Leonardi (2012) even argue that ISM will have profound consequences that will alter "socialization, information sharing and power processes in organizations" (p. 143). Employees are very knowledgeable about their work, and when organizations draw on their knowledge it should make for better decisions and practices, creating a more effective organization (Redding, 1972). Theoretically,

ISM can therefore be a transformative media in the internal communication strategy (Men et al., 2020) which will empower employees to become active communicators instead of passive receivers (Madsen, 2016).

Several researchers have pointed out the array of benefits that would result from introducing ISM into organizations, such as visible communication strengthening existing connections; the development of new horizontal and vertical connections; the increase in social capital among employees as competencies become more visible (Fulk & Yuan, 2013; Laitinen & Sivunen, 2020); the creation of enhanced knowledge-sharing capability (Vuori & Okkonen, 2012); and the improvement and acceptance of decisions (Madsen, 2016; Madsen & Johansen, 2019). Communication on ISM could furthermore be a key to create a sense of community (Laitinen & Sivunen, 2020; Uysal, 2016), which would help employees to display organizational citizen behavior (Madsen & Verhoeven, 2016). Other benefits include enhancing workplace productivity (Leftheriotis & Giannakos, 2014), improving ideation and innovation (Gode et al., 2019), and providing better customer service (Men & Bowen, 2016; Ruck, 2015) as employees can share thoughts and ideas about how to improve services, point out short-comings in existing offers and solve sudden and unexpected problems.

When organizational issues are discussed in the ISM communication arena, managers get a useful sense of the pulse of the organization. Managers at all levels can listen to the employees and understand how they make sense of internal communication. Managers can also engage in conversations with employees about organizational issues, which provides feedback about products, services, and work processes that can be richer than face-to-face discussions because they involve more participants. A CEO who communicates with employees will come across as more personal and amiable (Ewing et al., 2019), and when managers react, answer and provide additional explanations, the employees feel that they are heard and listened to (Madsen, 2016; Men et al., 2020). When organizational members discuss organizational issues on ISM, they are actually re-negotiating rules, norms, and organizational identity (Madsen, 2016; Uysal, 2016). This communication enhances organizational transparency and help employees identify with the organization (Madsen, 2018, 2020; Men et al., 2020). Participatory communication on ISM can thus involve and empower employees (Madsen, 2018; Men et al., 2020). There is a strong link between internal communication and engagement that especially seems to go through communication that involves, activates, and empowers employees (Men et al., 2020), which is precisely the promise of ISM (Men et al., 2020).

Challenges with Introducing ISM

Despite the benefits of using ISM in internal communication, several studies have found that organizations are far from unlocking the full potential of ISM (Madsen, 2017; Men & Hung-Baesecke, 2015; Ruck, 2015; Sievert & Scholz, 2017). Introducing ISM does not automatically introduce participatory communication. Many factors influence how employee communication on ISM will develop in an organization (see Fig. 4.1). The variability of the ISM organizational experience shows that, there are better and worse practices. The perception and the use of ISM differ not only from one organization to another, but, from one employee to another. The following sections will explore these factors.

The organizational context will influence the degree and quality of employee communication on ISM. The organization must be prepared to embrace participatory communication (Parry & Solidoro, 2013).

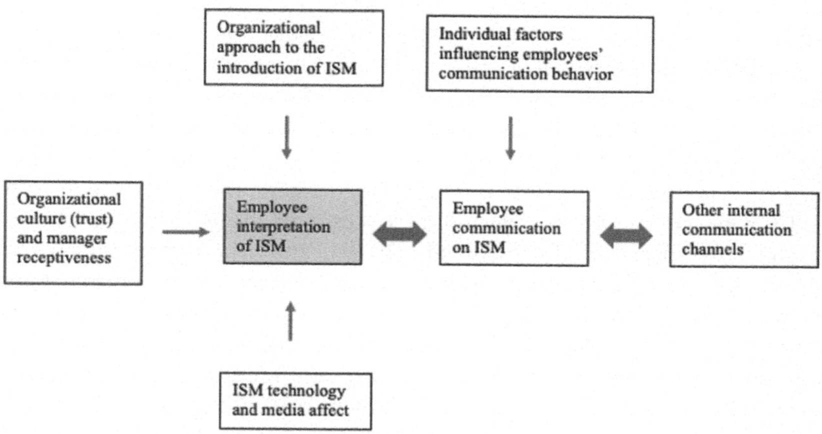

Fig. 4.1 Different factors influencing employee communication on ISM (slightly altered from Madsen [2017], with the permission of *Journal of Communication Management*)

Post-bureaucratic organizations with a flat structure and a tradition of involving employees in decision-making are therefore more likely to develop employee communication on ISM than a more hierarchical organization. A central issue is the conflict between the organization's need to control organizational communication and the nature of communication on social media as open and uncontrollable (Macnamara & Zerfass, 2012). Organizations may thus choose a "closed" or an "open" approach to ISM (Baptista & Galliers, 2012). In the closed approach the organization control the editorial content, and therefore restrict the range of commenting employees are allowed; in contrast, the open approach allows open debate and comments. These two options correspond to the success of the ISM as a communication arena. In the open case, communication is perceived as welcome, and thus enables a greater use and depth of employee communication, while in the closed case, employees will feel less welcome to communicate and will consequently avoid the ISM forum for any but pro forma communications (Baptista & Galliers, 2012; Pekkala, 2020). The open case is supported by several studies that have shown how important it is that managers listen to employee voices on ISM (Chin et al., 2015; Trimi & Galanxhi, 2014). Managerial receptiveness is not a matter of managers explicitly claiming to be receptive. It is rather a matter of managers conducting communicative practices such as actively engaging with employees on a regular basis and reacting to employee voice with respect, and for example provide additional explanations for managerial directives (Ellmer & Reichel, 2020). Furthermore, the organizational culture has to encourage employees to share their knowledge and opinions. A survey of 500 organizations in Germany found that organizational culture, especially the lack of trust, was a major impediment to integrating ISM (Sievert & Scholz, 2017). Huang et al. (2013) compared the use of ISM in three different organizations and found that ISM did not become multivocal in the organization that encouraged a competitive culture, while in the two others, which were more open, ISM did become multivocal as employees regardless of their role and position in the hierarchy trusted that they were welcome to participate. Employees are thus not only concerned about retaliation from managers but also comments and reactions from other coworkers (Madsen & Verhoeven, 2016). In this respect, as studies in employee voice have found the perceived safety and perceived efficacy of voice determines whether employees will voice their opinion in an organizational context (Morrison, 2014). Thus, the organizational context, style of leadership, management philosophy and managerial practices play a huge role in shaping the ISM experience, as norms and power struggles tend to move into the communication arena. If communication is contaminated with distrust and power struggles before ISM, these factors could even be enhanced by ISM (Denyer et al., 2011).

The process of introducing ISM often makes a difference as to whether communication on ISM become multivocal. ISM tends to fail when:

- the purpose of ISM is unclear (Denyer et al., 2011; Laitinen & Sivunen, 2020; Madsen, 2017; Manuti, 2016; Trimi & Galanxhi, 2014);
- ISM lacks support from (top) managers (Chin et al., 2015; Trimi & Galanxhi, 2014); or
- employees interpret and understand the social technology in a different way than anticipated (Högberg & Olsson, 2019; Madsen, 2017; Rice et al., 2017).

Broadly speaking the introduction of ISM can be treated as either a functionalistic technology project or as a change management project (Madsen, 2017). When it is treated as a technology project, employees tend to be unsure of what the new media should be used for, especially if there are other alternatives as emails, newsletters, meetings, and conversations with colleagues around the coffee machine. Successful ISM launches undertake it as a change management process, where employees get a clear picture of *how* and *why* ISM is being introduced and what is expected of them (Denyer et al., 2011). In other words, it is important to get employees on board (Madsen, 2017). In this process, communication professionals can play an important role as change agents, helping employees and managers make sense of the new media, provide training and help facilitate communication on ISM (Madsen, 2017).

The ISM technology provides a communication arena that make multivocal and participatory communication possible (Baptista & Galliers, 2012; Madsen, 2018). Especially the visibility of the communication makes it different from other types of organizational communication (Treem et al., 2020). Welch (2012) argue that organizations need to take *media affect* into account, and when an organization introduces ISM, employees will expect dialogue and interaction that they know from external social media, although they might also be concerned that the communication will be social and not work-related (Madsen, 2017). Scholars distinguish between lean and rich media where rich media include face-to-face communication, meetings, and lean media involve company magazines, electronic newsletters, bulletin boards, and intranet. Employees prefer rich media to lean media (Verčič & Špoljarić, 2020). One advantage of ISM is that it straddles the divide between lean and rich media. On one hand it consists of written text, which is characteristic of lean media, while on the other hand the writing is informal and conversational, and pictures of employees appear next to their post, which integrate elements from rich media (Ewing et al., 2019).

Where employees have many different information and communication channels, ISM must be positively presented as a different type of communication arena (Ellmer & Reichel, 2020), since employees may otherwise experience it as task overload (Cardon & Marshall, 2015; Chin et al., 2015; van Zoonen & Sivunen, 2020). In other words, employees' initial interpretation and sensemaking of ISM is crucial to how communication on ISM will develop (Ellmer & Reichel, 2020; Högberg & Olsson, 2019). Madsen (2017) found that many different organizational factors influence how employees interpret and understand communication on ISM (see Fig. 4.1). Apart from the overriding degree of openness in the organizational context, it mattered how communication among organizational members on ISM developed. If the communication appeared to be fruitful, interesting and valuable, it would in general be rated positively. However, if it appeared to be a "waste of time", this, too, would have prolonged effects (Madsen, 2017). In other words, employees communicating in the ISM arena can inspire other employees to do the same.

Three Types of Communication Arenas on ISM

Many different factors influence how communication on ISM develop. Madsen (2018) proposes three different types of communication arenas on ISM: a quiet arena, a knowledge-sharing arena and a participatory communication arena (see Fig. 4.2).

In the quiet arena, departments mainly use ISM as a one-way communication channel to inform employees. The latter may comment or like a post, but dialogue or threads are not encouraged. In the knowledge-sharing arena, employees share knowledge about customers, products and tasks horizontally across the organization. Finally, in the participatory

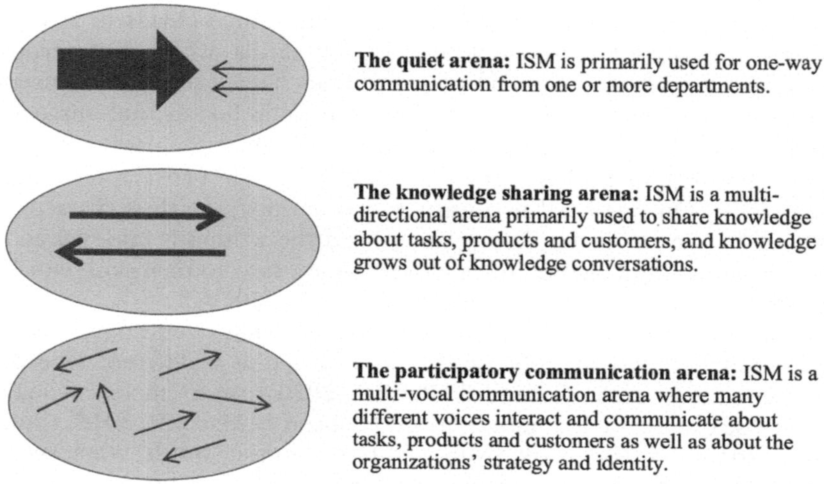

Fig. 4.2 Three types of communication arenas created by ISM (Madsen [2018], with the permission of *Corporate Communication: An international Journal*)

communication arena, organizational members share knowledge across the organization, and they discuss organizational identity and strategy with colleagues and managers. Thus, a horizontal, vertical and multi-vocal space is carved out for different voices and opinions. Participatory communication on ISM only seems to arise when employees perceive that they have a license to criticize organizational procedures and strategies without fearing comments and consequences from colleagues and managers. Participatory ISM is usually connected to a previously nourished culture of manager receptiveness. Madsen (2018) argues for the importance of the participatory communication arena, since it is here that ISM is different from other communication channels—and it is here that ISM has the potential to radically change internal communication.

Dynamics of Employee Communication on ISM

Employee communication on ISM is different from communication on external social media since employees have a contractual and psychological relationship with the organization (Frandsen & Johansen, 2011) which motivates and restrains their communication on ISM. Although empirical research on actual communication on ISM is still in its infancy, the following sketches out some of the dynamics that influence communication on ISM.

Madsen and Verhoeven (2016) found that employees were worried about providing low quality posts and comments, harming personal reputation, and violating unwritten rules, as well as receiving negative comments and reactions from other coworkers and managers. These risks made them consider their post carefully and apply seven self-censorship strategies: (a), postponing publishing content; (b), framing content in a constructive manner; (c), imagining responses from organizational members; (d), asking managers or colleagues for a second opinion; (e), using another channel; and (f), withdrawing or only writing positive comments. Self-censorship was a deliberate and ultimately prosocial tactic that helped create more valuable communication on ISM for other organizational members. It became a *social media skill* that developed over time. Some scholars argue that social media policies are necessary to guide employees about what to use the platform for (Ewing et al., 2019), while others argue that the norms of the organization tend to move onto the platform anyway (Uysal, 2016) and that explicit policies might just discourage employees from posting and commenting.

Employees can use ISM to raise issues and gain support from other organizational members, and it can develop into *a spiral of voice* as more organizational members comment or like the post (Madsen & Johansen, 2019). Due to the visibility of employee communication, the managers or staff who are responsible for the relevant issue have to react or risk the trap of double criticism as it has been defined in crisis communication (Frandsen & Johansen, 2017): the substantial issue raised by the original criticism provokes a second criticism, which is directed toward how the first criticism was (not) handled. Organizations often fear these spirals of voice, but Madsen and Johansen (2019) argue that if critical issues raised on ISM are explained and dealt with in a constructive manner in the ISM arena, it will contribute to creating a more open communication culture and lead to a more robust organization. When employees discuss, challenge and negotiate organizational issues on ISM, they construct organizational identity and acquire a deeper insight into organizational issues and decisions (Madsen, 2016). Madsen (2016) argues that this experience could make employees better prepared to face criticism from outsiders and act as organizational ambassadors.

Employee communication on ISM in open organizations connects frontline employees with top managers. This can make middle managers feel threatened and redundant (Koch et al., 2012), which on the one hand, flattens the hierarchy, and on the other hand, can lead to middle manager discontent. It makes it harder for middle managers or specialists to ignore issues of importance to employees (Madsen, 2020). Madsen (2021) found that communicative leadership on ISM was enacted not only by managers but also by knowledgeable individual organizational members, as well as being co-constructed by groups of employees. In this respect, employees can find solutions to problems and organizational issues without the mediation of managers. This strongly implies that easing the rules on ISM communication for and welcoming non-hierarchical cooperation works, creating quicker, better thought out feedback and decisions-making, with a considerable advantage to the organization in successfully engaging employees.

Prerequisites for Creating Open and Transparent Communication on ISM

As pointed out, the best strategic use of ISM in the organization springs from an open mindset among managers at different levels in the organization, most especially among top managers, and it depends on management's willingness to expose itself to criticism and feedback (Madsen, 2018; Madsen & Johansen, 2019). An open culture takes time to nourish: Employees have to learn how to feel free to speak their mind without aggressiveness or self-protective gestures, and managers have to learn not to confuse criticism with disobedience or ill-will. A first step is to appreciate that employees have competences and situated knowledge not necessarily possessed by management, and that making it safe and efficient to speak up is a net gain. Employees tend to remember how their viewpoints have been received in the past, which influences whether they will speak up again (Garner, 2013). If discussions or comments are ignored, employees will quickly stop posting.

When a situation with employee dissent on ISM is treated constructively, other employees will notice how it has benefitted the organization as well as the dissenter. This is likely to develop into an organizational story that creates incentives for employees to voice their opinions (Madsen, 2020).

Emerging Technologies in Internal Communication

ISM competes with other technologies populating the internal communication, such as machine learning and artificial intelligence (AI), which are increasingly used to optimize and automate work processes and knowledge-sharing. Machine learning is a computational method that classifies phenomena and identifies underlying patterns through statistical analyses on large data-sets (Provost & Fawcett, 2013). Artificial intelligence is based on what a computer have learned about the users of different digital tools. Machine learning can give managers and communication departments insights into how employees use different digital tools and communication channels. Using these tools in combination with ISM can uncover the interest and relevance of different types of content, which can help shape digital services such as chat-bots that can answer questions from employees or personalize the intranet frontpage so that it fits the needs of the individual employee. Machine translation is used in multinational organizations to automatically translate documents and news into the users' language, which can facilitate interactions on ISM between employees of different nationalities. Furthermore, machine learning can help identify and find employees with certain skills based on their communication and interaction of ISM.

Virtual reality is also becoming a tool for training employees and helping them acquire certain skills, and this will no doubt have massive effect on internal communication. However, as the technostructure is new, little research has been done on the use of these technologies in internal communication and how they can be used in relation to ISM. Surely future research will emerge in parallel with the proliferation of these tools and platforms, which will explore their real-time use, how employees interact with and perceive of them, as well as assess their benefits and negatives in relation to internal communication.

Future Research and Implications

ISM is on track to become a major component of the internal communication mix, and as such it comes heralded by employee expectation that it will make for more authentic and transparent internal communication. Some organization have even begun to use external social media as their internal communication channel, blurring the lines between internal and external communication in an attempt to make the organization seem more transparent to their customers or with citizens in general. In this respect, ISM requires managers to rethink organizational communication, bringing to the fore fundamental issues about transparency, open communications, privacy, decision-making hierarchies, and feedback. Future research will have to explore the positives and negatives—as well as the unexpected consequences—of increasing transparency on ISM and external social media, whether it influences managerial practices, whether it makes internal communication clearer and more democratic, and whether it produces greater employee engagement.

Two Practitioner's Perspectives

Mini-Case

The Catfish Discussion: Listening to the Employees

Jyske Bank is the third-largest bank in Denmark with approximately 3500 full-time employees divided between 98 different locations. Their internal social media is integrated with the intranet, hosting a discussion forum called "The Word is Free". All the employees can start, comment on, or like a discussion. The bank uses a catfish as an organizational symbol, a symbol of the bank's difference between itself and other banks, which became the topic of a memorable exchange between employees concerning the Bank's organizational identity.

The discussion started with a long and well-formulated post entitled: "Is the Catfish dead?". A bank adviser argued that, though the bank promoted itself as a different kind of bank from its competitors, it was hard to see any substance to this claim. He explained at length, and with several examples, that the bank was not delivering a different experience to its customers. The post received 43 comments and 900 likes. The first eight comments supported the bank adviser. Some just wrote "agree" or "agree—well written", while a lower-middle manager from a different branch supported the spirit in the post and commented: "I hope it is not an impossible fight". Then, a top manager entered the scene and wrote:

> Good and well-formulated post [name of initiator of the post]. This deserves a serious comment also here from the board of directors. 'We are working on the case' it says when you press a link here on the intranet. Actually, we are working on many initiatives and considerations in relation to your post, but the question is which one of them we will pursue. To

find the answer to that is I guess called the 'strategy process' according to theory books. Management will return to the question in the near future, but until then, it would be nice to hear the opinions and viewpoints from the readers.

This encouraging comment sparked 30 comments that supported the initial post and added more examples of frustrations, problems, and suggestions for improvement. Then, another senior manager commented that while he did not agree with everything in the initial post, he appreciated that the bank adviser wanted to act as a spokesperson on behalf of his coworkers. The post was then praised for being valuable and an inspiration to management: "I believe that your post is exactly what the CEO has hoped for and will cherish". This was followed by the comments of three more employees and a comment from one of the journalists from the communication department, who announced that the next issue of the monthly internal TV-program would be completely dedicated to the issue. The discussion turned into an organizational story known as "the catfish-discussion".

Professional Interview

Creating an Internal Culture Where Debate Is Welcome

In 2013 Jyske Bank launched a social intranet with news, debate and videos called JB United. Lasse Høgfeldt, Head of Communications, reflected in an interview on what it takes to develop participatory communication on ISM.

We call it our internal culture of debate, and it is a cornerstone of our internal communication. We are an organization scattered around almost 100 different locations and we have about 3500 employees, and if we want to be a value-based organization then we need an open democratic debate.

Historically it started when our present CEO was elected by the board. He felt that it was really difficult to know what was happening in the organization. He therefore initiated a culture of debate and a bottom-up culture where we can bring issues we have to the CEO. Employees can comment on JB United, and we as a communication department are expected to critically focus on things that do not function well. It is the CEO's choice to do something about it or leave it alone. But he can never say that he did not know. We also have top down communication where we "make our CEO shine". That is the other part of our job, but it is still in the context of our culture of debate. When we make a TV-spot with the board of directors or the CEO, it is always meant to serve as a starting point for a debate.

We have worked in this culture of debate for more than 20 years. Management and especially top management must appreciate that employees bring topics, stories, facts and emotions up to the surface so that we have to deal with them. On a regular basis the CEO responds to posts from employees even if he does not agree with them, and that it extremely important. As an employee you really risk something when you utter an opinion, which is why, as a communication department, our job is to do everything we can to support the employees so that they do not feel alone in their criticism. In our internal TV-department we will follow up on the story and find more perspectives to present it, challenging the managers to answer. We turn it into a journalistic story. We might also interview the person that initiated a post to recognize his or her courage and demonstrate to the organization that it is appreciated. Our journalistic approach is however always constructive. We cover many different perspectives to find solutions, not to blame someone. Our task is to create a good working environment.

Our model is that we have taken the talk that takes place around the coffee machine, across the lunch table or over a beer on a Friday afternoon and now the talk is shared across the organization on JB United (our ISM) as a democratic deliberating process. It gives employees a good sense of what is going on in the organization and they feel that they are able to influence things when they have ideas.

References

Baptista, J., & Galliers, R. D. (2012). *Social media as a driver for new rhetorical practices in organisations*. In 45th Hawaii International Conference on System Science, IEEE Computer Society (pp. 3540–3549). https://doi.org/10.1109/HICSS.2012.537.

Cardon, P. W., & Marshall, B. (2015). The hype and reality of social media use for work collaboration and team communication. *International Journal of Business Communication, 52*(3), 273–293. https://doi.org/10.1177/2329488414525446.

Chin, C. P. Y., Evans, N., Choo, R. K. K., & Tan, F. B. (2015). *What influences employees to use enterprise social networks? A socio-technical perspective*. In PACIS 2015 Proceedings (p. 54).

Denyer, D., Parry, E., & Flowers, P. (2011). "Social", "Open" and "Participative"? Exploring personal experiences and organisational effects of enterprise2.0 use. *Long Range Planning, 44*(5), 375–396. https://doi.org/10.1016/j.lrp.2011.09.007.

Ellmer, M., & Reichel, A. (2020). Mind the channel! An affordance perspective on how digital voice channels encourage or discourage employee voice. *Human Resource Management Journal*. https://doi.org/10.1111/1748-8583.12297.

Ewing, M., Men, L. R., & O'Neil, J. (2019). Using social media to engage employees: Insights from internal communication managers. *International Journal of Strategic Communication, 13*(2), 110–132. https://doi.org/10.1080/1553118X.2019.1575830.

Falkheimer, J., & Heide, M. (2014). Strategic communication in participatory culture. In D. Holtzhausen & A. Zerfass (Eds.), *The Routledge handbook of strategic communication* (pp. 337–349). Routledge.

Frandsen, F., & Johansen, W. (2011). The study of internal crisis communication: Towards an integrative framework. *Corporate Communications: An International Journal, 16*(4), 347–361. https://doi.org/10.1108/13563281111186977.

Frandsen, F., & Johansen, W. (2017). *Organizational crisis communication: A multivocal approach*. Sage.

Fulk, J., & Yuan, Y. C. (2013). Location, motivation, and social capitalization via enterprise social networking. *Journal of Computer-Mediated Communication, 19*(1), 20–37. https://doi.org/10.1111/jcc4.12033.

Garner, J. T. (2013). Dissenters, managers, and coworkers: The process of co-constructing organizational dissent and dissent effectiveness. *Management Communication Quarterly, 27*(3), 373–395. https://doi.org/10.1177/0893318913488946.

Gode, H. E., Johansen, W., & Thomsen, C. (2019). Employee engagement in generating ideas on internal social media. *Corporate Communications: An International Journal*. https://doi.org/10.1108/CCIJ-03-2019-0024.

Grunig, J. E. (2009). Paradigms of global public relations in an age of digitalisation. *Prism, 6*(2), 1–19.

Grunig, J. E., & Hunt, T. T. (1984). *Managing public relation's*. Holt.

Heide, M. (2015). Social intranets and internal communication. In W. T. Coombs, J. Falkheimer, M. Heide, & P. Young (Eds.), *Strategic communication, social media and democracy: The challenge of the digital naturals* (pp. 45–53). Routledge.

Heron, A. R. (1942). *Sharing information with employee's*. Stanford University Press.

Huang, J., Baptista, J., & Galliers, R. D. (2013). Reconceptualizing rhetorical practices in organizations: The impact of social media on internal communications. *Information & Management, 50*(2), 112–124. https://doi.org/10.1016/j.im.2012.11.003.

Högberg, K., & Olsson, A. K. (2019). Framing organizational social media: A longitudinal study of a hotel chain. *Information Technology & Tourism, 21*(2), 209–236.

Koch, H., Gonzalez, E., & Leidner, D. (2012). Bridging the work/social divide: The emotional response to organizational social networking sites. *European Journal of Information Systems, 21*(6), 699–717.

Laitinen, K., & Sivunen, A. (2020). Enablers of and constraints on employees' information sharing on enterprise social media. *Information Technology & People*. https://doi.org/10.1108/ITP-04-2019-0186.

Leftheriotis, I., & Giannakos, M. N. (2014). Using social media for work: Losing your time or improving your work? *Computers in Human Behavior, 31*(2), 134–142. https://doi.org/10.1016/j.chb.2013.10.016.

Leonardi, P. M., Huysman, M., & Steinfield, C. (2013). Enterprise social media: Definition, history, and prospects for the study of social technologies in organizations. *Journal of Computer-Mediated Communication, 19*, 1–19. https://doi.org/10.1111/jcc4.12029.

Macnamara, J., & Zerfass, A. (2012). Social media communication in organizations: The challenges of balancing openness, strategy, and management. *International Journal of Strategic Communication, 6*(4), 287–308. https://doi.org/10.1080/1553118X.2012.711402.

Madsen, V. T. (2016). Constructing organizational identity on internal social media: A case study of coworker communication in Jyske Bank. *International Journal of Business Communication, 53*(2), 200–223. https://doi.org/10.1177/2329488415627272.

Madsen, V. T. (2017). The challenges of introducing internal social media—The coordinators' roles and perceptions. *Journal of Communication Management, 21*(1), 2–16. https://doi.org/10.1108/JCOM-04-2016-0027.

Madsen, V. T. (2018). Participatory communication on internal social media—A dream or reality? Findings from two exploratory studies of coworkers as communicators. *Corporate Communications: An International Journal, 23*(4), 614–628. https://doi.org/10.1108/CCIJ-04-2018-0039.

Madsen, V. T. (2020). Crossing hierarchies in organizations: Making sense of employee dissent and circumvention on internal social media. *Globe: A Journal of Language, Culture and Communication, 9*, 57–72.

Madsen, V. T. (2021). Communicative leadership on internal social media: A way to employee engagement? In *Advances in public relations and communication management* (pp. 93–114). Emerald Group Publishing.

Madsen, V. T., & Johansen, W. (2019). A spiral of voice? When employees speak up on internal social media. *Journal of Communication Management, 23*(4), 331–347. https://doi.org/10.1108/JCOM-03-2019-0050.

Madsen, V. T., & Verhoeven, J. W. (2016). Self-censorship on internal social media: A case study of coworker communication behavior in a Danish bank. *International Journal of Strategic Communication, 10*(5), 387–409. https://doi.org/10.1080/1553118X.2016.1220010.

Manuti, A. (2016). Communicating the "social" organization: Social media and organizational communication. In *The social organization: Managing human capital through social media* (pp. 14–27). Palgrave Macmillan.

Men, L. R., & Hung-Baesecke, C. J. F. (2015). Engaging employees in China: The impact of communication channels, organizational transparency, and authenticity. *Corporate Communications: An International Journal, 20*(4), 448–467. https://doi.org/10.1108/CCIJ-11-2014-0079.

Men, R. L., & Bowen, S. A. (2016). *Excellence in internal communication management*. New York, NY: Business Expert Press.

Men, L. R., O'Neil, J., & Ewing, M. (2020). Examining the effects of internal social media usage on employee engagement. *Public Relations Review, 46*(2). https://doi.org/10.1016/j.pubrev.2020.101880.

Morrison, E. W. (2014). Employee voice and silence. *Annual Review of Organizational Psychology and Organizational Behavior, 1*(1), 173–197. https://doi.org/10.1146/annurev-orgpsych-031413-091328.

Parry, E., & Solidoro, A. (2013). Social media as a mechanism for engagement? In T. Bondarouk & M. R. Olivas-Lujan (Eds.), *Social media in human resources management* (Vol. 12, pp. 121–141). Emerald Group Publishing.

Pekkala, K. (2020). Managing the communicative organization: A qualitative analysis of knowledge-intensive companies. *Corporate Communications: An International Journal, 25*(3), 551–571. https://doi.org/10.1108/CCIJ-02-2020-0040.

Provost, F., & Fawcett, T. (2013). *Data science for business: What you need to know about data mining and data-analytic thinking*. O'Reilly Media.

Redding, W. C. (1972). *Communication within the organization: An interpretive review of theory and research*. Industrial Communication Council.

Rice, R. E., Evans, S. K., Pearce, K. E., Sivunen, A., Vitak, J., & Treem, J. W. (2017). Organizational media affordances: Operationalization and associations with media use. *Journal of Communication, 67*(1), 106–130. https://doi.org/10.1111/jcom.12273.

Ruck, M. K. (Ed.). (2015). *Exploring internal communication: Towards informed employee voice*. Gower Publishing.

Sievert, H., & Scholz, C. (2017). Engaging employees in (at least partly) disengaged companies. Results of an interview survey within about 500 German corporations on the growing importance of digital engagement via internal social media. *Public Relations Review, 43*(5), 894–903. https://doi.org/10.1016/j.pubrev.2017.06.001.

Treem, J. W., & Leonardi, P. M. (2012). Social media use in organizations: Exploring the affordances of visibility, editability, persistence, and association. In *Communication yearbook* (Vol. 36, pp. 143–189). Routledge.

Treem, J. W., Leonardi, P. M., & van den Hooff, B. (2020). Computer-mediated communication in the age of communication visibility. *Journal of Computer-Mediated Communication, 25*(1), 44–59. https://doi.org/10.1093/jcmc/zmz024.

Trimi, S., & Galanxhi, H. (2014). The impact of enterprise 2.0 in organizations. *Service Business, 8*(3), 405–424.

Uysal, N. (2016). Social collaboration in intranets the impact of social exchange and group norms on internal communication. *International Journal of Business Communication, 53*(2), 181–199.

van Zoonen, W., & Sivunen, A. (2020). Knowledge brokering in an era of communication visibility. *International Journal of Business Communication*. https://doi.org/10.1177/2329488420937348.

Verčič, A. T., & Špoljarić, A. (2020). Managing internal communication: How the choice of channels affects internal communication satisfaction. *Public Relations Review, 46*(3). https://doi.org/10.1016/j.pubrev.2020.101926.

Vuori, V., & Okkonen, J. (2012). Knowledge sharing motivational factors of using an intra-organizational social media platform. *Journal of Knowledge Management, 16*(4), 592–603. https://doi.org/10.1108/13673271211246167.

Welch, M. (2012). Appropriateness and acceptability: Employee perspectives of internal communication. *Public Relations Review, 38*(2), 246–254. https://doi.org/10.1016/j.pubrev.2011.12.017.

CHAPTER 5

Employee Advocates: Unlocking Their Power Through Internal Communication

Patrick D. Thelen

Scholars will frequently refer to employees as one of the most important publics for organizations (Grunig et al., 2002; Kang & Sung, 2017). In addition to their productive role, "employees are becoming the ultimate reputation makers or breakers in a world where every organization sells experiences rather than products and where the truth is more accessible and shareable than ever—particularly by those on the 'inside'" (Frank, 2015, p. 144). The in-depth knowledge they have of their organizations makes them credible sources of information for many publics, including customers (Dortok, 2006; Shinnar et al., 2004). Given employees' strong reputational role, the communication and business community are increasingly paying attention to a concept that has rapidly become a buzzword: employee advocacy.

Despite the interest generated by employee advocacy among communications and marketing practitioners, it remains an understudied topic

P. D. Thelen (✉)
San Diego State University, San Diego, CA, USA
e-mail: pthelen@sdsu.edu

L. R. Men and A. Tkalac Verčič (eds.), *Current Trends and Issues in Internal Communication*, New Perspectives in Organizational Communication, https://doi.org/10.1007/978-3-030-78213-9_5

in the public relations literature (Men, 2014). However, previous studies have begun to shed light on this research area (e.g., Lee & Kim, 2020; Men, 2014; Thelen, 2018, 2020; Walden & Kingsley Westerman, 2018). The impact that employees can have on an organization's reputation and relationship with external publics when they use their personal networks to promote their organizations has been recognized by scholars (Kim & Rhee, 2011; Men & Stacks, 2013). This understanding has led to the growing awareness of the necessity to develop strategies that can manage and guide employees' advocacy behaviors (e.g., Lee & Kim, 2020; Thelen, 2020; Walden & Kingsley Westerman, 2018). Drawing from this scholarship, this chapter seeks to answer the following four questions: (1) What is employee advocacy? (2) Why are employee advocacy behaviors important for organizations? (3) What factors drive employee advocacy? (4) How does strategic internal communication influence employee advocacy?

Defining Employee Advocacy

Although the literature on employee advocacy is scarce, there currently exist several definitions. Some have defined advocacy as "employees' willingness to act as 'part-time marketers' of the organization to both potential customers and potential employees" (Schweitzer & Lyons, 2008, p. 563). Similarly, Božac and colleagues have argued that advocacy refers to "the promotion of an organization by its employees, where the workforce acts as the voice of the company" (2017, p. 25). Advocacy is also understood as a boundary-spanning employee outcome that can help spread goodwill with external publics (Vlachos et al., 2017). What unites these definitions is that they view advocacy as a positive word-of-mouth behavior in which employees support their organizations to external publics by, for example, recommending their products and services or highlighting the work environment (Bettencourt & Brown, 2003; Schweitzer & Lyons, 2008; Tsarenko et al., 2018).

Other scholars have argued that in addition to positive word-of-mouth, employee advocacy also entails defending an organization from criticism (Men, 2014; Walden & Kingsley Westerman, 2018). As noted by Madsen and Verhoeven (2019), employees embody, promote, and defend their organizations externally. Employers are increasingly needing employees who can support them by defending their position when they are under scrutiny (Weber Shandwick, 2014). In other words, scholars who view employee advocacy as more than positive word-of-mouth, define this behavior as a "voluntary promotion or defense of a company, its products, or its brands by an employee externally" (Men, 2014, p. 262).

Despite these differences, most of the literature has consistently defined employee advocacy as a verbal behavior directed toward external publics. However, a recent study incorporated two additional elements to our understanding of employee advocacy (Thelen, 2020). First, it suggested that advocacy can also be expressed nonverbally. Two common nonverbal advocacy behaviors include using company swag (e.g., shirts, keychains) and volunteering in community relations activities. Second, the study highlighted that employee advocacy behaviors could also take place within an organization. In other words, advocacy behaviors can be directed to external publics (e.g., family, friends, and acquaintances) and internal audiences (e.g., other employees). As these two elements broaden the influence and scope of advocacy behaviors, the following definition was proposed: "Employee advocacy is a verbal (written and spoken) or nonverbal voluntary manifestation of support, recommendation, or defense of an organization or its products by an employee to either internal or external publics" (Thelen, 2020 p. 8).

The Importance of Employee Advocacy

When employees advocate and transmit an aspired brand image to diverse publics, they help organizations drive brand awareness. A survey conducted by Trapit, a company that enables social media content sharing by employees, found that 43% of employees state that their sharing helps increase their company's brand awareness (Springer, 2015). Employees' interactions with external publics can positively impact public relations outcomes such as reputation and organization-public relationships (Kim & Rhee, 2011).

Building high-quality relationships with employees who encourage behavioral outcomes such as employee advocacy contributes to organizational effectiveness and provides monetary value to the organization (Grunig et al., 2002). Scholars have argued that, for example, positive word-of-mouth impacts an organization's success and influences its growth and revenue (e.g., Godes & Mayzlin, 2004; Gremler et al., 2001). When employees are genuinely excited about their employer's products and service, they will be more likely to speak about them enthusiastically. As employees know the products of their organizations better than anyone else, they are in an ideal position to influence sales and growth. According to a study conducted by Hinge Research Institute and Social Media Today (2015), nearly two-thirds (64%) of organizations with formal employee advocacy programs in place state that they have helped them attract and develop new business (Frederiksen, 2015). At the same time, research has shown that when organizations acquire customers through employee endorsements, both the contribution margins and retention rates are higher (Schmitt et al., 2011; Villanueva et al., 2008). Given this reality, it is not surprising that empowering and motivating employees to engage in this behavior reinforces an organization's financial performance (Miles et al., 2011).

In addition to acquiring customers, employee advocacy positively impacts human capital in several ways. First, it helps organizations recruit suitable employees and attract highly skilled human capital (Cervellon & Lirio, 2017; Collins & Stevens, 2002). A study conducted by Wilden and colleagues (2010) found that prospective employees seek credible employer information through personal relationships and consider employee referrals as the most credible sources of information. Hence, having employees who are willing to act as brand ambassadors will help organizations share relevant brand messages to job seekers (Wilden et al., 2010). Second, advocacy also influences employee retention and engagement. Organizations with successful employee advocacy programs are not only 58% more likely to attract talent but also 20% more likely to retain employees (Levinson, 2018). Regarding engagement, research shows that employees feel more connected and enthusiastic about their organizations after sharing work-related content (Altimeter, 2016).

Finally, employees have the power to shape an organization's reputation when they describe their experiences within a company in a way that humanizes the brand and builds goodwill. When employees say positive things about their organization or volunteer on behalf of the organization they are building favorable perceptions and goodwill among community members that can have a positive effect when facing issues and even crises (Thelen, 2020).

Drivers of Employee Advocacy

Drivers of employee advocacy can be separated into three basic categories: individual, group, and organizational. Individual factors focus on individual differences in employees and are person-specific. Group factors are concerned with variables such as role, status, norms, and cohesiveness within groups of two or more individuals working for a particular objective. Finally, organizational factors are concerned with the structure and working culture of an organization.

Individual factors: Regarding individual factors, research has suggested that attitudes such as job satisfaction, organizational identification, and organizational commitment play an important role in driving employee advocacy (Thelen & Men, 2020). Committed employees feel identified, involved, and psychologically attached to their organizations and are willing to contribute to the organization's wellbeing by giving something of themselves (O'Reilly & Chatman, 1986; Tsarenko et al., 2018). Although in-role performance (i.e., those activities relevant to employees' formal job assignment) can be considered an antecedent of employees' commitment and satisfaction toward their organizations, extra-role performance (i.e., activities that aid the organization but are not explicitly required of employees) is expected to be a consequence of these attitudes (MacKenzie et al., 1998; O'Reilly & Chatman, 1986). Similarly, employees will engage in brand-building behaviors when they trust their organization (Punjaisri et al., 2013).

Feeling organizational pride and person-organization fit are two additional individual factors that can lead to employee advocacy behaviors (Thelen & Men, 2020). Working for successful companies or organizations with a meaningful purpose contributes to developing a sense of pride among employees. Finally, an individual's personality and whether or not they perceive advocacy as a means to some end (e.g., boosting their personal brand) may also play an important role in driving advocacy behaviors (Thelen & Men, 2020). Employees that desire positive recognition and are eager to promote themselves and their traits, may see online employee advocacy as an opportunity to share their organizational identities (e.g., Fieseler et al., 2015; Marwick & Boyd, 2011; van Zoonen et al., 2018). Having said this, it is important to note that a study conducted by Lee and Kim (2020) found that self-enhancement had no significant effect on an employee's willingness to advocate on behalf of their organization on social media. On the other hand, altruistic (i.e., helping the organization) and hedonic (i.e., enjoyment) motives increase advocacy intentions among employees (Lee & Kim, 2020).

Group-level factors: Group factors are a second broad area that can encourage advocacy behaviors. Among group factors, leader-member relationships, which refer to the degree of confidence, trust, and respect that subordinates have in their leader, can play a significant role in predicting advocacy behaviors (Thelen & Men, 2020). When leaders and supervisors exhibit a transformational style of leadership by, for example, acting as a coach and mentor, living the organization's brand values, expressing a unifying brand vision, and allowing employees to individually determine the role of a brand representative, they enable employees' motivation and increase their commitment, authenticity, and proactivity, which are referred to as the core characteristics of a brand advocate (Morhart et al., 2011). However, it is important to clarify that while scholars believe that the transformational approach is more effective in enhancing advocacy behavior than transactional leadership (MacKenzie et al., 2001; Morhart et al., 2009), research also suggests that leaders should not completely refrain from transactional leadership (Morhart et al., 2009, 2011).

A study conducted by Morhart et al. (2011) suggested that the best way to increase employee advocacy is by exhibiting a combination of a high level of transformational and a moderate level of transactional leadership behavior. Servant leadership, which has been described as a more people-centered and ethical theory of leadership (Clegg et al., 2007), has also been found to have a positive relationship with employee advocacy (Thelen, 2019). Finally, group cohesion is another factor that can play a role in advocacy behaviors (Thelen & Men, 2020). In other words, when group members support and validate one another while at work, they are more likely to advocate for the organization.

Organizational-level factors: Organizational factors also play a relevant role in generating advocacy behaviors. Among these organizational factors, top management and the culture of an organization are additional factors that can impact employees' willingness to advocate on behalf of their organizations (Thelen & Men, 2020). Additionally, internal communication and communication management (i.e., the way an organization communicates with its employees) can also influence advocacy behaviors.

Researchers have found that there is a positive relationship between internal branding and employee-related outcomes such as commitment (King & Grace, 2008) brand identification, loyalty (Punjaisri & Wilson, 2011), person-organization fit, and intention to stay (Matanda & Ndubisi, 2013). By educating employees on the organization's business proposition and brand values through communication and focusing on ensuring that employees adopt and deliver the brand promise to external publics (Foster et al., 2010), internal branding increases the likelihood that employees will advocate on behalf of the organization (Löhndorf & Diamantopoulos, 2014). Similarly, research has found a positive relationship between an employee's internal brand knowledge and their propensity to endorse their organization (Morokane et al., 2016). The formal and informal messages that employees receive from their organizations and internal communication teams increase employees' level of internal brand knowledge. These messages also help construct the psychological contract, defined as the perceptual, and often tacit, implicit, and subjective agreement of the exchange relationships that employees establish with their organizations (Conway & Briner, 2005; Mangold & Miles, 2007). Researchers have found that perceived psychological contract violations decrease employees' levels of trust, satisfaction, and commitment toward their organizations (e.g., Morrison & Robinson, 1997; Robinson & Morrison, 1995; Rousseau, 1995), and can therefore have an indirect negative effect on employee advocacy.

Strategic Internal Communication and Employee Advocacy

Research has shown that internal communication can help generate positive employee attitudes such as trust (Jo & Shim, 2005), job satisfaction (Gray & Laidlaw, 2004), and organizational identification (Smidts et al., 2001). These attitudes lead to outcomes such as favorable employee communication behavior (Kang & Sung, 2017; Kim & Rhee, 2011), higher productivity, and improved performance (Berger, 2008). A study conducted by Kim (2018) found that internal communication may increase organizational social capital and the likelihood that employees will have strong interpersonal relationships and share organizational information.

An exploratory study conducted by Thelen and Men (2020) looked at the role that internal communication plays in employee advocacy and what internal communicators should focus on to encourage this behavior. The results indicated that the factors could be separated into two layers: corporate communication strategies (macro-level) and employee advocacy management factors (micro-level). A visual display of the role played by internal communication in employee advocacy is found in Fig. 5.1.

Corporate communication strategies: The corporate communication strategies were separated into four categories. The first of these categories is *openness and transparency*. Public relations scholars have examined the

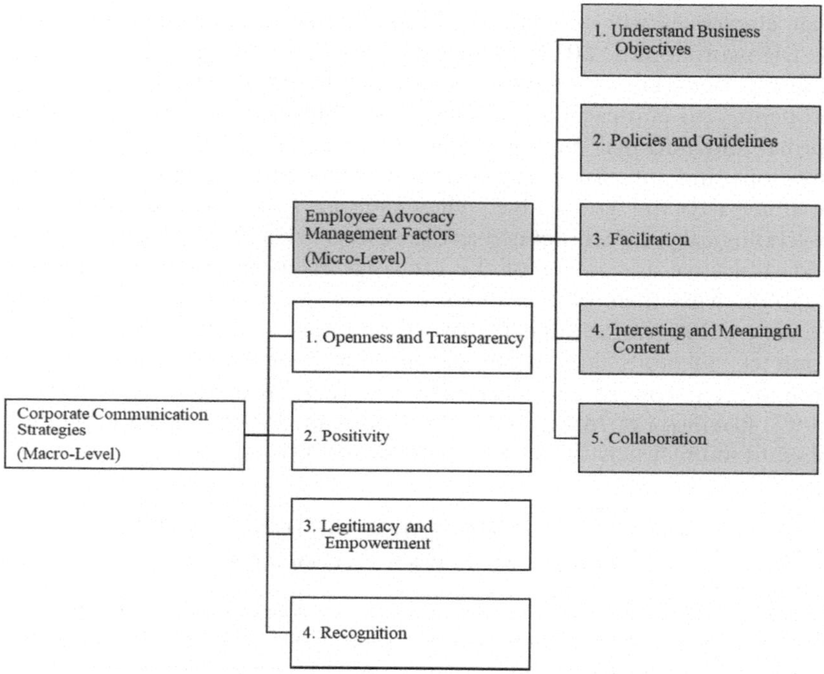

Fig. 5.1 Internal communication and employee advocacy behaviors

relationship that transparent communication (Rawlins, 2008, 2009)—an organization's intentional distribution of information that is truthful, substantial, and complete (Men & Bowen, 2017)—has with employee outcomes. As a result of these studies, a positive relationship between transparent communication and outcomes such as engagement (Jiang & Men, 2017) and EORs (Men & Stacks, 2014) has been established. J. E. Grunig (1992) proposed that symmetrical communication, which emphasizes "trust, credibility, openness, relationships, reciprocity, network symmetry, horizontal communication, feedback, adequacy of information, employee-centered style, tolerance for disagreement, and negotiation" (Grunig, 1992, p. 558), is one of the key components of an excellent internal communications program. He also suggested that excellent employee communications could lead to high-quality relationships with employees and supportive employee behaviors toward their employers (Grunig, 2001). Several studies have confirmed that an organization that communicates symmetrically with employees by emphasizing aspects such as openness, will be more likely to develop high-quality relationships with employees that can lead them to speak positively about their organizations (e.g., Kang & Sung, 2017; Kim & Rhee, 2011). The second category is *positivity*. In addition to being open and transparent, internal communicators should not forget to emphasize all of the positive things that are happening within an organization. This idea is related to the concept of positivity, which was conceptualized by Hon and Grunig (1999) as "anything the organization or publics do to make the relationship more enjoyable for the parties involved" (p. 14). By promoting the positive things occurring within an organization, employees may feel more proud of where they work, and as a result, more vocal about their place of work (Thelen & Men, 2020).

Legitimacy and empowerment is a third environmental category that was highly emphasized in Thelen and Men's study (2020). In other words, internal communicators need to focus on legitimizing employees' concerns by giving them a voice, listening to their needs, and asking for their feedback. Regarding empowerment, internal communicators need to facilitate the development of opportunities for employees to assume responsibilities in driving the conditions and experiences they desire in the workplace. These insights are aligned with research suggesting that the more opportunities employees are provided to get involved in decision-making processes, the more satisfied they will feel toward the work itself (Niehoff et al., 1990). By empowering employees and making them feel that they work in an inclusive environment where everyone has a voice, they will be more likely to advocate for the organization (Thelen & Men, 2020). The fourth environmental factor mentioned by the study is the importance of *recognition*, and the role that internal communication can play in developing a culture that acknowledges and appreciates the behaviors of employees in an organization (Nelson, 2005). As employee recognition has the potential to increase employee engagement and satisfaction (Gostick & Elton, 2007), it seems plausible that it can also be connected with employee advocacy behaviors.

Employee advocacy management factors: The micro-level employee advocacy management strategies were separated into five categories (Thelen & Men, 2020). The first category concerns *understanding the business strategy*. Internal communicators need to be focused on the drivers and objectives that are most important to an organization at a particular point in time. In addition to understanding the business objectives, the second category refers to ***developing or updating social media policies and guidelines*** and taking the time to educate employees on employee advocacy. The third category is ***facilitation.*** In other words, the organization needs to make sure that they are making it easy for employees to share and communicate (Cervellon & Lirio, 2017). As noted by Frank (2015), "we need to make the tools and channels simple and available, if we are to turn engaged employees into regular, active advocates" (p. 145). Given today's digital world, scholars have researched the best ways to encourage employee advocacy on social media. As many employees lack confidence in their social media competence and have developed psychological barriers toward engaging on social media, Cervellon and Lirio (2017) recommend encouraging digital natives to take the initiative and help their peers increase their proficiency in social media. In other words, peer-to-peer communication can play a role in increasing advocacy behavior.

The fourth category refers to the importance of ***creating interesting and meaningful content.*** If employees are to advocate on behalf of the organization, the organization needs to generate compelling, relatable, inspiring, or emotional stories that they will be excited to share (Cervellon & Lirio, 2017; Springer, 2015). A study conducted by Altimeter (2016) found that job postings, daily workplace life (e.g., office pictures), company accomplishments/news, community involvement, and product information are the five most popular types of content that employees share about their work-life through social channels. Finally, the fifth category emphasizes that internal communicators should ***collaborate and build synergistic relationships with other departments***, such as external communications and human resources. This will help them develop new opportunities for employee advocacy.

Conclusion

As employee advocacy is becoming such a relevant topic among organizations, additional empirical and theoretical research on this topic is necessary. This chapter examined the definition of employee advocacy, its importance, the drivers of this behavior, and the role that internal communication plays in influencing advocacy. Overall, this chapter suggests that employee advocacy is an extended behavioral outcome of internal communication. Employees will not genuinely and voluntarily praise, recommend, and defend their organization out of thin air. These behaviors are the result of a reputable organization that is engaging and building high-quality relationships with its employees via strategic internal communication.

Prior to the existence of social media, it would have been practically impossible to reward an employee's advocacy behavior. However, social media has given employers the opportunity to track what their employees are saying online (Altimeter Group, 2015). Several businesses offering employee advocacy programs are currently recommending companies to tangibly and intangibly reward employee advocates through monetary rewards (e.g., Amazon vouchers, movie tickets), learning opportunities (e.g., seminars and training programs), fun and wellness activities (e.g., hosting an off-site event), or employee recognition (e.g., congratulating employees) (Green, 2017). Hence, while offline, face-to-face advocacy seems harder to reward, some organizations are currently rewarding online advocacy. This situation presents a dilemma that requires further investigation: Should organizations reward employees for engaging in advocacy behaviors? Does it depend on the type of reward? Future research should answer these important questions, which may help practitioners implement successful employee advocacy programs.

Interview with Ethan McCarty (CEO, Integral Communications Group)

What should internal communicators focus on to encourage advocacy behaviors?

I typically shy away from the word "internal"—so let's say employee communications professionals. As a profession, we should focus on business strategy. Launching employee advocacy software is not going to help unless you're going to use it in a way that serves the business strategy. Communicators will often describe themselves as the storytellers of their organizations. There's nothing wrong with telling great stories; however, our role needs to go beyond that. We can start by asking ourselves: how will our programs change employees' behaviors, roll back into the business strategy, and enhance business outcomes?

What steps should organizations take when they begin to develop an employee advocacy program?

The first impulse that I typically see among organizations is to immediately start shopping for advocacy software as a tool to increase the number of employees sharing company news. That's the wrong approach. The most valuable first step will be listening. When communications teams read or listen to what their employees are saying online, they can gather relevant insights. For example, it can be very telling to see what employees do on LinkedIn. Do they have complete profiles? Do they follow your company's page? Did anyone comment or share anything? Companies can also look at what their competitors do in this same regard. The second step is to look at the company's social media policy and see if it needs revision. And finally, as I mentioned previously, the communication strategy needs to align with the business strategy. Why develop this employee advocacy program? Organizations generally promote employee advocacy to achieve one or more of three things: (1) to better sell or market the company, (2) to recruit and retain talent, and (3) to successfully address issues management. In other words, the advocacy program needs to align with the current needs of the organization.

What's your position on rewarding employees for engaging in advocacy behaviors?

If you create short-term incentives, you'll get short-term behaviors. For example, if a company gives out an iPad, they will definitely get employees to advocate on their behalf. But the minute they stop the incentive, they'll see the behaviors also come to an end. The more durable programs I've worked on with clients will have an intrinsic reward system. When I worked at Bloomberg, our company would reward employees for doing volunteer work through matched giving. If you did volunteer work for a certain number of hours each year, the company would write a check to the nonprofit of your choice. We also linked our social media advocacy program with that same idea. If you shared content about Bloomberg's philanthropic efforts and innovation programs, you could earn money for a charity of your choice by engaging in these social media activities. Finally, I think it's important to add that as a consultant, I would never advise an organization to set up any kind of advocacy program with a monetary reward without disclosure.

References

Altimeter. (2015, July 28). *The 2015 state of social business: Priorities shift from scaling to integrating*. Retrieved from http://mindersgroup.net/wp-content/uploads/2015/12/B14-The-2015-State-of-Social-Business-Priorities-Shift-From-Scaling-to-Integrating.pdf.

Altimeter. (2016, March 15). *Social media employee advocacy: Tapping into the power of an engaged social workforce*. https://www.prophet.com/2016/03/social-media-employee-advocacy-tapping-into-the-power-of-an-engaged-social-workforce/.

Berger, B. (2008, November 17). *Employee/organizational communications* [Web log post]. http://www.instituteforpr.org/topics/employee-organizational-communications/.

Bettencourt, L. A., & Brown, S. W. (2003). Role stressors and customer-oriented boundary-spanning behaviors in service organizations. *Journal of the Academy of Marketing Science, 31*(4), 394–408. https://doi.org/10.1177/0092070303255636.

Božac, M. G., Sušanj, Z., & Agušaj, B. (2017). Attitudinal and behavioral outcomes of P-O fit and work engagement in hotel staff. *Organizational Cultures: An International Journal, 17*(1), 21–38.

Cervellon, M., & Lirio, P. (2017). When employees don't 'like' their employers on social media. *MIT Sloan Management Review, 58*(2), 63–70.

Clegg, S., Kornberger, M., & Rhodes, C. (2007). Business ethics as practice. *British Journal of Management, 18*(2), 107–122. https://doi.org/10.1111/j.1467-8551.2006.00493.x.

Collins, C. J., & Stevens, C. K. (2002). The relationship between early recruitment-related activities and the application decisions of new labor-market entrants: A brand equity approach to recruitment. *Journal of Applied Psychology, 87*(6), 1121–1133. https://doi.org/10.1037//0021-9010.87.6.1121.

Conway, N., & Briner, R. B. (2005). *Understanding psychological contracts at work: A critical evaluation of theory and research*. Oxford University Press.

Dortok, A. (2006). A managerial look at the interaction between internal communication and corporate reputation. *Corporate Reputation Review, 8*, 322–338.

Fieseler, C., Meckel, M., & Ranzini, G. (2015). Professional personae: How organizationalidentification shapes online identity in the workplace. *Journal of Computer-Mediated Communication, 20*(2), 153–170.

Foster, C., Punjaisri, K., & Cheng, R. (2010). Exploring the relationship between corporate, internal and employer branding. *Journal of Product & Brand Management, 19*(6), 401–409. https://doi.org/10.1108/10610421011085712.

Frank, J. (2015). From engagement to empowerment—Employee advocacy in the social economy. *Strategic HR Review, 14*(4), 144–145. https://doi.org/10.1108/SHR-06-2015-0047.

Frederiksen, L. (2015, November 5). *Research shows firms with employee advocacy programs grow faster* [Web log post]. https://hingemarketing.com/blog/story/research-shows-firms-with-employee-advocacy-programs-grow-faster.

Godes, D., & Mayzlin, D. (2004). Using online conversations to study word-of-mouth communication. *Marketing Science, 23*(4), 545–560. https://doi.org/10.1287/mksc.1040.0071.

Gostick, A., & Elton, C. (2007). *The daily carrot principle: 365 ways to enhance your career and life*. Simon & Schuster.

Gray, J., & Laidlaw, H. (2004). Improving the measurement of communication satisfaction. *Management Communication Quarterly, 17*(3), 425–448. https://doi.org/10.1177/0893318903257980.

Green, B. (2017, May 16). *4 strategies to incentivize your employee advocates* [Web log post]. Retrieved from https://www.oktopost.com/blog/4-strategies-incentivize-employee-advocates/.

Gremler, D. D., Gwinner, K. P., & Brown, S. W. (2001). Generating positive word-of-mouth communication through customer–employee relationships. *International Journal of Service Industry Management, 12*(1), 41–59.

Grunig, J. E. (1992). Communication, public relations, and effective organizations: An overview of the book. In J. E. Grunig (Ed.), *Excellent public relations and communication management* (pp. 1–30). Lawrence Erlbaum Associates.

Grunig, J. E. (2001). Two-way symmetrical public relations: Past, present, and future. In R. L. Heath (Ed.), *Handbook of public relations* (pp. 11–32). Sage.

Grunig, L. A., Grunig, J. E., & Dozier, D. M. (2002). *Excellent public relations and effective organizations: A study of communication management in three countries*. Lawrence Erlbaum Associates.

Hinge Research Institute and Social Media Today. (2015). *Understanding employee advocacy on social media*. https://hingemarketing.com/uploads/hinge-research-employee-advocacy.pdf.

Hon, L. G., & Grunig, J. E. (1999). *Guidelines for measuring relationships in public relations*. The Institute for Public Relations.

Jiang, H., & Men, R. L. (2017). Creating an engaged workforce. *Communication Research, 44*(2), 225–243. https://doi.org/10.1177/0093650215613137.

Jo, S., & Shim, S. (2005). Paradigm shift of employee communication: The effect of management communication on trusting relationships. *Public Relations Review, 31*(2), 277–280. https://doi.org/10.1016/j.pubrev.2005.02.012.

Kang, M., & Sung, M. (2017). How symmetrical employee communication leads to employee engagement and positive employee communication behaviors.

Journal of Communication Management, 21(1), 82–102. https://doi.org/10.1108/JCOM-04-2016-0026.

Kim, D. (2018). Examining effects of internal public relations practices on organizational social capital in the Korean context; Mediating roles of employee-organization relationships. *Corporate Communications: An International Journal, 21*(1), 100–116. https://doi.org/10.1108/CCIJ-01-2017-0002.

Kim, J., & Rhee, Y. (2011). Strategic thinking about employee communication behavior (ECB) in public relations: Testing the models of megaphoning and scouting effects in Korea. *Journal of Public Relations Research, 23*(3), 243–268. https://doi.org/10.1080/1062726X.2011.582204.

King, C., & Grace, D. (2008). Internal branding: Exploring the employee's perspective. *Journal of Brand Management, 15*(5), 358–372. https://doi.org/10.1057/palgrave.bm.2007.48.

Lee, Y., & Kim, K. H. (2020). Enhancing employee advocacy on social media: the value of internal relationship management approach. *Corporate Communications: An International Journal*. https://doi.org/10.1108/CCIJ-05-2020-0088.

Levinson, K. (2018, March 13). *What is employee advocacy and how do marketers win with it?* [Web log post]. https://business.linkedin.com/marketing-solutions/blog/linkedin-elevate/2017/what-is-employee-advocacy--what-is-it-for--why-does-it-matter-.

Löhndorf, B., & Diamantopoulos, A. (2014). Internal branding: Social identity and social exchange perspectives on turning employees into brand champions. *Journal of Service Research, 17*(3), 310–325. https://doi.org/10.1177/1094670514522098.

MacKenzie, S. B., Podsakoff, P. M., & Ahearne, M. (1998). Some possible antecedents and consequences of in-role and extra-role salesperson performance. *Journal of Marketing, 62*(3), 87–98. https://doi.org/10.2307/1251745.

Mackenzie, S. B., Podsakoff, P. M., & Rich, G. A. (2001). Transformational and transactional leadership and salesperson performance. *Journal of the Academy of Marketing Science, 29*(2), 115–134. https://doi.org/10.1177/03079459994506.

Madsen, V. T., & Verhoeven, J. W. M. (2019). The big idea of employees as strategic communicators in public relation. In *Big ideas in public relations research and practice (advances in public relations and communication management, Vol. 4)* (pp. 143–162). Emerald Publishing Limited. https://doi.org/10.1108/S2398-391420190000004011.

Mangold, W. G., & Miles, S. J. (2007). The employee brand: Is yours an all-star? *Business Horizons, 50*(5), 423–433. https://doi.org/10.1016/j.bushor.2007.06.001.

Marwick, A. E., & Boyd, D. (2011). I tweet honestly, I tweet passionately: Twitter users, context collapse, and the imagined audience. *New Media and Society, 13*(1), 114–133.

Matanda, M. J., & Ndubisi, N. O. (2013). Internal marketing, internal branding, and organisational outcomes: The moderating role of perceived goal congruence. *Journal of Marketing Management, 29*(9/10), 1030–1055. https://doi.org/10.1080/0267257X.2013.800902.

Men, L. R. (2014). Why leadership matters to internal communication: Linking transformational leadership, symmetrical communication, and employee outcomes. *Journal of Public Relations Research, 26*(3), 256–279. https://doi.org/10.1080/1062726X.2014.908719.

Men, L. R., & Bowen, S. A. (2017). *Excellence in internal communication management*. Business Expert Press.

Men, L. R., & Stacks, D. W. (2013). The impact of leadership style and employee empowerment on perceived organizational reputation. *Journal of Communication Management, 17*(2), 171–192. https://doi.org/10.1108/13632541311318765.

Men, L. R., & Stacks, D. (2014). The effects of authentic leadership on strategic internal communication and employee-organization relationships. *Journal of Public Relations Research, 26*(4), 301–324. https://doi.org/10.1080/1062726X.2014.908720.

Miles, S. J., Mangold, W. G., Asree, S., & Revell, J. (2011). Assessing the employee brand: A census of one company. *Journal of Managerial Issues, 23*(4), 491–507.

Morhart, F. M., Herzog, W., & Tomczak, T. (2009). Brand-specific leadership: Turning employees into brand champions. *Journal of Marketing, 73*(5), 122–142. https://doi.org/10.1509/jmkg.73.5.122.

Morhart, F. M., Herzog, W., & Tomczak, T. (2011). Turning employees into brand champions: Leadership style makes a difference. *Gfk-Marketing Intelligence Review, 3*(2), 35–43. https://doi.org/10.2478/gfkmir-2014-0088.

Morokane, P., Chiba, M., & Kleyn, N. (2016). Drivers of employee propensity to endorse their corporate brand. *Journal of Brand Management, 23*(1), 55–66. https://doi.org/10.1057/bm.2015.47.

Morrison, E. W., & Robinson, S. L. (1997). When employees feel betrayed: A model of how psychological contract violation develops. *Academy of Management Review, 22*(1), 226–256. https://doi.org/10.5465/AMR.1997.9707180265.

Nelson B. (2005). *1001 Ways to reward employees* (2nd ed.). Workman Publishing.

Niehoff, B. P., Enz, C. A., & Grover, R. A. (1990). The impact of top management actions on employee attitudes and perception. *Group & Organization Studies, 14*(3), 337–352. https://doi.org/10.1177/105960119001500307.

O'Reilly, C., & Chatman, J. (1986). Organizational commitment and psychological attachment: The effects of compliance, identification, and internalization on prosocial behavior. *Journal of Applied Psychology, 71*(3), 492–499. https://doi.org/10.1037/0021-9010.71.3.492.

Punjaisri, K., Evanschitzky, H., & Rudd, J. (2013). Aligning employee service recovery performance with brand values: The role of brand-specific leadership. *Journal of Marketing Management, 29*(9–10), 981–1006. https://doi.org/10.1080/0267257X.2013.803144.

Punjaisri, K., & Wilson, A. (2011). Internal branding process: Key mechanisms, outcomes and moderating factors. *European Journal of Marketing, 45*(9/10), 1521–1537. https://doi.org/10.1108/03090561111151871.

Rawlins, B. (2008). Measuring the relationship between organizational transparency and employee trust. *Public Relations Journal, 2*(2), 1–21.

Rawlins, B. (2009). Give the emperor a mirror: Toward developing a stakeholder measurement of organizational transparency. *Journal of Public Relations Research, 21*(1), 71–99. https://doi.org/10.1080/10627260802153421.

Robinson, S. L., & Morrison, E. W. (1995). Psychological contracts and OCB: The effect of unfulfilled obligations on civic virtue behavior. *Journal of Organizational Behavior, 16*(3), 289–298. https://doi.org/10.1002/job.4030160309.

Rousseau, D. M. (1995). *Psychological contracts in organizations: Understanding written and unwritten agreements*. Sage.

Schmitt, P., Skiera, B., & Van den Bulte, C. (2011). Referral programs and customer value. *Journal of Marketing, 75*(1), 46–59. https://doi.org/10.1509/jmkg.75.1.46.

Schweitzer, L., & Lyons, S. (2008). The market within: A marketing approach to creating and developing high-value employment relationships. *Business Horizons, 51*(6), 555–565. https://doi.org/10.1016/j.bushor.2008.03.00.

Shinnar, R. S., Young, C. A., & Meana, M. (2004). The motivations for and outcomes of employee referrals. *Journal of Business and Psychology, 19*, 271–283.

Smidts, A., Pruyn, A. T. H., & van Riel, C. B. M. (2001). The impact of employee communication and perceived external prestige on organizational identification. *The Academy of Management Journal, 44*(5), 1051–1062. https://doi.org/10.2307/3069448.

Springer, R. (2015). What do your employees think about content marketing? *Econtent, 38*(10), 6–7.

Thelen, P. D. (2018). Supervisor humor styles and employee advocacy: A serial mediation model. *Public Relations Review, 45*(2), 307–318. https://doi.org/10.1016/j.pubrev.2019.02.007.

Thelen, P. D. (2019). *Nurturing employee advocacy: The determining role of internal communication*. Dissertation.

Thelen, P. D. (2020). Internal communicators' understanding of the definition and importance of employee advocacy. *Public Relations Review, 46*(4). https://doi.org/10.1016/j.pubrev.2020.101946.

Thelen, P. D., & Men, L. R. (2020). Commentary: The role of internal communication in fostering employee advocacy: An exploratory study. *International Journal of Business Communication*. https://doi.org/10.1177/2329488420975832.

Tsarenko, Y., Leo, C., & Tse, H. H. (2018). When and why do social resources influence employee advocacy? The role of personal investment and perceived recognition. *Journal of Business Research, 82*(C), 260–268. https://doi.org/10.1016/j.jbusres.2017.09.001.

van Zoonen, W., Bartels, J., van Prooijen, A. M., & Schouten, A. P. (2018). Explaining online ambassadorship behaviors on Facebook and LinkedIn. *Computers in Human Behavior, 87*, 354–362. https://doi.org/10.1016/j.chb.2018.05.031.

Villanueva, J., Yoo, S., & Hanssens, D. M. (2008). The impact of marketing-induced versus word-of-mouth customer acquisition on customer equity growth. *Journal of Marketing Research (JMR), 45*(1), 48–59. https://doi.org/10.1509/jmkr.45.1.48.

Vlachos, P. A., Panagopoulos, N. G., Bachrach, D. G., & Morgeson, F. P. (2017). The effects of managerial and employee attributions for corporate social responsibility initiatives. *Journal of Organizational Behavior, 38*(7), 1111–1129. https://doi.org/10.1002/job.2189.

Walden, J. A., & Kingsley Westerman, C. Y. (2018). Strengthening the tie: Creating exchange relationships that encourage employee advocacy as an organizational citizenship behavior. *Management Communication Quarterly, 32*(4), 593–611. https://doi.org/10.1177/0893318918783612.

Weber Shandwick. (2014, April 2). *Employees rising: Seizing the opportunity in employee activism*. https://www.webershandwick.com/uploads/news/files/employees-rising-seizing-the-opportunity-in-employee-activism.pdf.

Wilden, R., Gudergan, S., & Lings, I. (2010). Employer branding: Strategic implications for staff recruitment. *Journal of Marketing Management, 26*(1–2), 56–73. https://doi.org/10.1080/02672570903577091.

CHAPTER 6

Employee Voice and Internal Listening: Towards Dialogue in the Workplace

Kevin Ruck

This chapter starts with reviews of employee voice and internal listening, before exploring dialogue in the workplace. It then considers how voice, listening and dialogue lead to a redefinition of internal communication and how they add new perspectives to theory and practice.

Employee Voice

Employee voice is a well-established concern in human relations management literature (Marchington, 2015) which recognises the benefits that accrue from robust systems of employee involvement and participation. Satisfaction with employee voice is often discussed as driver of employee engagement (Ruck et al., 2017; Ruck & Welch, 2012; Truss et al., 2006). Rees et al. (2013) observe that employee voice was originally equated with trade union membership and collective bargaining,

K. Ruck (✉)
PR Academy, Maidstone, UK
e-mail: kevin.ruck@pracademy.co.uk

L. R. Men and A. Tkalac Verčič (eds.), *Current Trends and Issues in Internal Communication*, New Perspectives in Organizational Communication, https://doi.org/10.1007/978-3-030-78213-9_6

but it is now more frequently seen as a range of ways in which employees have a say about what goes on in their organisation. This is summarised as employees' 'speaking up' with constructive ideas that aim to improve or change the status quo. According to Van Dyne et al. (2003, p. 1369) the management literature contains two major conceptualizations. The first approach describes speaking up behaviour such as when employees proactively make suggestions for change. The second uses the term to describe procedures that enhance justice judgments and facilitate employee participation in decision-making. Wilkinson et al. (2004) developed a multi-dimensional approach to employee voice which is communication-oriented, highlighting exchanges of views, providing feedback on specific topics, the ability for employees to express their views to managers in an open environment and an expectation that employee views will be taken into account and may lead to changes in how decisions are made. While Truss et al. (2006) found that having opportunities to feed views upwards was one of the three most important factors for engagement, Purcell and Hall (2012, p. 3) assert that: 'Having a voice, and *being listened to*, is one of the most important antecedents of engagement' (emphasis added). Ruck et al. (2017) also report senior managers seeking employee views and responding to suggestions as antecedents of engagement. The literature suggests that opportunities for employees to have a say about what goes on should be complemented with active seeking of views and responses if the full benefits of associations with employee engagement are to be achieved.

Internal Listening

Macnamara (2016a) outlines seven canons of organisational listening: recognition, acknowledgement, attention, interpreting, understanding, consideration and responding. These highlight rational and emotional listening, taking what others say as receptively as possible, trying to understand others' perspectives and feelings, and providing a substantive response after considering what has been said. Macnamara (2020) argues that voice has no value without listening and proposes a turn from a focus on voice to active listening. The expectation of views being taken into account might not be sufficient. Voice without appropriate consideration and response can lead to negative effects such as disengagement and decreased productivity (Macnamara, 2016a). Listening is reviewed by Macnamara in the context of public communication and principles are posited to apply equally to a range of stakeholders. However, the dynamics of listening to employees are, as is argued in this chapter, notably different to those that are used for listening to other groups such as customers. This is because of specific barriers that might exist inside organisations that can make listening to employees more problematic. These barriers can include assumptions and expectations about the relative role of leaders and those they lead and the lack of emphasis on listening to employees in management education. Krais et al. (2019) suggest that there are four barriers to listening to employees: cultural (for example, employees can be concerned that they may potentially 'say the wrong thing'), the way leadership is understood (for example, a focus on the 'need to provide answers' rather than listen), an underinvestment in listening capability development, and a lack of structures and processes to support listening. Macnamara (2016b, p. 147) also emphasises a structured approach: 'organisational listening requires policies, processes and systems'. Edmondson (2019) argues that psychological safety, highlighted in the point above about employees being concerned about speaking out, is lacking in many organisations. In order to develop corporate climates where fears about psychological safety can be lessened, Krais et al. (2020, pp. 13–16) identify five core principles for listening to employees:

Openness—good listening requires an open mind.
Planning—good listening is the result of thorough planning across the organisation.
Distributed leadership—listening needs to be led at multiple levels.
Empathetic and creative feedback—good listening involves creating impactful and emotive feedback approaches.
Human—good listening is rooted in a humanistic approach to communication and change.

This section has outlined some of the concepts associated with listening to employees, where *listening* has more emphasis on understanding, consideration and responding than is sometimes found in the literature on *employee voice*. This is a useful differentiation although there a range of definitions for voice and the distinction between voice and listening is not clear cut. However, an emphasis on listening reinforces the requirement to respond to what is said and this is the basis for dialogue which is reviewed in more detail in the following section.

Dialogue in the Workplace

Before reviewing dialogue in the workplace, this section of the chapter firstly distinguishes dialogue from discussion. It then explores how dialogue is understood in the wider public relations literature and how dialogue is applied in the workplace. According to Senge (2006) a discussion is a process of exchanges of views, where pre-existing views are presented and defended. Dialogue is a process whereby alternative views are presented as a way to develop a new view. DeBussy and Suprawan (2015) provide a useful overview of the meaning of dialogue with reference to the twentieth-century Jewish theologian, Martin Buber who in 1932 argued that leaders should view organisations not as 'a mechanical structure with "organic servants"' but as 'an association of persons with faces and names and biographies' (Buber, 2002, p. 204). This led Buber to posit dialogue in workplaces being grounded in leaders understanding 'persons as persons'. In the public relations literature, Kent and Taylor (2002, pp. 24–25) set out five dimensions for dialogue:

> **Mutuality**—The acknowledgement that organisations and publics are inextricably linked.
> **Propinquity**—The willingness and capacity of publics to express their demands to the organisation, and the latter's ability to consult the former regarding matters of mutual interest.
> **Empathy**—The atmosphere or environment required for fruitful dialogue.
> **Risk**—The fact that the outcome of a dialogic process may be unpredictable.
> **Commitment**—The parties to the dialogue must be truly committed to real conversation.

These dimensions are suggested to apply to all stakeholders. Ruck (2017, p. 4) found that dialogue has to be authentic. Employees can sense when managers are 'smiling, but not with their eyes'. Gutiérrez-García et al. (2015) point out that although the term 'dialogue' has been part of the lexicon of public relations for many years, no clear consensus has yet emerged as regards its definition, and there has been little research into its applications or the management processes involved. This chapter aims to begin to address this point for dialogue with employees. As with an application of broad principles of listening to a range of stakeholder groups discussed in the previous section, dialogue in the workplace requires more localised consideration.

The term 'social dialogue' is often used in conjunction with collective bargaining on working conditions. It is defined by the International Labour Organisation (2018, p. 4) as 'all types of negotiation, consultation or information sharing among representatives of governments, employers and workers, or between those of employers and workers, on issues of common interest relating to economic and social policy'. Social dialogue in this context can take many different forms, from the relatively informal to more formal and institutionalised structures and mechanisms. The term 'dialogue in the workplace' is used in this chapter to convey a less formal and fluid process used for a wider range of defined and open topics. DeBussy and Suprawan (2015, p. 74) outline three key attributes for this:

> **Listening**—suspending one's own frame of reference.
> **Positive regard**—valuing people as people.
> **Willingness to change**—participants must enter into dialogue with the intent to reach an understanding.

Dialogue in the workplace therefore incorporates many of the aspects of voice and listening outlined in the previous sections, with the additional and notable points about positive regard and willingness to change. This requires empathy and commitment to developing deeper understandings.

This chapter has outlined broad definitions for voice, listening and dialogue. These can be considered to be separate, reasonably narrowly defined concepts, or as concepts with considerable overlap as illustrated in Table 6.1.

Table 6.1 Summary of voice, listening and dialogue in the workplace

Employee voice	*Listening to employees*	*Dialogue in the workplace*
Having a say about what goes on, making suggestions	Paying attention to what is said	Willingness to change
Speaking up, expressing views, exchanging views	Interpreting what is said and responding	Positive regard
Overlap: consideration of what is said	**Overlap:** suspending own frame of reference	

Finally, Taylor and Kent (2014, p. 395) argue that dialogue will not be possible until two related conditions are met: (a) public relations professionals are trained in how to facilitate dialogue and (b) management becomes convinced of its value. In the next section the way that dialogue in the workplace is incorporated into definitions of internal communication is considered before turning to the issues of internal communication education and capabilities.

Redefining Internal communication

Welch and Jackson (2007) suggest that internal communication is best situated within what is termed 'strategic public relations' alongside media relations, public affairs, environmental communication, investor relations, labour market communications (recruitment) and corporate advertising. In a response to other definitions that simplistically consider all employees as a single group, Welch and Jackson (2007, p. 184) propose a definition that identifies separate internal stakeholder groups:

> The strategic management of interactions and relationships between stakeholders within organisations across a number of interrelated dimensions including, internal line manager communication, internal team peer communication, internal project peer communication and internal corporate communication.

This definition notably moves away from 'communications transactions' to 'interactions and relationships'. The position taken for this chapter is that internal communication is a function that incorporates the distribution of information as a fundamental component for relationship building through voice and listening that leads to dialogue in the workplace. As Macnamara (2020) argues, corporate listening is an element of corporate communication that hereto has received relatively little attention. However, listening connects corporate communication to the large body of communication theory and research that emphasises two-way communication, dialogue, and engagement. With active, effective corporate listening, corporate communication extends beyond one-way, top-down information dissemination and gains insights, understanding, and engagement that lead to trust, loyalty and sustainable relationships. A revised definition for internal communication is proposed that connects it to corporate communication theory that emphasises dialogue and engagement:

> Keeping employees informed about what they need to know and what they are most interested in, giving them multi-faceted and regular opportunities to have a say about what goes on, and actively listening and responding to what is said with empathy and positive regard to them as human beings.

This definition acknowledges the importance of providing employees with the information that they want and need; the traditional, transactional, one-way, dissemination aspect of the role. However, it also incorporates voice and listening as critical components of any definition of practice. The combination of informing and listening is explored in more detail in the following section.

The Alignment-Voice-Identification-Dialogue (AVID) Framework

Effective employee voice is, to an extent, dependent on an understanding of the organisation's key priorities and in turn appreciating how an employee's work contributes to organisational success. Employee suggestions, views and feedback are grounded in (or constrained by) that knowledge. As Welch and Jackson (2007, p. 185) highlight in their internal communication matrix, the process of informing employees operates at many levels with strategic manager communication described as 'predominantly one-way'. Employee voice and listening can also be incorporated into all levels of internal communication. For example, it is not solely a line manager responsibility. According to Ruck (2020) employees expect line manager communication to be more oriented around local team tasks and explanations about how this aligned with corporate plans, whereas senior manager communication is expected to be more oriented in clear explanations about broader aims, plans and priorities of the organisation. When communication includes listening and responding, Ruck (2016) found strong associations with organisational engagement, defined by Welch (2020, p. 53) as:

> A dynamic, changeable psychological state which links employees to their organisations, manifest in employee role performances expressed physically, cognitively and emotionally, and influenced by organisation level internal communication.

More reactive
Rational
Business as usual

More proactive
Emotive
Change

	Passive	Active	Sensitive	Deep
Approach	Single survey: monitor for general trends	Multi-channel: identify common themes and respond	Listening culture: building trust	Listening for collaboration and innovation
Objective	Monitor and map the environment to identify trends and needs	Multi-channel: identify common themes and understand what's driving opinions	create a safe space to speak up	Listen to co-create, change ways of working and innovate
What characterizes the approach	*Interpret*: receptive and objective listening to what employees report	*Understand and respond*: listening for the reasons behind opinions to generate appropriate responses	*Consider seriously with emotional intelligence*: attention to psychological needs and safety, listening up so that people feel free to speak up	*Collaborate and innovate*: listening to synthesize perspectives and come up with new insights and ways of working
Approaches and tools	Annual survey	Pulse surveys, senior manager informal listening forums (F2F and online); trending topics in internal media (sentiment analysis); suggestion schemes	Local listening champions; line manager conversations; confidential counselling; employee support lines; representative groups; communities of practice	Big conversations; conferencing; open space; appreciative inquiry; solutions groups; task forces; engagement champions; cross-functional working
What's important to improve listening	Quantitative data, benchmarks, comparisons, anonymity, samples	Quantitative and qualitative data, explanations, action planning and responses	Confidentiality, empathy, freedom to speak out	Diversity of input, openness, curiosity, equal voice

Fig. 6.1 The employee listening spectrum (Krais et al., 2020)

Line manager communication can enable employees to ***align*** their work to the overall success of the organisation whereas senior manager communication can enable employees to ***identify*** with the broader organisation and to develop a sense of belongingness to it. Ruck's (2020) Alignment-Voice-Identification-Dialogue (AVID) Framework sets out this distinction between line and senior manager communication and incorporates employee voice and dialogue (see Fig. 6.1). The framework was developed from research conducted with 2066 employees in the UK in 2016 (Ruck, 2016). The components of the framework are reviewed in the following sections.

Alignment

According to Robinson and Hayday (2009), the top two behaviours cited by team members for an engaging line manager are firstly making it clear what is expected from the team and secondly listening to team members. Gatenby et al. (2009) conclude that it is important for most managers to focus on doing the 'simple' things well, including communicating clear work objectives that employees can understand. This emphasises the focus on communication about team tasks. However, as Men (2014) highlights, a symmetrical communication environment is typified by managers who listen and align individual goals with organisational goals. The challenge for line manager communication is therefore to connect the micro to the macro. This is not straightforward. Indeed, Baumruk (2006) suggests that line managers may not be the best people to communicate about strategy as senior managers believe that they have problems with 'complexity' and 'strategic stuff'. It is therefore unrealistic to expect line managers to communicate about strategy *per se*. Instead, they should be informed enough about 'strategic stuff', with the support of their managers (the middle management layer in organisations), to be able to make meaningful connections that resonate with their team at a time when it is most appropriate to do so—in an unforced and authentic manner.

Voice

Employee voice has been explored in previous sections of this chapter. The term 'voice' within the AVID framework is based on a broader understanding of voice that includes consideration of what is said and responding. It operates at line and senior manager levels and is underpinned by a systemic, multi-method, approach to listening throughout the organisation. This approach to voice and listening can be extended into a spectrum, as outlined by Krais et al. (2020) ranging from passive to deep, as illustrated in Fig. 6.2. The shift from passive to active listening requires a step-change in approach in many organisations. However, practice is evolving in this direction as listening and dialogue are now increasingly perceived as important activities with 80% of internal communication manager respondents agreeing that they are involved with 'two-way communication with employees' (Gatehouse, 2020, p. 7). As Macnamara (2020, p. 381) highlights, 'in the era of online digital communication, natural language processing, machine learning content and textual analysis applications, voice to text (VTT) software, and other sense-making tools, expressions of voice can be listened to 24/7, compared with traditional employee engagement surveys that are usually conducted once a year'. Madsen and Johansen (2019) found that employees are now making use of internal social media platforms to raise concerns which were, generally, treated seriously by managers who either accepted or rejected the issue raised. If they did not accept it, they typically supplied a long and well-supported explanation of why things were the way they were.

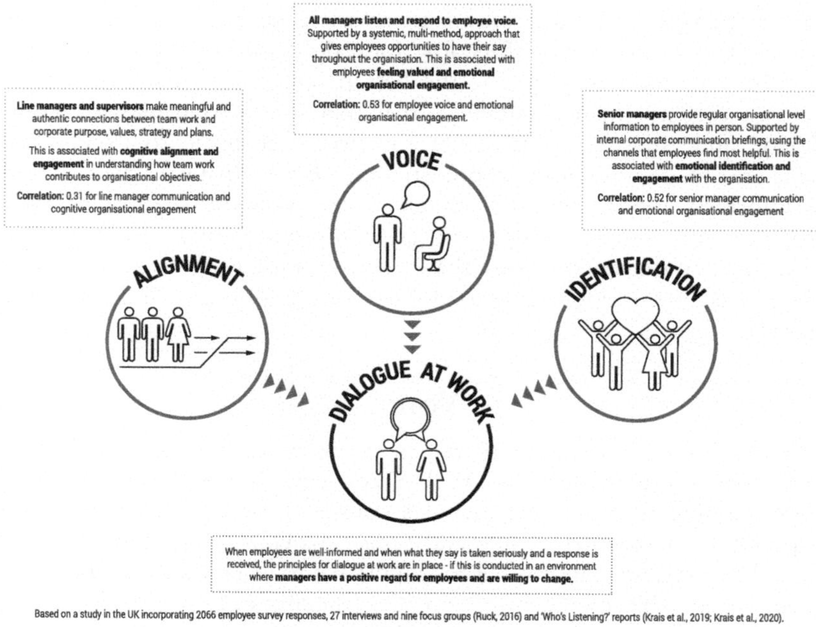

Based on a study in the UK incorporating 2066 employee survey responses, 27 interviews and nine focus groups (Ruck, 2016) and 'Who's Listening?' reports (Krais et al., 2019; Krais et al., 2020).
Correlations are significant at 0.01 level (2-tailed).

Fig. 6.2 The alignment, voice, identification, dialogue (AVID) framework for internal communication

Identification

Identification with an organisation stems from organisation engagement, as defined by Welch (2020) in the previous section. Engagement is not simply with one's work. As Kahn (2010, pp. 27–30) observes, employees also engage with leaders and aspects of the organisation itself: 'Leaders needed to learn to dismantle the obstacles to engagement—structures, processes, and, for some, themselves—and create new patterns of interaction with and among employees. They had to create learning forums that were safe enough for employees to tell them the truth of their experiences'.

Millward and Postmes (2010) report that the fact that identification with the superordinate grouping of 'the organisation' was particularly relevant to performance is important for theoretical, empirical, and pragmatic reasons. Fleck and Inceoglu (2010, p. 38) outline two separate dimensions for organisational engagement: identification—a sense of belonging, and alignment—the congruence between employees' beliefs about where the organisation should be heading, what the goals and aspirations of the organisation should be, and the actual direction of the organisation. They argue that identification is affective and alignment is cognitive. This conceptual differentiation underpins the AVID framework, with an important distinction being made between the communication role for line managers (for alignment) and for senior managers (for identification). According to Galunic and Hermreck (2012), although local job conditions matter, senior management has a unique voice and understanding of strategy, and this may help explain the substantial influence they have on strategic embeddedness when they engage with employees.

Identification is dependent on symmetrical internal communication, which focuses on 'employee-centric values and organisations' genuine care and concern for employees' interests' (Men & Bowen, 2017, p. 174). This includes meaning making and empathy which, according to Yue et al. (2020) enhances organisational identification. Men and Yue (2019) found that when the desire to be heard is satisfied and when this takes place in open and equal communication, employees can be happy, proud, appreciative, and affectionate. This is a relational perspective of leadership (Fairhurst & Uhl-Bien, 2012) where it is seen not as a trait or behaviour, but as a phenomenon generated in the interactions among people acting in context. At the core of this view is the assumption that leadership is co-constructed in social interaction processes that include employee voice and listening. CEOs should communicate in a 'responsive, warm, friendly, empathetic, sincere, caring, and interested manner to demonstrate their concern for their employees, openness, and willingness to listen' as this is positively associated with employee-organisation relationships (Men, 2015, p. 469). Furthermore, Walker and Aritz (2014, p. 13) suggest that this approach to leadership means that communication becomes 'the primary concern rather than a secondary or tertiary consideration'.

Dialogue

Dialogue in the workplace has been explored in a previous section of this chapter. The term 'dialogue' within the AVID framework is based on a willingness to change and a positive regard for all employees. This can be further extended to the ways that organisations, as Deetz (2005, pp. 85–86) puts it, 'allow greater democracy and more creative and productive cooperation among stakeholders'. This view is representative of the pursuit of alternative, critical, communication practices that underpin this chapter. It can be associated with the wider literature on employee involvement and participation (Miller, 2009) which has also been extended by some critical theorists (Cheney, 1995) to a general concept of workplace democracy, based on humanistic principles about how people should be treated in society, including in organisations.

Incorporating Voice, Listening and Dialogue into the Role of the Internal Communication Manager

In this final section of the chapter, implications for incorporating voice, listening and dialogue into the role of the internal communication manager are considered. In a review of internal communication knowledge foundations and post-graduate education, Welch (2013, p. 616) argues that 'In medicine, general practitioners have valuable knowledge, but specialists have in-depth knowledge of particular disciplines or branches of medicine. Just as we wouldn't expect our family doctor to perform brain surgery, perhaps we should not assume that general PR and communication management knowledge is enough to equip internal communication specialists'. Throughout this chapter, the requirement to extend and adapt broad communication concepts to the particular context of communication inside organisations has been stressed. This can now be extended to specialist role descriptions, training and education that reflect a broader approach to internal communication that includes voice, listening and dialogue.

The Global Alliance for Public Relations and Communication Management's Global Capability Framework (2020) incorporates listening within a broader relationship facilitation capability, set out as follows: 'You identify, analyse and listen to stakeholders and their communication needs'.

This suggests that listening is restricted to understanding 'communication needs' rather than listening being related to organisational issues. The UK Institute of Internal Communication (IoIC) describes listening as a personal behaviour (together with other behaviours such as 'tenacity' and 'curious') rather than a professional area of activity in its profession map (IoIC, 2020) where listening to employees receives minimal attention. This brief overview of capabilities raises two concerns. Firstly, broad corporate communication capability frameworks fail to recognise the specialist nature of internal communication. Secondly, where specialist profession maps exist, they may currently have a limited appreciation of how voice, listening and dialogue underpin good practice.

The rationale for the internal communication manager taking responsibility for establishing robust processes and systems for listening to employees is that this is a natural corollary to keeping employees informed. Adopting the listening and dialogue principles outlined in this chapter requires internal communication managers to take on a primary responsibility, collaborating with other functions, for implementing organisation-wide listening channels, processes and systems. This entails analysis of the views, issues and concerns that employees raise with expert input from data analysts. It is the analysis that generates insights and trends that may go beyond individual employees. The analysis forms the basis of management reporting that enables leaders to consider and reflect more deeply on what is being said and then provide meaningful responses that leads to wider trust in the listening process.

In practical terms, this requires an internal communication plan that includes regular listening activities as outlined in the Employee Listening Spectrum that are led by senior managers and which make the best use of a wide range of methods. The emphasis on embedding organisation-wide listening into planning does not require a significant budget. Instead, it will often require a redistribution of the time devoted to 'sending-out-stuff' so that more time is devoted to listening.

Finally, listening to employees is also an essential component of good practice. Listening to employees is 'good' in the sense that it has numerous benefits for organisations and it is also associated with employee wellbeing (CIPD, 2019). There is also a social justice perspective to listening to employees. As organisations increasingly understand the requirement for good governance, integrated reporting (Wang et al., 2019) and responsible leadership (Muff et al., 2020) so the recognition of listening and dialogue in the workplace will increase. Not to listen to employees in a systemic way or in active, sensitive and deep ways potentially leads to employee cynicism with what might be perceived as persistent one-way management-oriented propaganda.

Professional Interview with Martin Flegg

Kevin Ruck is the co-founder of PR Academy and the editor and co-author of Exploring Internal Communication: Towards Informed Employee Voice published by Routledge.

Martin Flegg, Chart.PR has been an internal communication practitioner for over 20 years working in-house and as a consultant in government, financial services, legal services and higher education. He is the 2021 Committee Chair for CIPR Inside and the founder of The IC Citizen.

What is your perception of the way organisations listen to employees?
I think it's quite mechanistic. There are events during the year where listening is done through surveys, particularly an annual employee engagement, which might be bolstered with periodic pulse surveys. Then there are change programmes where project managers want to get feedback from employees on what they're proposing to do, whether that's structural, terms and conditions, IT implementations, or process changes and they run co-creation workshops and focus groups for this.

Where do you think you get the best insights from listening to employees?
I'm a big believer in gathering feedback that's actionable. Just asking the open question, 'What do you think at the moment?' means that you get a lot of unstructured feedback which is difficult to analyse and feed in to governance processes that determine the decision-making in the organisation at the top table.

What about listening to employees on internal digital platforms?
Internal social media platforms are a great source of how people are feeling, what they're talking about, what the issues of the day are, what they're interested in, gossip in the organisation, the office politics, all that sort of stuff. I don't think internal comms people have got to grips with how to harness the power of that information—to brigade it in a way that makes it actionable.

How does listening affect the role of the internal communication manager?
Listening is allied to measurement and evaluation quite a lot. Internal comms people are told to measure everything. But I don't feel that there is a lot of continuous listening outside of those events that I've talked about where you might have some kind of consultation going on. I do think there's a gap between what employers and recruiters look for and what professional bodies and professional frameworks say that we should know and be able to do and one of those gaps is definitely listening.

What do organisations need to do to get the most from listening?
Listening should feed into a governance process. It falls between the cracks at the moment. There should be a collaboration between market insight, process and governance—if that exists in the organisation—with internal comms and HR there in a consultative and advisory capacity. The other component that's really important for internal comms is they can inform the other part of the loop which is the 'we did' bit and then the cycle goes round again. So, 'you gave us this feedback, we did this, we told you this, did that work', and so on.

References

Baumruk, A. (2006). Why managers are crucial to increasing engagement, identifying steps managers can take to engage their workforce. *Strategic HR Review*, *5*(2), 24–27. https://doi.org/10.1108/14754390680000863.

Buber, M. (2002). From 'dialogue' (1932). In A. D. Biemann (Ed.), *The Martin Buber reader*. Palgrave Macmillan.

Cheney, G. (1995). Democracy in the workplace: Theory and practice from the perspective of communication. *Journal of Applied Communication Research*, *23*(3), 167–200. https://doi.org/10.1080/00909889509365424.

CIPD. (2019, February). Chartered Institute of Personnel and Development. *Talking about voice: Employees' experience*. Report.

DeBussy, N. M., & Suprawan, L. (2015). Employee dialogue: A framework for business success. In K. Ruck (Ed.), *Exploring internal communication* (3rd ed.). Gower Publishing.

Deetz, S. (2005). Critical theory. In S. May, & D. K. Mumby (Eds.), *Engaging organisational communication theory and research*. Sage.

Edmondson, A. C. (2019). *The fearless organisation: Creating psychological safety in the workplace for learning, innovation and growth*. Wiley.

Fairhurst, G. T., & Uhl-Bien, M. (2012). Organisational discourse analysis (ODA): Examining leadership as a relational process. *The Leadership Quarterly, 23*(6), 1043–1062. https://doi.org/10.1016/j.leaqua.2012.10.005.

Fleck, S., & Inceoglu, I. (2010). A comprehensive framework for understanding and predicting engagement. In A. Albrecht (Ed.), *Handbook of employee engagement, perspectives, issues, research and practice*. Edward Elgar.

Galunic, C., & Hermreck, I. (2012, December). How to help employees "get" strategy. *Harvard Business Review*.

Gatehouse. (2020). State of the sector 2020. Vol 12. *The definitive global survey of the internal communication landscape*. Gatehouse: A Gallagher Company.

Gatenby, M., Alfes, K., Truss, K., & Soane, E. (2009, October 3). *Harnessing employee engagement in UK public services*. Paper presented at Public Management Research Association Conference, Columbus, Ohio.

Global Alliance for Public Relations and Communication Management. (2020). *Global capability framework*. Global Alliance for Public Relations and Communication Management. Retrieved from https://www.globalalliancepr.org/capabilitiesframeworks.

Gutiérrez-García, E., Recalde, M., & Piñera-Camacho, A. (2015). Reinventing the wheel? A comparative overview of the concept of dialogue. *Public Relations Review, 41*(5), 744–753. https://doi.org/10.1016/j.pubrev.2015.06.006.

Institute of Internal Communication. (2020). *Profession map*. Milton Keynes, UK. Retrieved from https://www.ioic.org.uk/professional-development/ioic-profession-map-2.

Kahn, W. A. (2010). The essence of engagement: Lessons from the field. In S. L. Albrecht (Ed.), *Handbook of employee engagement, perspectives, issues, research and practice*. Edward Elgar.

Kent, M. L., & Taylor, M. (2002). Toward a dialogic theory of public relations. *Public Relations Review, 28*(1), 21–37. https://doi.org/10.1016/S0363-8111(02)00108-X.

Krais, H., Pounsford, M., & Ruck, K. (2019). *Who's listening? A small-scale research project exploring how organisations listen to employees*. PR Academy, Couravel & IABC UK.

Krais, H., Pounsford, M., & Ruck, K. (2020). *Who's listening? Update: Good listening practice*. PR Academy, Couravel & IABC UK.

International Labour Organisation. (2018). *The impact of social dialogue and collective bargaining on working conditions in SMEs*. International Labour Office, Enterprises Department.

Macnamara, J. (2016a). *Organisational listening: The missing essential in public communication*. Peter Lang.

Macnamara, J. (2016b). Organisational listening: Addressing a major gap in public relations theory and practice. *Journal of Public Relations Research, 28*(3–4), 146–169. https://doi.org/10.1080/1062726X.2016.1228064.

Macnamara, J. (2020). Corporate listening: Unlocking insights from VOC, VOE and VOS for mutual benefits. *Corporate Communications: An International Journal, 25*(3), 377–393. https://doi.org/10.1108/CCIJ-08-2019-0102.

Marchington, M. (2015). Analysing the forces shaping employee involvement and participation (EIP) at organisation level in liberal market economies (LMEs). *Human Resource Management Journal, 25*(1), 1–18. https://doi.org/10.1111/1748-8583.12065.

Madsen, V. T., & Johansen, W. (2019). A spiral of voice? When employees speak up on internal social media. *Journal of Communication Management, 23*(4), 331–347. https://doi.org/10.1108/JCOM-03-2019-0050.

Men, L. R. (2014). Strategic internal communication: Transformational leadership, communication channels, and employee satisfaction. *Management Communication Quarterly, 28*(2), 264–284. https://doi.org/10.1177/0893318914524536.

Men, L. R. (2015). The internal communication role of the chief executive officer: Communication channels, style, and effectiveness. *Public Relations Review, 41*(4), 461–471. https://doi.org/10.1016/j.pubrev.2015.06.021.

Men, R. L., & Bowen, S. A. (2017). *Excellence in internal relations management*. Business Expert Press.

Men, R. L., & Yue, C. A. (2019). Creating a positive emotional culture: Effect of internal communication and impact on employee supportive behaviors. *Public Relations Review, 45*(3), 101764. https://doi.org/10.1016/j.pubrev.2019.03.001.

Miller, K. S. (2009). *Organisation communication approaches and processes* (5th ed.). Wadsworth Cengage Learning.

Millward, L., & Postmes, T. (2010). Who we are affects how we do: The financial benefits of organisational identification. *British Journal of Management, 21*(2), 327–339. https://doi.org/10.1111/j.1467-8551.2009.00667.x.

Muff, K., Liechti, A., & Dyllick, T. (2020). How to apply responsible leadership theory in practice: A competency tool to collaborate on the sustainable development goals. *Corporate Social Responsibility and Environmental Management, 27*, 2254–2274. https://doi.org/10.1002/csr.1962.

Purcell, J., & Hall, M. (2012). *Voice and participation in the modern workplace: Challenges and prospects*. Future of Workplace Relations Discussion Paper Series. Acas.

Rees, C., Alfes, A., & Gatenby, M. (2013). Employee voice and engagement: Connections and consequences. *The International Journal of Human Resource Management, 24*(14), 2780–2798. https://doi.org/10.1080/09585192.2013.763843.

Robinson, D., & Hayday, S. (2009). *The engaging manager, report 470*. The Institute for Employment Studies.

Ruck, K. (2016). *Informed employee voice: The synthesis of internal corporate communication and employee voice and the associations with organisational engagement*. Ph.D. thesis, University of Central Lancashire, UK.

Ruck, K. (2017, December). *Smiling, but not with his eyes: Authentic employee voice for inclusive organisations*. Paper presented at CIPD Applied Research Conference, Glasgow. https://www.cipd.co.uk/learn/events-networks/applied-research-conference/2017-papers.

Ruck, K. (2020). The AVID framework for good and ethical practice. In K. Ruck (Ed.), *Exploring internal communication, towards informed employee voice* (4th ed.). Routledge.

Ruck, K., & Welch, M. (2012). Valuing internal communication: Management and employee perspectives. *Public Relations Review, 38*(2), 294–302. https://doi.org/10.1016/j.pubrev.2011.12.016.

Ruck, K., Welch, M., & Menara, B. (2017). Employee voice: An antecedent to organisational engagement? *Public Relations Review, 43*(5), 904–914. https://doi.org/10.1016/j.pubrev.2017.04.008.

Senge, P. (2006). *The fifth discipline* (2nd ed.). Random House.

Taylor, M., & Kent, M. L. (2014). Dialogic engagement: Clarifying foundational concepts. *Journal of Public Relations Research, 26*(5), 384–398. https://doi.org/10.1080/1062726X.2014.956106.

Truss, C., Soane, E., Edwards, C., Wisdom, K., Croll, A., & Burnett, J. (2006). *Working life: Employee attitudes and engagement 2006*. Research Report. Chartered Institute of Personnel and Development.

Van Dyne, L., Ang, S., & Botero, I. C. (2003). Conceptualizing employee silence and employee voice as multidimensional constructs. *Journal of Management Studies, 40*(6), 1359–1392. https://doi.org/10.1111/1467-6486.00384.

Walker, R., & Aritz, J. (2014). *Leadership talk: A discourse approach to leader emergence*. Business Expert Press.

Wang, R., Zhou, S., & Wang, T. (2019). Corporate governance, integrated reporting and the use of credibility—Enhancing mechanisms on integrated reports. *European Accounting Review, 29*(4), 631–663. https://doi.org/10.1080/09638180.2019.1668281.

Welch, M. (2013). Mastering internal communication: Knowledge foundations and post-graduate education. *Public Relations Review, 39*(5), 615–617. https://doi.org/10.1016/j.pubrev.2013.04.003.

Welch, M. (2020). Dimensions of internal communication and implications for employee engagement. In K. Ruck (Ed.), *Exploring internal communication, towards informed employee voice* (4th ed.). Routledge.

Welch, M., & Jackson, P. R. (2007). Rethinking internal communication: A stakeholder approach. *Corporate Communications: An International Journal, 12*(2), 177–198. https://doi.org/10.1108/13563280710744847.

Wilkinson, A., Dundon, T., Marchington, M., & Ackers, P. (2004). Changing patterns of employee voice: Case studies from the UK and the Republic of Ireland. *Journal of Industrial Relations, 46*(3), 298. https://doi.org/10.1111/j.0022-1856.2004.00143.x.

Yue, C. A., Men, R. L., & Ferguson, M. A. (2020). Examining the effects of internal communication and emotional culture on employees' organisational identification. *International Journal of Business Communication, 58*(2), 169–195. https://doi.org/10.1177/2329488420914066.

CHAPTER 7

Employee Activism and Internal Communication

Arunima Krishna

On September 23, 2020, Sam Anderson, a senior training specialist at the social media management platform Hootsuite wrote a series of tweets drawing attention to the company's deal with the controversial United States federal agency, Immigration and Customs Enforcement (ICE hereafter; Moreno, 2020). Anderson claimed that the three-year deal between Hootsuite and ICE had been signed over the objections and protests of over a hundred employees, including some in Mexico City who reported having been harassed by ICE officials (Sandler, 2020). The internal concerns about the deal quickly spilled over to Hootsuite's external environment, with several social media managers, Hootsuite's client base, announcing that they would be reconsidering their use of the platform (Moreno, 2020). What followed was a swift and public policy reversal from Hootsuite. Within 24 hours of Anderson's tweets Hootsuite's CEO issued a public statement, acknowledging that the deal has "sparked a

A. Krishna (✉)
Boston University, Boston, MA, USA
e-mail: arunimak@bu.edu

L. R. Men and A. Tkalac Verčič (eds.), *Current Trends and Issues in Internal Communication*, New Perspectives in Organizational Communication, https://doi.org/10.1007/978-3-030-78213-9_7

great deal of internal conversation" and that the company would no longer be going ahead with the deal with ICE (Moreno, 2020).

Hootsuite's capitulation to employee pressure is only one of many recent examples of heightened employee activism. The last few years, in particular, have seen the rise of employees giving voice to their opposition to organizational policies, particularly related to controversial social issues, and mobilizing to form social movement organizations within their employer organizations to sue for change (Scully & Segal, 2002). From the Wayfair walkout to protest the company's dealings with ICE (Hames, 2019), the multiple employee walkouts, and organized protests at Google against their handling of sexual harassment cases in 2018 (Wakabayashi et al., 2018) and then to protest what was viewed as retaliation against two employees who were activist organizers (Ghaffrey, 2019), to Amazon (Wingard, 2020) and Walmart (Gurchiek, 2019), recent instances of employee activism abound. Indeed, a 2019 report by public relations agency, Weber Shandwick found that 4 in 10 employees (38%) say they have "spoken up to support or criticize their employers' actions over a controversial issue that affects society" (Gaines Ross, 2019). Weber Shandwick's executive chairman, Andy Polanksy, attributed this finding to the increasing number of Millennials in the workforce who believe it their right to criticize their employers on controversial issues (Wingard, 2020).

Such activism stemming from within an organization presents an internal and external communication challenge, as organizations' leaders try to balance mindfully addressing employee activists' demands before and after they become public with the organization's own values and interests. Public relations nightmares resulting from poorly handled employee activism, as was the case with Google and Wayfair's employee walkouts, remind us of the important role played by public relations functions in communicating and negotiating between organizational leaders and internal activists (McCown, 2007). The present chapter presents a review of the literature on activism and employee activism within public relations scholarship and beyond, followed by industry perspectives on employee activism. A theoretically driven and practically sound definition of employee activism is advanced, followed by recommendations for future research on employee activism and internal communication.

Activism in Public Relations Scholarship

The study of activism enjoys a long history in public relations scholarship. Defined by L. A. Grunig et al. (2002) as "a group of two or more individuals who organize in order to influence another public or publics through action that may include education, compromise, persuasion, pressure tactics, or force" (p. 446), activist groups are important constituencies for public relations practitioners to consider when formulating their communication strategy (Grunig & Grunig, 1997). However, too often in public relations scholarship activists and activism have been cast in a negative light, as efforts that inhibit public relations practice (Dozier & Lauzen, 2000) and therefore need to be limited and controlled (Dougall, 2005). Dozier and Lauzen (2000) criticized the "intellectual myopia" associated with public relations scholarship which is dominated by former practitioners at large organizations, who see activists as the "other" and thus a force to be thwarted (p. 7).

Since then, scholars have embraced Dozier and Lauzen's (2000) call to understand activism, helping build a robust body of literature understanding organized activist groups and their communicative strategies (e.g., Anderson, 1992; Reber & Kim, 2006; Taylor et al., 2001; Werder, 2006), as well as individual-level activism (e.g., Krishna, 2017). However, much of the public relations scholarship on activism tends to focus on external activists, particularly organized activist groups and their relationship building efforts to advance their agenda (e.g., Taylor et al., 2001). Few studies have focused on the role of internal activists (e.g., Curtin, 2016; McCown, 2007) in bringing about organizational change and even forcing changes in organizational policy. With employee activism on the rise (Gurchiek, 2019) and becoming a crucial piece of corporations' employee engagement efforts ("Employees Rising: Seizing the Opportunity in Employee Activism," n.d.), it behooves public relations scholarship to examine employee activism and its impact on internal communication and corporate strategy. The next section presents a review of the literature on internal and employee activism, in public relations and beyond, to unpack the differences between external, internal, and employee activism.

Theoretical Perspectives on Employee Activism

As noted in the previous section, much of the public relations scholarship on activism has focused on external organized activist groups, such as environmental groups (e.g., Taylor et al., 2001) as well as organic, issue-specific activism (e.g., Krishna, 2017; Vardeman & Sebesta, 2020). Relatively understudied, however, are instances of internal activism, particularly those initiated and carried out by employees. Although McCown (2007) noted that "...employee activism should inform future public relations practice" (p. 47), theoretical explications of employee activism and internal activism in public relations scholarship are few and far between and tend to be primarily qualitative explorations of specific instances of internal activism in the form of case studies. For example, Luo and Jiang (2014) interviewed employee activists at a large multinational food company in China to understand the various empowerment strategies they adopted to force the reversal of an unpopular policy. Similarly, Curtin (2016) adopted a case study approach to understand the discourses adopted by internal activists, in this case, Girl Scout members, to pressure the manufacturer of Girl Scout cookies, the Kellogg Company to use only palm oil from responsible sources.

In organizational studies and management literature, however, internal activism has received more attention. Briscoe and Gupta (2016), for example, articulated the different types of social activism experienced within and around organizations and differentiated between "insider" and "outsider" activists (p. 671). Whereas "outsider" activists or external activists exist outside the organization as non-members, such as social movement organizations like Greenpeace, "insider" activists are members of an organization. Briscoe and Gupta (2016) further differentiated between types of insider activists by envisioning a continuum of activist types, i.e., an insider–outsider continuum, with non-members or external activists at one end and employees as full members of the organization at the other. Such envisioning of activist types on a spectrum helps account for partial members of organizations, including students, as internal members of their schools and institutions, and shareholders, who although have an interest in the organization do not enjoy the level of access that employees do. Two key factors, i.e., resource dependence and target organization knowledge, characterize groups' classification into activist types (Briscoe & Gupta, 2016). For example, employee activists experience a high level of resource dependence with their organization, particularly as they risk retaliation and career damage (Taylor & Raeburn, 1995). At the same time, they also enjoy knowledge not only about informal social structures in the organization that may facilitate organizing and the strategic deployment of activism efforts but also of internal culture (Baron & Diermeier, 2007). Shareholders, as partial members, are highly resource-dependent on the organization but lack the requisite knowledge of internal culture and social structures to effectively organize and drive change from within. The insider–outsider continuum, a function of resource dependency and target organization knowledge, thus, helps distinguish between employee activists and other types of internal and external activists.

Early theorizing on employee activists described these individuals as "tempered radicals" (Meyerson, 2001; Meyerson & Scully, 1995, p. 585), who must balance their commitment to their chosen social cause, and thus critique their organization's policies and practices, with their commitment to the organization and the rewards and benefits that ensue when the organization succeeds. Historically, labor unions tended to be cast as protagonists in the fight for workplace equality and equity (Western & Rosenfeld, 2011), fighting for fairer wages and income equity within their organizations as well as lobbying legislative bodies. However, with union membership on a steady decline (Maiorescu, 2017) an alternate form of employee activism has recently gained traction. Specifically, scholars have noted the emergence of issue-specific employee groups that have been able to successfully lobby their organizations to take concrete action on issues ranging from LBGT policy and activism (e.g., Githens & Aragon, 2009; Maks-Solomon & Drewry, 2020) to environmental issues (e.g., Skoglund & Böhm, 2020). Recent upheavals in the tech industry, including employee protests and walkouts at Google, Amazon, and Wayfair (Gautam & Carberry, 2020) in response to what the employees considered inappropriate corporate policies regarding controversial social issues point to a more organic form of employee organizing and activism in response to perceived corporate missteps on crucial sociopolitical issues. Such employee activism is even more evident in instances when employees perceive there to be a disconnect between organizational values and organizational action (Stuart, 2020).

Scully and Segal (2002) posit three reasons for the manifestation of employee activism in the workplace. First, given that many of the issues that form the target of social activism can be directly attributed to corporate (in)action, such as inequality, injustice, and discrimination (Baron,

1984), employees experience the effects of these inequalities firsthand, and thus are more motivated to address them. Second, as noted earlier, having an intimate knowledge of the internal culture of the organization and the informal (power) structures that characterize it facilitate the mobilization and distribution of information and attitudes. Third, the proximity afforded by a workplace as well as the shared experience of inequity may also facilitate the mobilization and organizing of groups, as well as the recruitment of new members to help address the issues faced by the collective.

Industry Perspectives on Employee Activism

As is evidenced by extant theorizing on employee activism reviewed so far, such efforts are conceptualized to be inwardly directed. That is, employee activism is considered to be efforts organized and negotiated by individual employees and/or groups of employees directed toward organizational leadership to change organizational policy or direction. However, outside of the academy in the practice, employee activism is defined more broadly than just inwardly directed. For example, Rouse (2020) defined employee activism as "actions taken by workers to speak out for or against their employers on controversial issues that impact society" and noted that it is characterized by "actions performed intentionally to generate social change" (para. 1). However, such activism is not necessarily inwardly directed. Instead, "employee activists use various social activism methods, including social media campaigns, staged walkouts, and protests, to make their actions visible and generate social change" (Nataros, 2020, para. 4). In other words, unlike extant theorizing, industry understanding of employee activism involves not only lobbying for change within the organization to top leadership but also the use of public relations strategies to garner external attention and support for the employees' agenda. Indeed, Peachey (n.d.) attributed the recent increase in high-profile instances of employee activism to the advancements in technology that allow individuals and employee groups to reach large audiences easily, thus adding external social pressure on organizations in addition to the internal pressure.

Additionally, whereas theoretical accounts of employee activism tend to focus on employees campaigning against organization action (e.g., Luo & Jiang, 2014; McCown, 2007), or to urge the organization to implement changes in existing policy and action (e.g., Curtin, 2016) in practice employee activism may also involve employees speaking out for or in support of their organizations. For example, in the wake of Nike's controversial ad campaign featuring Colin Kaepernick, the equally controversial activist quarterback, Nike's employees reported having "more respect for our company than we have in the past" and feeling "a big swell of pride that we stood up for something meaningful" despite fielding a volley of abuse from upset customers (Saincome, 2018, para. 6). Indeed, an industry study found that over 87% of employees want their organizations to take a stand on social issues that are relevant to its business (Bryan, 2019), and such corporate advocacy shown to foster employee engagement.

Advancing a Theoretically and Practically Sound Definition of Employee Activism

Taken together, the academic and industry perspectives on employee activism offer insights into elements that characterize the concept. Combining these perspectives, a definition of employee activism is advanced in this chapter. Employee activism is defined as *goal-oriented efforts organized and negotiated by individual and/or groups of employees to internally and/or externally advocate for or against organizational policy and/or decision making to generate social change*. This definition captures the various features of employee activism as discussed earlier. First, it acknowledges that employee activism encompasses organized and negotiated efforts (Gautam & Carberry, 2020), undertaken by formal, organized groups such as unions (Western & Rosenfeld, 2011) or by individuals motivated about an issue (Krishna, 2017). Second, per industry perspectives on employee activism is conceptualized as being internally directed as well as externally focused, such that employee activism may involve making use of social activism tactics to garner external support for their agenda, thereby exerting both internal and external pressure on the organization. Third, this definition positions employee activism as an act of *advocacy*, such that it may manifest in the form of support for or opposition to organizational policy or action. Whereas most academic discussions on employee activism center on it being an oppositional force against the employer, this definition refocuses the potential of employee activism as also being a positive force for the employer, where employee activism may manifest in the form of employee advocacy and external promotion of organizational action for positive social change.

Employee activism, then, may be divided into two sub-concepts depending on the valence of employees' actions and attitudes vis-à-vis the organization's policy. When employee activists' efforts are aimed against or criticize organizational action or decision that the employees believe to be against social good, they may be considered *adversary activists*. On the other hand, when their efforts seek to support or praise an organization's stance or position that does generate positive social change, employee activists may be termed *advocate activists*. This typology of employee activists follows and complements discussions of employees' communicative behaviors during crises as discussed by public relations scholars (e.g., Lee, 2019; Mazzei et al., 2019). Just as employees may act as external advocates or adversaries for their organizations in times of crises, so too may they engage in advocacy or adversarial activism, and act as advocate activists or adversarial activists when trying to encourage the organization to behave in certain ways regarding controversial social issues. It is important to note, however, that whether employee activists are advocates or adversaries may be situational, rather than static.

This last aspect of employee activism discussed in the previous paragraph bears some similarity to the concept of *megaphoning* in public relations literature (see Kim & Rhee, 2011). Megaphoning refers to employees' external communicative behaviors about their employers. Similar to employee activism, these behaviors may manifest in the form of positive megaphoning or negative megaphoning. In other words, megaphoning refers to employees' sharing of positive or negative opinions about their organization to those outside the organization. Such opinion sharing about an organization by its own members has been shown to impact individuals' attitudes about the organization (Vibber & Kim, 2019). A similar concept to megaphoning is that of employee advocacy. Defined as "the voluntary promotion or defense of a company, its products, or its brands by an employee externally" (Men, 2014, p. 262), employee advocacy captures employees' actions to support and defend their employers against criticisms, not just promote or criticize them. Thelen (2020) clarified the concept of employee advocacy, defining it as "Verbal (written and spoken) or nonverbal voluntary manifestation of support, recommendation, or defense of an organization or its products by an employee to either internal or external publics" (p. 9). Much like megaphoning, employee advocacy is generally considered beyond the scope of an employee's job responsibilities and is not tied explicitly to rewards and job performance (Walden & Kingsley Westerman, 2018).

However, the key difference between employee megaphoning, employee advocacy, and the communicative dimension of employee activism lies in their respective goals of the two activities. Although both employee megaphoning and the communicative aspect of employee activism may involve speaking for or against the employees' organization, the goal of employee activism is to generate social change by either changing or reinforcing organizational policy. No such social change-based goal is conceptualized to underpin megaphoning or employee advocacy efforts. Indeed, megaphoning is conceptualized merely as employees' show of support for or against their employer with no other motive than to vent (Kim & Rhee, 2011), whereas employee advocacy serves to support or defend the organization against criticism regardless of context, and includes nonverbal actions (Thelen, 2020). Importantly, whereas the subject of employee advocacy and megaphoning is the organization, the subject of advocacy activism and adversarial activism is the organization's stance on a controversial social issue and the issue itself.

Employee Activism and Internal Communication

Several opportunities for theory development and future research related to employee activism and internal communication emerge from this review of the literature. Indeed, industry experts have acknowledged the crucial role played by internal communication in helping engage with employee activists to ensure mutually beneficial outcomes (Comcowich, 2019). This section offers scholars questions for future research to further explicate employee and workplace activism and to advance theory building on the concept. For example, scholars may want to explore the concepts of advocate activism and adversary activism, presenting empirical, theoretically driven explanations of the conditions under which organizations may encourage advocacy activism, and even adversary activism in certain cases. Would symmetrical communication and relationship cultivation encourage more advocacy activism and perhaps discourage adversary activism, as it does with positive and negative megaphoning, respectively, in times of crisis (Lee, 2020)? What other internal communication strategies and organizational factors encourage or inhibit employees' organizing and activism behaviors? Furthermore, what kinds of individual- and group-level activism may be expected when organizations engage in or attempt to take a stand on controversial social issues?

Additionally, a key question for public relations and organizational studies scholars to consider is this: is adversary activism inherently bad? Or perhaps is the answer more nuanced? Indeed, how adversary activism can help improve organizational decision-making and policies, and, eventually, contribute to the betterment of society, is also a worthy area of research. The strategies, discourses, and tactics used by adversary activism that have found success would help shed light on how other employee groups may also successfully organize for change in their own organizations, as well as build knowledge on activism and organizing. Such scholarship would contribute to and complement extant literature on employee organizing related to unionizing (e.g., Badigannavar & Kelly, 2005), change management (e.g., Goodall, 1992), and organizational systems and management (e.g., Hoogervorst, 2017).

Furthermore, for scholars interested in the intersection of internal communication, digital media, and social networks, employee activism as discussed in this chapter presents opportunities for research. How do employee groups and activists leverage their internal and external social networks to facilitate organizing and mounting external pressure on organizations? What role do digital media and social networks play in enabling the amplification and employee activists' agendas, thus facilitating the spillover of internal issues into external environments? Are there certain issues that garner more social amplification than others? These and other questions may be valuable areas for scholarship.

To answer these questions and more, scholars may consider adopting extant theoretical frameworks that have been successfully applied to understand activism and activists, writ large, and integrate these frameworks with internal communication scholarship. For example, the situational theory of problem solving has found application in explaining activists' communicative behaviors (e.g., Chen et al., 2017; Krishna, 2017) as well as supportive behaviors in times of crises (e.g., Krishna & Kim, 2020). The anger activism model, which proposes that "anger facilitates attitude and behavior change when (a) the target audience is pro-attitudinal, (b) the anger is intense, and (c) the audience has strong perceptions of efficacy" (Turner et al., 2006, p. 3) has found use predicting rage-fueled donation behaviors (Austin et al., 2020).

Critical-cultural perspectives too have been advanced to further the scholarship on activism, as scholars have called for a shift in how activist public relations is considered in ways that "acknowledges alternative articulations and power as fluid" and not "rigidly hierarchical" (Ciszek, 2015,

p. 451). Curtin and Gaither's (2005) cultural-economic model provides one such model which provides a critical-cultural alternative to conceptualizing activism and public relations. Dialogic approaches to activism too have found use in identifying how best activists can harness information technology tools to advance their causes (e.g., Sommerfeldt et al., 2012). These and other theoretical frameworks on activism and conflict resolution may be useful in furthering our understanding of employee activism and internal communication.

Conclusion

Although research on employee activism is in its infancy, especially in public relations, extant theoretical and industry perspectives offer several avenues for future scholarship, as discussed in the previous section. The present chapter offered a theoretically and practically driven definition of employee activism and proposed two sub-concepts to describe both pro-organization and anti-organization efforts, i.e., advocate activism and adversary activism respectively. This chapter serves as a call to scholars across disciplines to further examine employee activism. The research questions as well as the definition of employee activism posited in this chapter serve as a starting for future scholarship, within public relations and beyond.

Employee Activism and Internal Communication

Practitioner's Perspective (Interview)
Raymond L. Kotcher
Professor of the Practice
Boston University College of Communication

Q: What is employee activism? What is the role of the modern-day communicator in addressing employee activism?
A: Today, employees are central to corporate strategy. They are a powerful force. As advocates, they can help companies gain strategic and competitive advantage. They can support and accelerate transformation, even enable companies to become disruptors themselves. Keeping employees engaged and building community and culture are a crucial part of the modern-day communicator's job. However, rapidly shifting social, economic, technological, and generational changes have complicated the

employee–employer dynamic, making the job of communicators complex. One key factor contributing to this complexity is employees' expectations of their employers. Gone are the days when an employee's relationship with their employer was limited to a transaction with an employee simply providing services in exchange for a salary. Instead, employees want their employers to behave in ways that match their own values and expectations—organizations that don't fulfill these expectations can end up facing employees as activists, even strong adversaries.

Q: What are some factors that have contributed to the recent rise of employee activism?

A: One factor that has spurred on employee expectations is the generational shift in the workforce. Millennials, who now constitute half the American workforce and grew up during the Great Recession of 2008, are witness to the income and social inequalities that persist around the world. They are acutely aware of the impending climate crisis and, as we all are, of the dreadful pandemic and its economic impact. They want more than just a job. They want to be part of organizations that stand for something larger. They want jobs that contribute to the greater good on issues such as health, social justice, diversity and inclusion, the environment, education, and labor practices, among others. And they are not afraid of speaking out when they are unhappy with their employers' actions. Their voices are fast becoming a force for social change, one company at a time.

Q: Are these developments and expectations new? How can employee expectations and employee activism manifest, particularly against the backdrop of the Covid-19 pandemic?

A: This change had been coming to the workplace for quite some time. In the not-so-distant past, what happened inside a company stayed inside a company. Not anymore. Communication technologies have lowered the boundaries separating the internal and the external. Employees and their expectations and demands now resonate, often simultaneously, on the inside and the outside. Employees ask their companies to stand tall and lead, as have activist employee groups at Google and Facebook; they ask their companies to be moral leaders, and are unafraid to express their displeasure when they believe their employers have violated moral expectations, as Wayfair and Hootsuite found out. Today's workforce expects purpose with action and will engage actively if expectations are not met. The Covid-19 health crisis and the social justice movement have only intensified employees' expectations and demands of their employers' behaviors on both the inside and the outside.

Ray Kotcher is a professor of the practice, public relations, at Boston University's College of Communication, and the former CEO and chairman of Ketchum, one of the world's largest and most awarded public relations agencies.

References

"Employees Rising: Seizing the Opportunity in Employee Activism." (n.d). *Weber Shandwick*. https://www.webershandwick.com/uploads/news/files/employees-rising-seizing-the-opportunity-in-employee-activism.pdf.

Anderson, D. S. (1992). Identifying and responding to activist publics: A case study. *Journal of Public Relations Research, 4*, 151–165. https://doi.org/10.1207/s1532754xjprr0403_02.

Austin, L., Overton, H., McKeever, B. W., & Bortree, D. (2020). Examining the rage donation trend: Applying the anger activism model to explore communication and donation behaviors. *Public Relations Review, 46*(5), 1–8. https://doi.org/10.1016/j.pubrev.2020.101981.

Badigannavar, V., & Kelly, J. (2005). Why are some union organizing campaigns more successful than others? *British Journal of Industrial Relations, 43*(3), 515–535. https://doi.org/10.1111/j.1467-8543.2005.00367.x.

Baron, J. B. (1984). Organizational perspectives on stratification. *Annual Review of Sociology, 10*, 37–69. https://doi.org/10.1146/annurev.so.10.080184.000345.

Baron, D. P., & Diermeier, D. (2007). Strategic activism and nonmarket strategy. *Journal of Economics & Management Strategy, 16*(3), 599–634. https://doi.org/10.1111/j.1530-9134.2007.00152.x.

Briscoe, F., & Gupta, A. (2016). Social activism in and around organizations. *The Academy of Management Annals, 10*(1), 671–727. https://doi.org/10.1080/19416520.2016.1153261.

Bryan, J. (2019, July 3). *Corporate advocacy of social issues can drive employee engagement*. Smarter with Gartner. https://www.gartner.com/smarterwithgartner/corporate-advocacy-of-social-issues-can-drive-employee-engagement/.

Chen, Y. R. R., Hung-Baesecke, C. J. F., & Kim, J. N. (2017). Identifying active hot-issue communicators and subgroup identifiers: Examining the situational theory of problem solving. *Journalism & Mass Communication Quarterly, 94*(1), 124–147. https://doi.org/10.1177/1077699016629371.

Ciszek, E. L. (2015). Bridging the gap: Mapping the relationship between activism and public relations. *Public Relations Review, 41*(4), 447–455. https://doi.org/10.1016/j.pubrev.2015.05.016.

Comcowich, W. (2019, August 8). 5 ways communicators can prep for—And respond to—Employee activism. *Ragan's PR Daily*. https://www.

ragan.com/5-ways-communicators-can-prep-for-and-respond-to-employee-activism/.

Curtin, P. A. (2016). Exploring articulation in internal activism and public relations theory: A case study. *Journal of Public Relations Research, 28*(1), 19–34. https://doi.org/10.1080/1062726X.2015.1131696.

Curtin, P., & Gaither, T. K. (2005). Privileging identity, difference, and power: The circuit of culture as a basis for public relations theory. *Journal of Public Relations Research, 17*, 91–115. https://doi.org/10.1207/s1532754xjprr1702_3.

Dougall, E. (2005). Revelations of an ecological perspective: Issues, inertia, and the public opinion environment of organizational populations. *Public Relations Review, 31*(4), 534–543. https://doi.org/10.1016/j.pubrev.2005.08.013.

Dozier, D. M., & Lauzen, M. M. (2000). Liberating the intellectual domain from the practice: Public relations, activism, and the role of the scholar. *Journal of Public Relations Research, 12*(1), 3–22. https://doi.org/10.1207/S1532754XJPRR1201_2.

Gaines Ross, L. (2019, September 20). 4 in 10 American workers consider themselves social activists. *Quartz at Work*. https://qz.com/work/1712492/how-employee-activists-are-changing-the-workplace.

Gautam, N., & Carberry, E. (2020). Understanding employee activism in the high-tech sector: A comparative case analysis. In *Academy of Management Proceedings* (Vol. 2020, No. 1, p. 20523). Academy of Management.

Ghaffrey, S. (2019, November 22). Google employees protest the company's "attempt to silence workers." *Vox*. https://www.vox.com/recode/2019/11/22/20978537/google-workers-suspension-employee-activists-protest.

Githens, R. P., & Aragon, S. R. (2009). LGBT employee groups: Goals and organizational structures. *Advances in Developing Human Resources, 11*(1), 121–135. https://doi.org/10.1177/1523422308329200.

Goodall, H. L. (1992). Empowerment, culture, and postmodern organizing: Deconstructing the Nordstrom employee handbook. *Journal of Organizational Change Management, 5*(2), 23–30. https://doi.org/10.1108/09534819210014850.

Grunig, J. E., & Grunig, L. A. (1997, July). *Review of a program of research on activism: Incidence in four countries, activist publics, strategies of activist groups, and organizational responses to activism*. Paper presented to the Fourth Public Relations Research Symposium, Lake Bled, Slovenia.

Grunig, L. A., Grunig, J. E., & Dozier, D. M. (2002). *Excellent public relations and effective organizations: A study of communication management in three countries*. Lawrence Erlbaum Associates Inc.

Gurchiek, K. (2019, September 2019). Employee activism is on the rise. *SHRM*. https://www.shrm.org/hr-today/news/hr-news/pages/employee-activism-on-the-rise.aspx.
Hames, A. (2019, July 2). The rise of employee activism: Lessons from the Wayfair walkout. *Employee Benefit News*. https://www.benefitnews.com/opinion/wayfair-walkout-exemplifies-importance-of-company-culture.
Hoogervorst, J. (2017). The imperative for employee-centric organizing and its significance for enterprise engineering. *Organizational Design and Enterprise Engineering, 1*(1), 43–58. https://doi.org/10.1007/s41251-016-0003-y.
Kim, J. N., & Rhee, Y. (2011). Strategic thinking about employee communication behavior (ECB) in public relations: Testing the models of megaphoning and scouting effects in Korea. *Journal of Public Relations Research, 23*(3), 243–268. https://doi.org/10.1080/1062726X.2011.582204.
Krishna, A. (2017). Motivation with misinformation: Conceptualizing lacuna individuals and publics as knowledge deficient, issue-negative activists. *Journal of Public Relations Research, 29*(4), 176–193. https://doi.org/10.1080/1062726X.2017.1363047.
Krishna, A., & Kim, S. (2020). Understanding customers' reactions to allegations of corporate environmental irresponsibility. *Journalism & Mass Communication Quarterly*, 1–24. https://doi.org/10.1177/1077699020958756.
Lee, Y. (2019). Crisis perceptions, relationship, and communicative behaviors of employees: Internal public segmentation approach. *Public Relations Review, 45*(4), 1–10. https://doi.org/10.1016/j.pubrev.2019.101832.
Lee, Y. (2020). A situational perspective on employee communicative behaviors in a crisis: The role of relationship and symmetrical communication. *International Journal of Strategic Communication, 14*(2), 89–104. https://doi.org/10.1080/1553118X.2020.1720691.
Luo, Y., & Jiang, H. (2014). Empowerment and internal activism during organizational change: A relocation story in China. *International Journal of Strategic Communication, 8*(1), 1–28. https://doi.org/10.1080/1553118X.2013.810628.
Maiorescu, R. D. (2017). Using online platforms to engage employees in unionism. The case of IBM. *Public Relations Review, 43*(5), 963–968. https://doi.org/10.1016/j.pubrev.2017.07.002.
Maks-Solomon, C., & Drewry, J. M. (2020). Why do corporations engage in LGBT Rights Activism? LGBT employee groups as internal pressure groups. *Business and Politics*, 1–29. https://doi.org/10.1017/bap.2020.5.
Mazzei, A., Kim, J. N., Togna, G., Lee, Y., & Lovari, A. (2019). Employees as advocates or adversaries during a corporate crisis. The role of perceived authenticity and employee empowerment. *Sinergie Italian Journal of Management, 37*(2), 195–212. https://doi.org/10.7433/s109.2019.10.

McCown, N. (2007). The role of public relations with internal activists. *Journal of Public Relations Research, 19*(1), 47–68.

Men, L. R. (2014). Why leadership matters to internal communication: Linking transformational leadership, symmetrical communication, and employee outcomes. *Journal of Public Relations Research, 26*(3), 256–279. https://doi.org/10.1080/1062726X.2014.908719.

Moreno, J. E. (2020, September 24). Hootsuite reverses after criticism of contract with ICE. *The Hill*. https://thehill.com/policy/technology/518091-hootsuite-reverses-after-criticism-of-contract-with-ice.

Meyerson, D. (2001). *Tempered radicals: How everyday leaders inspire change at work*. Harvard Business School Press.

Meyerson, D. E., & Scully, M. A. (1995). Tempered radicalism and the politics of ambivalence and change. *Organization Science, 6*(5), 585–600. https://doi.org/10.1287/orsc.6.5.585.

Nataros, T. (2020, August 20). How to respond to employee activism. *FAMA*. https://blog.fama.io/how-to-respond-to-employee-activism.

Peachey, R. (n.d.). The 2020s: Decade of employee activism. *The HR Director*. https://www.thehrdirector.com/the-2020s-decade-of-employee-activism/.

Reber, B. H., & Kim, J. K. (2006). How activist groups use websites in media relations: Evaluating online press rooms. *Journal of Public Relations Research, 18*(4), 313–333. https://doi.org/10.1207/s1532754xjprr1804_2.

Rouse, M. (2020). Employee activism. *TechTarget*. https://searchhrsoftware.techtarget.com/definition/employee-activism#:~:text=Employee%20activism%20is%20actions%20taken,intentionally%20to%20generate%20social%20change.

Saincome, M. (2018, September 8). What it was like inside a Nike call center after the Colin Kaepernick ad dropped. *Rolling Stone*. https://www.rollingstone.com/culture/culture-features/colin-kaepernick-controversy-nike-call-center-720713/.

Sandler, R. (2020, September 24). Hootsuite drops ICE contract after employee backlash. *Forbes*. https://www.forbes.com/sites/rachelsandler/2020/09/24/hootsuite-drops-ice-contract-after-employee-backlash/#4e7f59d51c50.

Scully, M., & Segal, A. (2002). Passion with an umbrella: Grassroots activists in the workplace. *Research in the Sociology of Organizations, 19*(2), 125–168. https://doi.org/10.1016/S0733-558X(02)19004-5.

Skoglund, A., & Böhm, S. (2020). Prefigurative partaking: Employees' environmental activism in an energy utility. *Organization Studies, 41*(9), 1257–1283. https://doi.org/10.1177/0170840619847716.

Sommerfeldt, E. J., Kent, M. L., & Taylor, M. (2012). Activist practitioner perspectives of website public relations: Why aren't activist websites fulfilling the dialogic promise? *Public Relations Review, 38*(2), 303–312. https://doi.org/10.1016/j.pubrev.2012.01.001.

Stuart, P. (2020, February 10). The rise of employee activism: A defining issue for HR in 2020. *HRZone*. https://www.hrzone.com/lead/culture/the-rise-of-employee-activism-a-defining-issue-for-hr-in-2020.

Taylor, M., Kent, M. L., & White, W. J. (2001). How activist organizations are using the Internet to build relationships. *Public Relations Review, 27*, 263–284. https://doi.org/10.1016/S0363-8111(01)00086-8.

Taylor, V., & Raeburn, N. C. (1995). Identity politics as high-risk activism: Career consequences for lesbian, gay, and bisexual sociologists. *Social Problems, 42*(2), 252–273.

Thelen, P. D. (2020). Internal communicators' understanding of the definition and importance of employee advocacy. *Public Relations Review, 46*(4), 1–11. https://doi.org/10.1016/j.pubrev.2020.101946.

Turner, M. M., Bessarabova, E., Hambleton, K., Sipek, S., Weiss, M., & Long, K. (2006). *Does anger facilitate or debilitate persuasion? A test of the anger activism model*. Presented at the Annual Conference of the International Communication Association.

Vardeman, J., & Sebesta, A. (2020). The problem of intersectionality as an approach to digital activism: The Women's March on Washington's attempt to unite all women. *Journal of Public Relations Research, 32*(1–2), 7–29. https://doi.org/10.1080/1062726X.2020.1716769.

Vibber, K., & Kim, J.-N. (2019). Advocates or adversaries? Explicating within-border foreign publics' role in shaping soft power through megaphoning and echoing. *Place Branding and Public Diplomacy*, 1–18. https://doi.org/10.1057/s41254-019-00156-0.

Wakabayashi, D., Griffith, E., Tsang, A., & Conger, K. (2018, November 1). Google walkout: Employees stage protest over handling of sexual harassment. *The New York Times*. https://www.nytimes.com/2018/11/01/technology/google-walkout-sexual-harassment.html.

Walden, J. A., & Kingsley Westerman, C. Y. (2018). Strengthening the tie: Creating exchange relationships that encourage employee advocacy as an organizational citizenship behavior. *Management Communication Quarterly, 32*(4), 593–611. https://doi.org/10.1177/0893318918783612.

Werder, K. P. (2006). Responding to activism: An experimental analysis of public relations strategy influence on attributes of publics. *Journal of Public Relations Research, 18*(4), 335–356. https://doi.org/10.1207/s1532754xjprr1804_3.

Western, B., & Rosenfeld, J. (2011). Unions, norms, and the rise in US wage inequality. *American Sociological Review, 76*(4), 513–537. https://doi.org/10.1177/0003122411414817.

Wingard, J. (2020, January 10). Employee activism is the new normal. So why is Amazon leadership freaking out? *Forbes*. https://www.forbes.com/sites/jasonwingard/2020/01/10/employee-activism-is-the-new-normal-so-why-is-amazon-leadership-freaking-out/#3110658827f1.

CHAPTER 8

Beyond Internal Corporate Social Responsibility Communication (ICSRC): Creating a Purposeful Organization

Ganga S. Dhanesh

Corporate social responsibility (CSR) is broadly defined as businesses meeting their social responsibilities toward diverse stakeholders. From a functionalist perspective, it is critical to communicate an organization's socially, environmentally, legally, ethically, and economically responsible policies and actions to stakeholders to garner desirable organizational outcomes while from a constitutive, constructivist perspective, it is critical to engage in CSR communication to co-create meanings and understandings of CSR among organizations and their stakeholders (Crane & Glozer, 2016; Schoeneborn et al., 2020). Even though employees have been highlighted as a critical stakeholder in CSR communication,

G. S. Dhanesh (✉)
College of Communication and Media Sciences, Zayed University, Dubai, United Arab Emirates
e-mail: Ganga.Dhanesh@zu.ac.ae

L. R. Men and A. Tkalac Verčič (eds.), *Current Trends and Issues in Internal Communication*, New Perspectives in Organizational Communication, https://doi.org/10.1007/978-3-030-78213-9_8

research on internal stakeholders lags behind that on external stakeholders and scholars continue to call for more research on internal CSR communication (ICSRC) from constitutive and functionalist perspectives to reflexively interrogate and co-create meanings of CSR, and generate significant returns such as ethical employer brand identity, employer attractiveness, employee engagement, and employee identification, ultimately leading to employees becoming CSR advocates and ambassadors (Duthler & Dhanesh, 2018; Edinger-Schons et al., 2019; Jiang & Luo, 2020; Schaefer et al., 2019, 2020; Verčič & Ćorić, 2018; Wang & Pala, 2020).

In addition to engendering these outcomes, ICSRC has been called upon to inspire employees to contribute to building a purpose-driven organization. Although organizational purpose has become a buzzword in practice, and practitioners across management, marketing, and communication have begun to link the concepts of CSR and purpose, there is hardly any academic literature that theorizes connections between ICSRC and purpose. Accordingly, this chapter reviews the literature on ICSRC; defines organizational purpose, connects it to extant understandings of CSR; and offers a theoretical framework that leverages ICSRC to engage employees in building a purposeful organization.

Internal CSR Communication (ICSRC)

Definitions

Prior to defining ICSRC, it is important to define related concepts such as CSR, internal CSR, internal communication, and integrated CSR communication.

CSR and Internal CSR

According to one of the most widely cited definitions, CSR refers to "the simultaneous fulfillment of the firm's economic, legal, ethical, and philanthropic responsibilities" (Carroll, 1991, p. 42). Most discussions of internal CSR mirror these dimensions. For instance, to Maignan et al. (1999) internal CSR includes monitoring employee productivity, honoring employees' contractual obligations, encouraging workforce diversity, and policies that support work-life balance. In addition, to Weder et al. (2019) internal CSR includes employee volunteering programs. This chapter adopts the view that while the concept of internal

CSR provides a tidy label to CSR activities that are related to employees, this conceptualization is problematic because as organizational members, employees have a ringside view of their organization's CSR efforts related to multiple stakeholders. They are also exposed to external CSR communication and articulations of corporate ethical identities, which can contribute to a holistic assessment of their organization's CSR philosophies and activities, and not just one based on internal aspects (Carlini et al., 2019).

Internal Communication
Internal communication includes intra-organizational communication that encompasses informal watercooler chats as well as formal, managed communication (Vercic et al., 2012; Welch & Jackson, 2007). According to Welch and Jackson (2007) formal, internal communication management is "the strategic management of interactions and relationships between stakeholders at all levels within organisations" (p. 183). Internal communication has four dimensions of which internal corporate communication, mostly based on one-way communication between managers and employees, is employed to communicate organization-wide goals, objectives, and achievements, making it an ideal vehicle to communicate CSR (Duthler & Dhanesh, 2018). However, since social media platforms have amplified employee word-of-mouth communication, particularly with regard to CSR, in addition to strategically managing formal internal corporate communication, organizations will need to consider employees' informal word-of-mouth CSR communication as well (Lee & Tao, 2020).

Integrated CSR Communication
Scholars have challenged the siloed notion of internal communication directed at one set of stakeholders with the concept of auto-communication, which argues that as organizational boundaries blur, communication directed externally could influence internal stakeholders too, and have supported the notion of integrated communication (Cornelissen, 2020). Building on the theory of auto-communication and organizational identification, Morsing (2006) proposed that CSR communication is a vital process of auto-communication for member identification. Arguing that the trends of mediatization, digitalization, media convergence, and demographic developments behooves breaking down silos among public relations, advertising, branding etc., Diehl et al. (2017) defined integrated CSR communication as "the harmonization

of all CSR-related communication strategies and activities, whereby CSR is understood as the company's attitudes and behaviors with regard to its perceived obligations and responsibility toward its stakeholders and society" (p. v).

Internal CSR Communication (ICSRC)
Since employees are exposed to diverse aspects of CSR, internal, external, and auto CSR communication, articulations of their employer's ethical organizational and corporate identities, and because they engage in informal word-of-mouth CSR communication, employees become producers and consumers of CSR communication. Hence, this chapter defines internal CSR communication (ICSRC) as ***holistic intra-organizational and auto-communication related to diverse dimensions of CSR, disseminated by organizations and constructively constituted by employees***.

While CSR communication faces issues such as audience skepticism, ICSRC faces specific obstacles due to the relatively intimate nature of employer–employee relationships. Employees have an insider view of the organization; they receive internal and external CSR communication; they have deep knowledge of the company's CSR practices; can better assess CSR action-communication gaps; and as a result, could fall on a continuum that ranges from being highly skeptical to being advocates and ambassadors of CSR (Carlini et al., 2019; Edinger-Schons et al., 2019). The following section will review theoretical frameworks of ICSRC created to address some of these issues.

Theoretical Frameworks to Examine ICSRC

A thorough review of literature on ICSRC across public relations, marketing, advertising, management, accounting, and organizational communication revealed only a handful of theoretical frameworks for ICSRC. These include Maignan and Ferrell (2001) who considered CSR as an internal marketing strategy; Carlini et al. (2019) who offered a theoretical model for the CSR employer brand process; and Du et al. (2010), Crane and Glozer (2016), and Morsing and Schultz (2006) who offered CSR communication frameworks and strategies that are relevant for internal and external stakeholders.

According to Maignan and Ferrell's (2001) conceptualization of corporate citizenship as internal marketing, three aspects of internal and external corporate citizenship communication (intensity, accuracy, and value congruence) influence (a) the relationship between corporate citizenship practices and employee evaluations of corporate citizenship, and (b) the relationship between employee evaluation of corporate citizenship and outcomes such as organizational commitment and *esprit de corps*. Further, individual characteristics such as personal values, stage of cognitive moral development, and socio-demographics can also moderate these relationships.

More recently, Carlini et al. (2019) synthesized literatures from CSR and employer branding to create a conceptual model that addressed the CSR employer branding process from the perspectives of potential and existing employees. According to the model based on signaling theory, external CSR signals (CSR conduct, which in turns affects uncontrolled communication) are antecedents for potential employees' CSR journey, while CSR employer brand identity is an antecedent for the CSR journey of potential and current employees. For potential employees, external CSR signals can affect the perceived sincerity of CSR signaling, which can moderate the relationship between CSR employer brand identity and potential employee perception, which can influence intention to apply. For current employees, CSR employer brand identity can affect employee perception of CSR experience (such as CSR socialization, workplace benefits, corporate ethical empowerment, and equitable human resource practices, considered as internal CSR signals), which can lead to positive and negative employee outcomes. Further, the relationship between employee perception of CSR experience and outcomes will be moderated by the perceived gap between employees' CSR expectations and experiences. The authors proposed that firms need to achieve CSR consistency in terms of embeddedness of CSR values (embedded vs peripheral), and levels of internal CSR (high vs. low) and offered a typology of organizations that includes CSR employer brand, Underperformers, Internal focused, and Greenwashers that can enable managers to create a CSR employer brand identity, which can create a high-quality talent pool, and generate positive affective, cognitive and behavioral employee outcomes.

However, one of the greatest obstacles of CSR communication has been stakeholder skepticism, to address which Du et al. (2010) proposed a framework that dealt with the influence of message content (issue importance; commitment, impact, motives and fit of the CSR initiatives), and message channel (corporate, independent) on internal outcomes (awareness, attributions, attitudes, identification, and trust) and external outcomes from the perspective of customers (purchase, loyalty, and advocacy), employees (productivity, loyalty, citizenship behavior, advocacy) and investors (amount of invested capital, loyalty). This relationship can be moderated by stakeholder characteristics (stakeholder types, issue support, social value orientation) and company characteristics (reputation, industry, marketing strategies).

More recently, Crane and Glozer (2016) conducted a review of CSR communication literature, proposed a framework that distinguished research across two dimensions—internal/external stakeholders, and functionalist/constitutive paradigms, and identified four sets of CSR communication research. These included research on employees within the functionalist paradigm called CSR Integration, while research within the constitutive paradigm was called CSR Interpretation. After noting the limited research on CSR Integration, the authors suggested that functionalist research could adopt theoretical perspectives such as social identity theory and organizational justice to connect diverse disciplinary perspectives. Scholarship on CSR Interpretation could examine the role of CSR communication in new forms of organization such as social enterprises, and multi-stakeholder initiatives. Rupturing silos of work on ICSRC, the authors suggested research that spans internal and external stakeholders. For instance, research on externally focused CSR identity can be extended to internal audiences; or theories of sensemaking used to explore internal CSR meaning-making can be extended to understand how internal meaning-making can influence external sense-giving.

Finally, Morsing and Schultz (2006) offered three CSR communication strategies to engage with stakeholders—the stakeholder information strategy built on the public information model; the stakeholder response strategy based on the two-way asymmetrical communication model; and the stakeholder involvement strategy built on the two-way symmetrical model of communication. Although companies could adopt all three models for CSR communication, it is important to develop CSR communication strategies based on two-way symmetrical communication processes.

To summarize, while Maignan and Ferrell's (2001) early model conceptualized ICSRC only as a moderator between CSR practices and employee CSR evaluations; and between employee CSR evaluations and outcomes, later models (Carlini et al., 2019; Du et al., 2010) considered the effects of ICSRC on diverse employee outcomes. Overall, theoretical frameworks have offered various antecedents such as

CSR conduct/practices, moderators such as stakeholder and company characteristics, CSR expectation–experience gap; perceived sincerity of CSR signaling; and outcomes such as intention to apply, organizational commitment, esprit de corps, loyalty, citizenship behavior, and advocacy. Finally, Crane and Glozer's (2016) work acknowledged typologies of research on ICSRC across stakeholder types and research paradigms, while Morsing and Schultz (2006) offered a typology of CSR communication strategies that can be applied to both internal and external stakeholders.

Empirical Research on ICSRC

Scholars have conducted more work within the functionalist than the constitutive perspective. Functionalist scholarship includes examining antecedents of ICSRC such as CSR communication strategies (Duthler & Dhanesh, 2018; Jiang & Luo, 2020), message valence of employee word-of-mouth related to CSR (Lee & Tao, 2020), and potential employees' perceptions of CSR and employer brand (Verčič & Ćorić, 2018).

Limited research has identified moderators such as frequency and transparency of CSR communication over social media (Wang & Pala, 2020), and employee involvement in CSR (Schaefer et al., 2019) and mediators such as the evaluation of perceived organizational CSR engagement (Schaefer et al., 2020), CSR social media and job engagement, and employee perceptions of CSR motives (Jiang & Luo, 2020), and authenticity (Lee & Tao, 2020).

Finally, scholarship has examined multiple outcomes such as job satisfaction due to CSR, organizational pride, and word-of-mouth about CSR (Schaefer et al., 2020), consumers' corporate attitudes and purchase intentions (Lee & Tao, 2020), employee engagement (Duthler & Dhanesh, 2018; Jiang & Luo, 2020), employee identification (Wang & Pala, 2020), perceived authenticity of CSR engagement (Schaefer et al., 2019) and corporate reputation from the perspective of potential employees (Verčič & Ćorić, 2018).

In addition, a handful of studies has examined ICSRC from a constitutive perspective. For instance, Girschik (2020) examined how CSR managers fulfil an internal activist role by framing CSR activities to influence understandings of CSR, while Wagner (2019) demonstrated how employees might withdraw from CSR processes when organizations follow strong sense-giving, informational, and persuasive approaches.

To summarize, empirical research on ICSRC within the functionalist paradigm has been scattered, examining a multitude of antecedents, moderators, mediators, and outcomes, indicative of an emergent and productive area of research, while research within the constitutive paradigm is limited. While research on these streams needs to be strengthened, a new direction of research across functionalist and constitutive approaches is to examine articulations of interconnections between ICSRC and organizational purpose.

ICSRC to Build a Purposeful Organization

Defining Purpose and Connecting It to CSR

Kantar Consulting (2018) defined purpose as "why you exist: and the positive impact in people's lives and the world they live in" (p. 12) in their report, *Purpose 2020*. The report distinguishes purpose from vision, mission, and CSR. While *purpose* refers to the organization's positive impact in the world; *vision* refers to where the organization is headed; *mission* refers to how the organization is going to get there; and CSR refers to what the organization does to help protect the world. Most business/trade journals also distinguish between *cause* and *purpose*. While cause refers to an issue a company might address, purpose lies at the heart of the business model and is the reason for being. Vila and Bharadwaj (2017) argued that some brands, whom they called *social purpose natives,* have built social purpose into their business models, such as TOMS and Patagonia. The societal benefits they offer are so deeply intertwined with their products and services that one cannot separate the two. However, for those they called *social purpose immigrants*, established brands that are committed to social and environmental causes, but may not have a consciously articulated social purpose, they proposed exploring social purpose through the brand's heritage, customer tensions, and product externalities. Exploring a brand's heritage and the core reason for its existence can offer clues to the social needs the brand is positioned to address. Similarly, examining issues that are pertinent to the organization's customers, especially those related to the brand's heritage, and identifying externalities caused by the brand or the industry can also help to identify social purpose.

Academic scholarship on purpose also seems to concur with these ideas. Basu (1999) argued that corporate purpose represents the ultimate priority of the organization. The needs of the organization's key stakeholders, the macro environment of the organization, and the cultural beliefs and values of the organization influence corporate purpose. White et al. (2017), reporting an interview with Antony Jenkins, ex-CEO/chairman at Barclays, wrote that a number of CEOs use the word *purpose* to refer to the "underlying issues and practices of rethinking how corporations work, and also rethinking the basic relationship between corporations and society" (p. 101).

To Hollensbe et al. (2014), purpose refers to the reason for which business is created or exists, its meaning and direction. They argued that a focus on organizational purpose highlights the interdependence of business and society, a notion that is also reflected in the literature on CSR. They proposed that the values of dignity (that considers the whole person), solidarity (recognizing that other people matter), plurality (valuing diversity), subsidiarity (promoting accountability at all levels by proper delegation of decision-making), reciprocity (building mutual trust and trusted relationships), and sustainability (being stewards of people, values, and resources) are potential mechanisms to help organizations build trust and better businesses.

Similarly, Karns (2011) argued that the purpose of business is to contribute to *human flourishing*, which is about individual and communal well-being with economic, psycho-social, spiritual, and physical dimensions as reflected in the United Nations Millennium Development Goals. Karns (2011) suggested the stewardship model where the purpose of business is to serve society by contributing to the flourishing of humankind. Indeed, Cone/Porter Novelli's Purpose study (2018) found that to 89% of Americans, implementing CSR programs was one of the major ways companies could demonstrate their purpose.

The discussions reviewed above establish *purpose as the reason for existence of organizations, and meeting organizations' social and environmental responsibilities (CSR) as a way of delivering purpose, thus making a clear connection between organizational purpose and responsibilities.*

Organizations have been paying attention to the conceptualization, enactment, and communication of their purpose and responsibilities for multiple reasons such as the generation of relational, reputational, and legitimacy capitals and because people increasingly want to work for companies that create positive value. According to Cone/Porter Novelli's

Purpose study (2018), 68% said they would work for a company leading with purpose. Despite these encouraging statistics, research findings on whether stakeholders, particularly current and prospective employees, care about organizational purpose and CSR have been mixed. Consequently, scholars have highlighted the need to acknowledge the role of employee characteristics in the conceptualization and enactment of CSR communication, particularly the emergence of a socially and environmentally conscious generation of employees (Dhanesh, 2020; Diehl et al., 2017; Weder et al., 2019).

Changes in Employee Characteristics and Organizational Responses

Scholars have examined the CSR attitude–behavior gap or the claim by stakeholders that they harbor positive attitudes toward socially responsible companies, but do not translate those positive attitudes to behavior (Johnstone & Tan, 2015). However, scholars have also found that stakeholders care for socially responsible companies, especially millennials, who represent the largest generation in the labour force since 2016 (White et al., 2017). Beyond this demographic categorization of stakeholders who care about organizational purpose and CSR, Dhanesh (2020) proposed that the concept of hypermodernity might offer a new segmentation of publics that care for purpose and CSR.

Adapting Lipovetsky's (2005) ideas of hypermodernity, Dhanesh (2020) argued that characteristics of hyper-individualism such as (a) a paradoxical focus on self and others, (b) the need to actively construct exemplary individual identities (c) a penchant for emotional and experiential consumption (d) a love of hyperspectacles and (e) a paradoxical obsession with enjoying the present while being racked with anxiety about the future, might drive hypermodern individuals' deep interest in engaging with purpose-led, socially and environmentally responsible companies.

Hypermodern organizations, or organizations based on excessive levels of speed, characterized by hyper-flexibility to meet market conditions; and focus on the short term exert undue pressures on employees, and create a climate of risk and uncertainty. Further, widespread adoption of communication technologies has ensured constant connectivity between employees and their organizations, placing excessive stress and an expectation of never being completely disconnected from work (Roberts & Armitage, 2006).

Dhanesh (2020) suggested that to address such issues and to adapt purpose and CSR for hypermodern employees, organizations should create employee well-being programs that rearticulate core work hours and increase organizational awareness of the negative consequences of an always-on mentality. Organizations can also create emotive, experiential CSR programs aligned with organizational purpose that hypermodern employees can engage with as volunteers. Finally, organizations can create visual hyperspectacles that can help to create ethical corporate identities built on the enactment of purpose-aligned CSR programs. Dhanesh (2020) argued that engaging in experiential CSR programs could help hypermodern employees to connect multiple dots—their longing for rich, qualitative experiences; desire to contribute to a humane world; and need to belong to a community which could help them craft unique personal identities. Establishing these connections could meet higher-order needs of employees and enable employee identification.

This approach of creating purpose-aligned CSR initiatives for employees that could improve employee outcomes augments Karns' (2011) idea of purpose as contributing to the flourishing of humankind through individual and communal well-being. Offering initial empirical support for the interconnections of purpose and CSR from an employee perspective, Bhattacharya et al. (2019) found that employee awareness of their company's higher purpose could positively impact reduction in justification strategies of their lack of ownership of CSR, which could, in turn, lead to sustainable behaviors in the workplace. However, scholarship is yet to deal with the role of ICSRC in engaging employees to build a purposeful organization, which the next section addresses with a proposed theoretical framework.

Framework for Purpose-Aligned ICSRC

This chapter builds on the literature reviewed and proposes a framework for purpose-aligned ICSRC (see Fig. 8.1). According to this framework, organizations need to employ communication strategies of engagement and involvement to create conversations among employees on purpose-aligned CSR, straddling topics such as issues and causes to focus on, probable motives and objectives, company-purpose-cause fit, extent and duration of input, and intended impact. This meaning-making process could not only help to collaboratively construct meanings of purpose-led social responsibilities within the organization but could also inform the

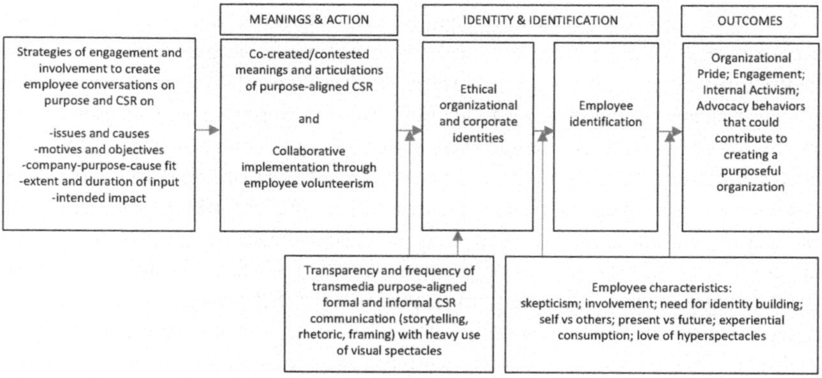

Fig. 8.1 Framework for purpose-aligned ICSRC

crafting of ethical organizational and corporate identities. Given trends such as media convergence, and employees enthused by hyperspectacles, the move from shared articulations and collaborative implementation to creating ethical organizational and corporate identities could be moderated by the extent of transmedia rhetoric, framing, and storytelling employing spectacular visuals. These ethical organizational and corporate identities could meet hypermodern employee needs for identity building, which could be moderated by employee characteristics such as skepticism, or the paradoxical hypermodern feature of being both self- and other-focused simultaneously. Employee identification could generate outcomes such as organizational pride, engagement, advocacy behavior, or internal activism, all of which can contribute to creating a reflexive, responsible, purposeful organization.

Future research can examine each of these variables using both functionalist and constitutive approaches to ICSRC. While organizations tend to adopt top-down, one-way models of communication, research can examine how communication strategies of engagement and involvement can foster both co-created and contested meanings of CSR, and how the two can coexist as organizational members continue to dynamically debate and discuss evolving meanings and articulations of what it means to be a purpose-led, responsible organization. Research can also examine various forms of transmedia storytelling related to purpose and CSR that encompasses both formal internal and external corporate communication, and informal word-of-mouth employee communication and how processes of auto-communication can moderate the association between CSR practices and creation of ethical identities. Much more research needs to be done on examining the processes through which organizational and corporate ethical identities can meet employee identity needs and achieve identification. Most importantly, how do changing employee characteristics such as those of hypermodern employees affect this process of employee identification, and finally how do these characteristics influence the generation of outcomes from employee identification.

Interview with Alex Malouf, Corporate Communications Director MEA, Schneider Electric

How would you define organizational purpose? Is it a fad or a meaningful trend? And why?

For me, organizational purpose should be about what people are there to do in their organizations. Is it making great food? Is it solving problems using technology? Is it connecting people? It's the goal that everyone at that organization is working towards. And it's always been a part of every company and it's the reason companies exist (tell me of a single company that started out with the aim of paying shareholders). What's happened is that this concept has morphed into "positive purpose". Let me give you an example—a fast food company's purpose may have gone from selling great burgers to selling nutritious meals. Pepsi's atrocious Black Lives Matter ad is a great example of this—the company sells tasty drinks and snacks. But they wanted to be seen in the light of a social movement. And this doesn't always work, because that isn't true organizational purpose.

What are your thoughts on the relationship between CSR and organizational purpose?

CSR isn't often long-term—strategies get changed year-in, year-out. And ideas shift. Without long-term planning and execution, CSR isn't as effective as it could be. If CSR is to be truly sustainable, it has to be linked to organizational purpose. Employees need to feel that CSR is part of the company, management even more so if we expect them to support CSR long-term. And stakeholders should see an alignment between CSR and organizational purpose. The two notions feed off and amplify one another. They help people to see the other much more clearly.

How can internal CSR communication help to engage employees in building a purposeful organization? Could you share an example?

We had one wonderful group in a previous company (Procter & Gamble). They were from the same function, the same team, and they set up a social group. Part of their activities included one CSR activity every quarter. They'd discuss within themselves their big ideas which were linked to what the company did. They'd talk with the communications team about these ideas, to see if they were feasible and if the comms team could craft stories around the activities. Because these were their ideas, they were always engaged, committed, and would do whatever they needed to do to make the activity happen (be it with funding or getting products). I didn't see this level of energy or enthusiasm when ideas were imposed from the top. And the team was the closest, the friendliest in the organization.

What are some of the factors that help and/or hinder the use of internal CSR communication to engage employees in contributing to building a purposeful organization?

Internal CSR can't be top-down. There must be some employee engagement—employees need to feel they have something to give and do in the process of coming up with ideas and execution, otherwise it can just feel like work. Ask your employees, seek out their opinion, preferably in small groups (up to 20 people). Anything larger and it'll often be the management who will seek to lead (at least in patriarchal, top-down societies). Bring in external voices, such as customers and community members, who can speak about societal issues and help educate your internal audience. Use visuals and video, and ask the beneficiaries to tell their own story, especially after the event, so you can emphasize the impact of the good work being done.

Alex Malouf, a marketing communications executive who has spent the last 17 years in the Middle East has lived across the region, working for the public and private sectors in a variety of communications roles. He is the Corporate Communications Director for the Middle East and Africa at Schneider Electric.

References

Basu, S. (1999). *Corporate purpose: Why it matters more than strategy*. Routledge.

Bhattacharya, C. B., Sen, S., & Edinger-Schons, L. M. (2019). How corporate purpose affects employees' sustainable behaviors: The moderating role of autonomy and culture. In R. Bagchi, L. Block, & L. Lee (Eds.), *Advances in consumer research* (pp. 456–458). Association for Consumer Research.

Carlini, J., Grace, D., France, C., & Lo Iacono, J. (2019). The corporate social responsibility (CSR) employer brand process: Integrative review and comprehensive model. *Journal of Marketing Management, 35*(1–2), 182–205. https://doi.org/10.1080/0267257x.2019.1569549.

Carroll, A. B. (1991). The pyramid of corporate social responsibility: Toward the moral management of organisational stakeholders. *Business Horizons, 34*(4), 39–48.

Cone/Porter Novelli. (2018). *How to build deeper bonds, amplify your message, and expand your consumer base*. http://www.conecomm.com/research-blog/2018-purpose-study.

Cornelissen, J. (2020). *Corporate communication* (6th ed.). Sage.

Crane, A., & Glozer, S. (2016). Researching corporate social responsibility communication: Themes, opportunities and challenges. *Journal of Management Studies, 53*(7), 1223–1252. https://doi.org/10.1111/joms.12196.

Dhanesh, G. S. (2020). Who cares about organizational purpose and corporate social responsibility, and how can organizations adapt? A hypermodern perspective. *Business Horizons, 63*(4), 585–594.

Diehl, S., Karmasin, M., Mueller, B., Terlutter, R., & Weder, F. (Eds.). (2017). *Handbook of integrated CSR communication*. Springer.

Du, S., Bhattacharya, C. B., & Sen, S. (2010). Maximizing business returns to corporate social responsibility (CSR): The role of CSR communication. *International Journal of Management Reviews, 12*(1), 8–19.

Duthler, G., & Dhanesh, G. S. (2018). The role of corporate social responsibility (CSR) and its internal communication in predicting employee engagement: Perspectives from the United Arab Emirates (UAE). *Public Relations Review, 44*(4), 453–462.

Edinger-Schons, L. M., Lengler-Graiff, L., Scheidler, S., & Wieseke, J. (2019). Frontline employees as corporate social responsibility (CSR) ambassadors: A quasi-field experiment. *Journal of Business Ethics, 157*(2), 359–373. https://doi.org/10.1007/s10551-018-3790-9.

Girschik, V. (2020). Shared responsibility for societal problems: The role of internal activists in reframing corporate responsibility. *Business & Society, 59*(1), 34–66. https://doi.org/10.1177/0007650318789867.

Hollensbe, E., Wookey, C., Hickey, L., & George, G. (2014). Organizations with Purpose. *Academy of Management, 57*(5), 1227–1234.

Jiang, H., & Luo, Y. (2020). Driving employee engagement through CSR communication and employee perceived motives: The role of CSR-related social media engagement and job engagement. *International Journal of Business Communication*. Published online first.

Johnstone, M., & Tan, L. P. (2015). Exploring the gap between consumers' green rhetoric and purchasing behaviour. *Journal of Business Ethics, 132*(2), 311–328.

Kantar Consulting. (2018). *Purpose holds the key to igniting brand growth*. https://consulting.kantar.com/news-events/purpose-holds-the-key-to-igniting-brand-growth/.

Karns, G. L. (2011). Stewardship: A new vision for the purpose of business. *Corporate Governance: The International Journal of Business in Society, 11*(4), 337–347. https://doi.org/10.1108/14720701111159190.

Lee, Y., & Tao, W. (2020). Employees as information influencers of organization's CSR practices: The impacts of employee words on public perceptions of CSR. *Public Relations Review, 46*(1), 101887. https://doi.org/10.1016/j.pubrev.2020.101887.

Lipovetsky, G. (2005). *Hypermodern times*. Polity Press.

Maignan, I., & Ferrell, O. C. (2001). Corporate citizenship as a marketing instrument: Concepts, evidence and research directions. *European Journal of Marketing, 35*(3/4), 457–484.

Maignan, I., Ferrell, O. C., & Hult, G. T. M. (1999). Corporate citizenship: Cultural antecedents and business benefits. *Journal of the Academy of Marketing Science, 27*(4), 455–469.

Morsing, M., & Schultz, M. (2006). Corporate social responsibility communication: Stakeholder information, response and involvement strategies. *Business Ethics: A European Review, 15*, 323–338.

Morsing, M. (2006). Corporate social responsibility as strategic auto-communication: On the role of external stakeholders for member identification. *Business Ethics, 15*(2), 171–182. https://doi.org/10.1111/j.1467-8608.2006.00440.x.

Roberts, J., & Armitage, J. (2006). From organization to hypermodern organization: On the accelerated appearance and disappearance of Enron. *Journal of Organizational Change Management, 19*(5), 558–577.

Schaefer, S. D., Terlutter, R., & Diehl, S. (2019). Is my company really doing good? Factors influencing employees' evaluation of the authenticity of their company's corporate social responsibility engagement. *Journal of Business Research, 101*, 128–143. https://doi.org/10.1016/j.jbusres.2019.03.030.

Schaefer, S. D., Terlutter, R., & Diehl, S. (2020). Talking about CSR matters: Employees' perception of and reaction to their company's CSR communication in four different CSR domains. *International Journal of Advertising, 39*(2), 191–212. https://doi.org/10.1080/02650487.2019.1593736.

Schoeneborn, D., Morsing, M., & Crane, A. (2020). Formative perspectives on the relation between CSR communication and CSR practices: Pathways for walking, talking, and T(w)alking. *Business & Society, 59*(1), 5–33. https://doi.org/10.1177/0007650319845091.

Verčič, A. T., & Ćorić, D. S. (2018). The relationship between reputation, employer branding and corporate social responsibility. *Public Relations Review, 44*(4), 444–452. https://doi.org/10.1016/j.pubrev.2018.06.005.

Vercic, A. T., Vercic, D., & Sriramesh, K. (2012). Internal communication: Definition, parameters and the future. *Public Relations Review, 38*, 223–230.

Vila, O. R., & Bharadwaj, S. (2017). Competing on social purpose. *Harvard Business Review*. https://hbr.org/2017/09/competing-on-social-purpose.

Wagner, R. (2019, September 18–20). Activating employees for sustainability: The importance of narrative and sensemaking in a salutogenic approach to internal CSR communication. In *Proceedings of the 5th International CSR Communication Conference*, Stockholm School of Economics, Stockholm.

Wang, Y., & Pala, B. (2020). Communicating philanthropic CSR versus ethical and legal CSR to employees: Empirical evidence in Turkey. *Corporate Communications: An International Journal*. Ahead-of-print. https://doi.org/10.1108/CCIJ-01-2020-0014.

Weder, F., Einwiller, S., & Eberwein, T. (2019). Heading for new shores: Impact orientation of CSR communication and the need for communicative responsibility. *Corporate Communications, 24*(2), 198–211. https://doi.org/10.1108/CCIJ-02-2019-0020.

Welch, M., & Jackson, P. R. (2007). Rethinking internal communication: A stakeholder approach. *Corporate Communications: An International Journal, 12*(2), 177–198.

White, A., Yakis-Douglas, B., Helanummi-Cole, H., & Ventresca, M. (2017). Purpose-led organization: "Saint Antony" reflects on the idea of organizational purpose, in principle and practice. *Journal of Management Inquiry, 26*(1), 101–107.

CHAPTER 9

Enhancing Employee Well-Being Through Internal Communication

Justin A. Walden

Employee well-being has come into sharp focus in industry and academic realms in recent years as it is associated with a number of organization and employee-favorable outcomes. Knowing the importance of helping employees maintain their health, scholars from several disciplines have examined both the organizational and personal influences on employee well-being and the outcomes that develop when employees feel that their various needs are being met in the workplace.

As it will be explored in detail in this chapter, employee well-being generally consists of workers' social, physical, and psychological health (Grant et al., 2007). From the employee's perspective, psychological well-being is linked to job satisfaction, employee engagement, affective commitment to one's employing organization, and employee turnover intentions (Brunetto et al., 2012). Research has found that physical well-being is associated with decreased workers' compensation costs

J. A. Walden (✉)
North Dakota State University, Fargo, ND, USA
e-mail: justin.walden@ndsu.edu

L. R. Men and A. Tkalac Verčič (eds.), *Current Trends and Issues in Internal Communication*, New Perspectives in Organizational Communication, https://doi.org/10.1007/978-3-030-78213-9_9

for firms (Hodges et al., 2004) and decreased organizational expenditures on employee health in general (Keller et al., 2009). Evidence further suggests that psychological well-being predicts supervisory performance ratings (Wright et al., 2007) and employee retention/withdrawal decisions (Wright & Bonett, 1992/2007).

Three intersecting areas are relevant to contemporary discussions of employee well-being in light of the COVID-19 pandemic declaration: Remote work/telework trends; employees' responses to pandemic-related stressors; and managing employees amid the pandemic-caused economic downturn. The push toward increased worker flexibility through telework and work from home arrangements was remarkable even before the pandemic declaration. One industry study indicated that the number of people who engaged in telecommuting in the U.S. jumped 115 percent from 2005 to 2015 (Global Workplace Analytics and Flexjobs, 2017). COVID-19 further pushed this trend in a dramatic fashion across the world. For example, in the immediate aftermath of the pandemic, employment in the United States fell considerably in those occupations in which telework was not feasible (Dey et al., 2020). Meanwhile, it was estimated that 40 percent of European Union workers began to telework full-time because of the pandemic (Milasi et al., 2020).

To the second major change associated with the pandemic, workers suddenly had to contend with several new or exacerbated mental health issues in 2020. Concerns were raised about workers' overall levels of anxiety associated with forced at-home work arrangements, worries about job security, and their ability to juggle domestic responsibilities with their children at home because of school closures (Eurofound, 2020). Pre-COVID-19, scholars noted that a "practical paradox of technology" was shaping workplace communication and workers' interactions with each other in and out of the workplace (Ter Hoeven et al., 2016). This paradox suggests that the use of communication technology for work fosters greater efficiency and accessibility in work communication, while also contributing to interruptions that can cause burnout and decreases in work engagement (Ter Hoeven et al., 2016). These tensions were heightened in our post-COVID landscape through telework.

Potentially compounding employees' work experiences is that in many corners of the world, there were sharp rises in 2020 in unemployment, major disruptions to key local industries, and dramatic market volatility that put many countries at risk of economic recession (Jones et al., 2020). It was not just stress from work that employees felt, many employees' livelihoods were disrupted. In the aftermath of the Coronavirus outbreak, scholars from management, organizational psychology, and communication had begun to examine the effects of the sudden and mass transition to telework.

The impact of the tumultuous events of 2020 will be felt for years. However, even before the world turned upside down because of the global pandemic, employee well-being had been a significant concern for managers and scholars. The question moving forward is not whether firms *should* address employee well-being, rather it is imperative to reflect on how firms can address the multitude of stressors that employees are contending with and to help bring out the best in employees.

This chapter takes a look at the intersection of internal communication and employee well-being and some of the emerging opportunities for research collaboration between scholars and practitioners. Such an analysis allows for an extension of theory and a better understanding of employees' experiences at work from the vantagepoint of both strategic/internal communication and organizational management.

What Are We Discussing?

To provide meaningful context to this discussion, to give direction for future research, and to outline a roadmap for professionals for implementing well-being and wellness programs, I want to first define some key concepts.

A notable definition of "internal communication" comes from Welch and Jackson (2007, p. 183), who defined it as "the strategic management of interactions and relationships between stakeholders at all levels within organisations." This involves manager communication, peer communication on teams and projects, and internal corporate communication (Welch & Jackson, 2007). The latter element falls under the traditional realm of public relations and marketing. Worth noting is that among PR professionals in Brazil, concerns about employee well-being are more likely to be handled by low-level practitioners than their high-ranking peers (Molleda & Ferguson, 2004). Although a considerable amount of discussion on internal communication and employee well-being has occurred among practitioners, there is a need for more scholarly research on how practitioners view their roles in contributing to employee well-being. Of the definitions of internal communication that I have encountered, Welch and Jackson (2007) offer the most accessible, practitioner-oriented, and comprehensive description of managed communication within firms. This is important because internal communication provides frontline employees with crucial information about their organization, jobs, and peers (Walden et al., 2017). Welch and Jackson's definition frames the role that internal communication practitioners have in shaping employee well-being, along with organizational leaders, peers, and human-resource teams.

The other focal concept of this chapter, employee well-being, is best understood as the quality of an employee's workplace experiences and their functioning at work (Warr, 1987). Though there is the potential to conflate employee well-being with job satisfaction, the two are distinct concepts. Well-being includes job satisfaction and satisfaction with the tangible and intangible elements of work (Brunetto et al., 2012).

Well-being involves individuals' work-related psychological, physical, and social health (Grant et al., 2007). This definition encompasses many crucial elements of employee health and its subdimensions allow for focused studies of employees' experiences. Breaking this down further, the psychological dimensions of well-being include satisfaction, self-respect, agency, and capabilities as they relate to work (Grant et al.). The social dimensions include helping others, becoming involved in the community, and having public acceptance (Grant et al.). Finally, the physical dimensions of well-being include shelter, healthcare, clothing, mobility, and nourishment (Grant et al., 2007). It is about feeling good inside, being physically well, and knowing that we are supported by peers who understand us. Although it is possible to expand upon the specific attributes of physical, psychological, and economic health, this framework is inclusive of the broader dimensions of employee well-being.

Scholars have also separated well-being into two classifications, hedonic and eudaemonic (Ilies et al., 2005). The former involves a subjective assessment of life as it relates to approaching pleasure and avoiding pain, the latter reflects personal growth, self-realization and a general fulfillment of an individual's true nature (Ilies et al., 2005).

Conditions for Well-Being

A review of the literature on internal communication and employee well-being reveals two noticeable takeaways. One, scholars from outside of strategic communication have published work that have direct implications for employee well-being and professional practice. Yet some of these articles do not make connections to strategic internal communication (e.g., Janicke et al., 2018; Zeng & Chen, 2020; Zeng et al., 2020). A second major idea from the literature is that those strategic communication scholars who have researched well-being have tended to consider separate elements of well-being without addressing well-being in its totality (e.g., Jiang & Shen, 2013; Lee & Li Queenie, 2020; Men & Robinson, 2018).

To start this review, I turn to the research of Cheng Zeng, who found through two different international studies (Zeng & Chen, 2020; Zeng et al., 2020) that employees express more latent dissent (vocalizing concerns to one's coworkers) when they are emotionally fatigued. Thus, under phycological duress, employees are inclined to complain to each other. Un-managed or misdirected, this venting can have serious consequences for employee–organization relationships. Zeng and his colleagues' work is not PR-focused. However, this research is relevant to practitioners given the potential reputation repercussions that can come when stressed employees voice concerns about work externally and given practitioners' promotion of employee wellness programs internally.

An experiment by Janicke et al. (2018) revealed one way to contribute to employee well-being during the workday. The research team exposed employees to videos that were either meaningful (feelings of elevation or gratitude), funny, or neutral in tone (control condition). Among the study's key findings, meaningful content increased levels of energy at work and satisfaction came from watching funny videos that made employees feel relaxed. Although the Janicke et al. study did not involve internal communication, their research can be extended to this area of practice. It reveals the potential for organization-produced content to help employees feel good at work, while also demonstrating the need for organizations to not be heavy-handed in policing external media content that their employees consume during the workday.

Employee wellness and health promotion programs can be ideal conduits for addressing workers' physical/cognitive, emotional, and social health needs (Nöhammer et al., 2011). Yet in starting these programs, firms must answer a number of important questions. Firms have to determine which employee health issues to address and how to market those programs (Keller et al., 2009). Additionally, firms need empirical evidence and metrics to justify their wellness program costs (Keller et al., 2009). Both the composition of the workforce and the size of the organization predicts the effectiveness and engagement in wellness programs, according to Keller et al. Moreover, when employees feel a connection to their employing organization such that they identify with it, they will be inclined to participate in workplace wellness programs (Zhu & Dailey, 2019).

This research points to the initial investment that is needed to secure participation in wellness programs. Yes, firms see financial benefits when employees are healthy and yes, these programs can be instrumental in contributing to employee health. Yet resources are needed to develop effective wellness programs, communicate about them, and assess them. More research is needed to understand the types of well-being messages that employees respond to and how small group and one-to-one meetings may complement company-wide wellness messages.

Research on the relationship between internal communication and employee–organization relationship (EOR) perceptions has implications for employee well-being. For example, Men and Robinson (2018) investigated employees' psychological needs. They found that an organization's emotional culture (as characterized by joy, happiness, excitement and companionate love, affection, and warmth) can meet employees' psychological need for mutual respect, connection, and reliance on one another in an organization. Authentic organizational leaders that truly care about their employees' well-being can establish lasting relationships with followers (Men & Stacks, 2014). Meanwhile, Lee and Li Queenie (2020) found that employees who have quality relationships with their organizations are likely to see more benefits and perceive fewer risks of sharing private health issues in the workplace. This reveals how a strong EOR that is influenced by internal communication can contribute to employee well-being. Notably, Ćorić et al. (2020) found a relationship between internal communication satisfaction and life satisfaction. Though not addressing all dimensions of employee well-being, the study by Ćorić et al. considered a major aspect of well-being—which is one's overall cognitive assessment of their life through life satisfaction. Organizations should not only pay attention to personal characteristics and non-work issues with their employees, they should also foster positive internal communication climates as a means of contributing to employees' life satisfaction (Ćorić et al., 2020).

Navigating Trouble Spots-

Just as organizations have realized the potential to enhance employee well-being through internal communication and internal relationship management, there are risk points that to be addressed. Recall the practical paradox of technology. This idea holds that employee well-being can be enhanced through the use of communication technologies that enhance accessibility to peers and work-related efficiency, while well-being is also diminished by technologies that increase workplace interruptions and unpredictability (Ter Hoeven et al., 2016). Similar points have been raised about PR practitioners' own work-life boundary experiences and use of social media for work (Jiang et al., 2017). Technologies that connect us to work at off-hours or to work in spaces that are generally work-free (i.e., home), may contribute to burnout. This blurring of boundaries can harm employees' psychological health—a point that was brought to dramatic light in 2020 when the Coronavirus sent millions of people home to work.

Information has a critical role in shaping well-being. However, internal communicators face difficulties in fostering positive everyday talk in organizations when organizational members engage in unjust behaviors that either mislead members or are outright dishonest (Omilion-Hodges & Baker, 2014). Furthermore, information exchange in organizations is limited when leaders claim to have an open-door policy but do not actually commit to it, and when leaders do not interact with all members of their organizations (Omilion-Hodges & Baker, 2014).

Additionally, conflict is possible between the various facets of employee well-being. We might at times feel good about our psychological health at work (through engagement and productivity), yet spend so much time at work that we experience physical health problems. There also might be instances when we are supported in the workplace and yet experience psychologically-limiting dissatisfaction with general workplace practice or management. In a study of PR practitioners, Jiang and Shen (2013) found that work–life conflict was positively linked to practitioners' salary. The more conflict between work and home, the more one earned (Jiang & Shen, 2013). This puts one aspect of psychological health (work–life balance) at odds with one's financial standing (which could address a different element of psychological health).

We should also not assume that organizations will always act in their employees' best well-being interests and that mistakes will not be made, particularly in internal communication. As more wellness programs are implemented in the workplace, employees will be subject to increasing levels of surveillance. The same organizational tools that make it easy for employees to keep track of their wellness goals through work could, in the wrong hands, be used as tools of control, humiliation, and exploitation. As Zhu and Dailey (2019) noted, employees do not participate in workplace health promotion programs for a variety of reasons, including confidentiality concerns, embarrassment, and lack of time. To build on this, scholars and practitioners should look at the dark side of employee wellness programs and organizations' attempts to meet their employees physical, social, and psychological health needs.

A Framework for Researching Employee Well-Being

One perspective to help us understand the development and outcomes of employee well-being is job demands-resources theory and the related job-demands resources (J-DR) model from the management literature (Bakker & Demerouti, 2018; Demerouti et al., 2001; Schaufeli & Bakker, 2004). This model suggests that perceived job demands can harm employee health and that perceived job resources can, alternately, help employees cope with work-related stressors (Bakker & Demerouti, 2018). Job demands are physical organizational, or social elements of one's job that require a sustained mental effort (Demerouti et al., 2001). Demands are associated with psychological and physiological costs such as burnout (Demerouti et al., 2001). On the flip side, job resources are the organizational, physical, social, or psychological elements of one's job that may help someone achieve their work goals, reduce job demands, or stimulate personal development and growth (Demerouti et al., 2001). Demands are hindering job characteristics, while resources are enabling job characteristics that are often in conflict (Shen & Jiang, 2019).

Critical to this model is job engagement, which is an employee's immersion in their work. At the risk of a messy definitional discussion, employee engagement takes on different forms depending on the scholar and practitioner. Those who draw on the J-DR model tend to view engagement as some combination of vigor, dedication, and absorption in one's job (Schaufeli & Bakker, 2004). Job demands can hinder engagement, while job resources contribute to engagement (Schaufeli & Bakker, 2004). When we are supported at work and when those obstacles to getting work completed are managed, it is natural to assume that we will throw ourselves into the job through engagement. With engagement and burnout as focal concepts, this model suggests that two psychological processes occur. On one hand, job demands can exhaust employees and tax them mentally. Yet according to Schaufeli and Bakker (2004), job resources can also serve a motivational role by either fostering employees' personal growth (intrinsically motivating) or helping them achieve work goals (which is extrinsically motivating).

Interestingly, one of the leading contributors to the development of the J-DR model, Wilmar Schaufeli noted in a case study that the model itself is communicative. The model can provide common language to organizational members to discuss work and well-being (Schaufeli, 2017). Because of its breadth, the J-DR model represents an ideal framework for understanding how public relations-counseled information-sharing policies and public relations-related internal messages can act as communication resources that help employees manage their psychological, physical, and social health (Walden, 2020). In viewing job resources through the J-DR framework, supervisor support, communication, and work environment are thus critical for helping employees deal with job demands and stress and for helping foster employee growth and engagement (Jiang & Men, 2017).

There are untapped areas for research about communication-related phenomena (i.e., leader-membership exchanges, supervisor support, office gossip) in the form of job demands and job resources as predictors of burnout and engagement. As my co-authors and I note in one article that drew on this model, PR practitioners are responsible for helping ensure the adequate and quality flow of information through organizations. Thus, information can serve as a valuable currency (or job resource) that drives engagement (Walden et al., 2017). Conversely, there are new areas to explore employees' communication behaviors as outcomes of burnout and engagement. The work by Zeng et al. (2020) and Zeng and Chen (2020) could be a helpful point for scholars to look at the voice-related reputational issues that can stem from unhappy and burned out employees.

Additionally, a notable contribution that has been influenced by the JD-R model comes from Shen and Jiang (2019), who focused on the engagement strategies that organizations take with employees. These strategies include sharing enough information with employees and encouraging them to disclose their thoughts about organizations;

demonstrating efforts to build partnerships and employees' professional networks; and organizations expressing care for employee concerns. This research showed that organizations' engagement strategies predicted employee engagement, which in turn predicted employee performance and employees' voice behaviors (Shen & Jiang, 2019). My takeaway from Shen and Jiang—and they point to this as a future direction for research in their study—is that engagement has the potential to contribute to employee well-being.

When we feel engaged at work, we feel good about work and therefore our psychological well-being is addressed. Extending this, if we are doing absorbed, dedicated, and vigorous work with others, we should connect and communicate with our peers in ways that meet our social needs.

Concluding Thoughts

Regardless of how one defines it, it is important to acknowledge that employee well-being is not a unidimensional construct and nor is it static. There are a host of elements that comprise well-being and it can be challenging for organizations to meet *all* of these needs through internal communication. Likewise, these elements are subject to influence from organizational and peer communication and these elements can, in turn, have implications for employee communication behaviors.

Providing ample amounts of information, having managers support employees, and creating a positive internal communication climate can represent job resources that may contribute to well-being. Yet employee well-being can also be threatened, either intentionally or unintentionally, by organizations. The key is to have privacy-respecting wellness programs and well-being assessment plans in place and to realize that workers are facing considerable stressors. This is where research should take priority.

Professional organizations such as Public Relations Society of America, PR Academy, the Institute for Public Relations, and International Association of Business Communicators serve as helpful interfaces between industry and the academy. Meaningful discussion on practice is happening in these groups. Given what is at stake (employee well-being) and given the drastic changes that have occurred because of the COVID-19 pandemic, there needs to be more collaboration between practitioners and scholars on research. The pandemic thrust employee well-being to the forefront of managers' concerns—yet employee well-being needs to remain a priority for organizations even post-COVID. Research to date is definitive in revealing that internal communication can support employees in their personal and professional lives. Moving forward, we need to take a harder look at how communication practitioners interact with HR teams and leadership on issues involving well-being and at how research can more directly inform practice.

Practitioner Profile

With 9 hospitals, 27,000 employees, an affiliated health plan, and a medical school, Geisinger Health System is one of the largest integrated healthcare providers in the United States. Headquartered in the central Pennsylvania town of Danville, Geisinger provides service across most of that state and into parts of New Jersey.

Their clinical, support, and administrative staff were put on high-alert with the COVID-19 pandemic declaration in March, 2020. Geisinger has cared for thousands of sick patients and been on the front lines of researching the Coronavirus, its spread, and treatment.

Geisinger's marketing and communications department (with more than 100 employees) has also been tested early in the pandemic. Having worked in public relations for Geisinger from 2006 to 2009, I was well aware of the department's expertise.

To shed light on internal communication and employee well-being during a crisis, I interviewed Geisinger Chief Marketing and Communications Officer Don Stanziano, APR. The following is an abridged version of our conversation from Sept. 2020.

WALDEN: What internal communication plans were in place to help you deal with the expected crisis?

STANZIANO: It came on like a tidal wave for all of us. When you work in healthcare delivery, there are some things that are very specific to our world. We were working throughout and had to show up. And a lot of our workforce is directly taking care of these people who have Covid. That's a very different dynamic than in other types of organizations. Employees are high risk because of their risk of exposure. In the early days, we didn't know a lot about the disease. Communications with employees, a major consideration was protecting them and getting [personal protective equipment]. Also, communication was on handwashing, social distancing, masking. We did infographics, we did videos and then constant reinforcement.

WALDEN: What are the greatest challenges that your team has encountered?

STANZIANO: The greatest challenge was the massive amount of information that needed to be shared in a short amount of time and the fact that it was so dynamic. We were updating and changing materials sometimes daily. We were meeting three times a day with the Covid taskforce. It wasn't just about wellness. It was about operational changes, clinic closures. We had to figure out a structure for working from home. What worked well was that we were singularly focused, everything else went away. From an organizational perspective it gave my team an opportunity to show what they could do. In normal circumstances, we're doing a lot of things people don't really see. But everyone was so focused on Covid that they saw all of it. They saw the internal communications, they saw the media relations work, they saw the collateral materials.

WALDEN: What are you most proud of through the early part of the pandemic?

STANZIANO: That the work was high quality. It was responsive to the needs of the organization. Our employee engagement on our internal communications [platforms] is up significantly. That tells me that it's valuable to the workforce and we're putting out quality information. We learned some things in terms of what people want and how to communicate. I'm proud that folks showed up and did great work. Covid created an opportunity to demonstrate the value of employee communications.

WALDEN: What lessons can you share with other practitioners when it comes to employee well-being, and especially during a crisis?

STANZIANO: Frequency, transparency, multiple channels, and listening. We used questions that came [from employees during townhall sessions] as content ideas for other channels. Just when you think you've said it too many times... it's probably the right number of times.

Don Stanziano, MHA, APR, is Chief Marketing & Communications Officer for Geisinger, an integrated health system based in Danville, Pennsylvania, recognized as a national leader in healthcare innovation. Don is responsible for all marketing and communications across the Geisinger enterprise, including brand and growth marketing, internal and external communications and issues management, and digital customer and employee engagement across a robust marketing technology stack.

References

Bakker, A. B., & Demerouti, E. (2018). Multiple levels in job demands-resources theory: Implications for employee well-being and performance. In E. Diener, S. Oishi, & L. Tay (Eds.), *Handbook of well-being*. DEF Publishers. nobascholar.com.

Brunetto, Y., Teo, S. T. T., Shacklock, K., & Farr-Wharton, R. (2012). Emotional intelligence, job satisfaction, well-being and engagement: Explaining organisational commitment and turnover intentions in policing. *Human Resource Management Journal, 22*(4), 428–441.

Ćorić, D. S., Vokic, N. P., & Verčič, A. T. (2020). Does good internal communication enhance life satisfaction? *Journal of Communication Management, 24*(4), 363–376.

Demerouti, E., Bakker, A. B., Nachreiner, F., & Schaufeli, W. B. (2001). The job demands-resources model of burnout. *Journal of Applied Psychology, 86*(3), 499–512. https://doi.org/10.1037/0021-9010.86.3.499.

Dey, M., Frazis, H., Loewenstein, M. A., & Sun, H. (2020, June). Ability to work from home: Evidence from two surveys and implications for the labor market in the COVID-19 pandemic. *Monthly Labor Review*. Retrieved from: https://www.bls.gov/opub/mlr/2020/article/ability-to-work-from-home.htm.

Eurofound. (2020). Regulations to address work–life balance in digital flexible working arrangements. *New forms of employment series*. Publications Office of the European Union, Luxembourg. Retrieved from: https://www.eurofound.europa.eu/sites/default/files/ef_publication/field_ef_document/ef19046en.pdf.

Global Workplace Analytics and Flexjobs. (2017, June 22). *115 Percent Increase in Telecommuting since 2005, According to Global Workplace Analytics Report sponsored by Flexjobs* [Press release]. Retrieved from: https://globalworkplaceanalytics.com/brags/news-releases.

Grant, A. M., Christianson, M. K., & Price, R. H. (2007). Happiness, health, or relationships? Managerial practices and employee well-being tradeoffs. *Academy of Management Perspectives, 21*(3), 51–63.

Hodges, L. C., Satkowski Harper, T., Hall-Barrow, J., & Tatom, I. D. (2004). Reducing overall health care costs for a city municipality. *Aaohn Journal, 52*(6), 247–253.

Ilies, R., Morgeson, F., & Nahrgang, J. (2005). Authentic leadership and eudaemonic well-being: Understanding leader-follower outcomes. *The Leadership Quarterly, 16*(3), 373–394. https://doi.org/10.1016/j.leaqua.2005.03.002.

Janicke, S. H., Rieger, D., Reinecke, L., & Connor, W. (2018). Watching online videos at work: The role of positive and meaningful affect for recovery experiences and well-being at the workplace. *Mass Communication and Society, 21*(3), 345–367. https://doi.org/10.1080/15205436.2017.1381264.

Jiang, H., & Men, R. J. (2017). Creating an engaged workforce: The impact of authentic leadership, transparent organizational communication, and work-life enrichment. *Communication Research, 44*(2), 225–243.

Jiang, H., & Shen, H. (2013). Toward a theory of public relations practitioners' own conflict: Work versus life. *Journal of Public Relations Research, 25*(3), 259–279.

Jiang, H., Luo, Y., & Kulemeka, O. (2017). Strategic social media use in public relations: Professionals' perceived social media impact, leadership behaviors, and work-life conflict. *International Journal of Strategic Communication, 11*(1), 18–41. https://doi.org/10.1080/1553118X.2016.1226842.

Jones, L., Palumbo, D., & Brown, D. (2020, June 29). Coronavirus: A visual guide to the economic impact. *BBC News*. Retrieved from: https://www.bbc.com/news/business-51706225.

Keller, P. A., Lehmann, D. R., & Milligan, K. J. (2009). Effectiveness of corporate well-being programs. *Journal of Macromarketing, 29*(3), 279–302.

Lee, Y., & Li Queenie, J.-Y. (2020). The value of internal communication in enhancing employees' health information disclosure intentions in the workplace. *Public Relations Review, 46*(1). https://doi.org/10.1016/j.pubrev.2019.101872.

Men, L. R., & Robinson, K. L. (2018). It's about how employees feel! Examining the impact of emotional culture on employee–organization relationships. *Corporate Communications: An International Journal, 23*(4), 470–491.

Men, L. R., & Stacks, D. W. (2014). The effects of authentic leadership on strategic internal communication and employee-organization relationships. *Journal of Public Relations Research, 26*(4), 301–324.

Milasi, S., González-Vázquez, I., & Fernández-Macías, E. (2020). Telework in the EU before and after the COVID-19: Where we were, where we head to. *European Commission*. Retrieved from: https://ec.europa.eu/jrc/sites/jrcsh/files/jrc120945_policy_brief_-_covid_and_telework_final.pdf.

Molleda, J.-C., & Ferguson, M. A. (2004). Public relations roles in Brazil: Hierarchy eclipses gender differences. *Journal of Public Relations Research, 16*(4), 327–351. https://doi.org/10.1207/s1532754xjprr1604_1.

Nöhammer, E., Stummer, H., & Schusterschitz, C. (2011). Improving employee well-being through worksite health promotion? The employees' perspective. *Journal of Public Health, 19*(2), 121–129. https://doi.org/10.1007/s10389-010-0364-4.

Omilion-Hodges, L. M., & Baker, C. R. (2014). Everyday talk and convincing conversations: Utilizing strategic internal communication. *Business Horizons, 57*(3), 435–445.

Schaufeli, W. B. (2017). Applying the Job demands-resources model: A 'how to' guide to measuring and tackling work engagement and burnout. *Organizational Dynamics, 46*(2), 120–132.

Schaufeli, W. B., & Bakker, A. B. (2004). Job demands, job resources, and their relationship with burnout and engagement: A multi-sample study. *Journal of Organizational Behavior, 25*(3), 293–315. https://doi.org/10.1002/job.248.

Shen, H., & Jiang, H. (2019). Engaged at work? An employee engagement model in public relations. *Journal of Public Relations Research, 31*(1–2), 32–49.

Ter Hoeven, C. L., van Zoonen, W., & Fonner, K. L. (2016). The practical paradox of technology: The influence of communication technology use on employee burnout and engagement. *Communication Monographs, 83*(2), 239–263. https://doi.org/10.1080/03637751.2015.1133920.

Walden, J. (2020, October 30). Linking communication to job demands and resources. *Institute for Public Relations blog*. Retrieved from: https://instituteforpr.org/linking-communication-to-job-demands-and-resources.

Walden, J., Jung, E., & Westerman, C. Y. K. (2017). Employee communication, job engagement, and organizational commitment: A study of members of the Millennial Generation. *Journal of Public Relations Research, 29*(2–3), 73–89.

Warr, P. (1987). *Work, unemployment, and mental health*. Clarendon Press.

Welch, M., & Jackson, P. R. (2007). Rethinking internal communication: A stakeholder approach. *Corporate Communications: An International Journal, 12*(2), 177–198. https://doi.org/10.1108/13563280710744847.

Wright, T. A., & Bonett, D. G. (1992). The effect of turnover on work satisfaction and mental health: Support for a situational perspective. *Journal of Organizational Behavior, 13*(6), 603–615.

Wright, T. A., & Bonett, D. G. (2007). Job satisfaction and psychological well-being as nonadditive predictors of workplace turnover. *Journal of Management, 33*(2), 141–160.

Wright, T. A., Cropanzano, R., & Bonett, D. G. (2007). The moderating role of employee positive well being on the relation between job satisfaction and job performance. *Journal of Occupational Health Psychology, 12*(2), 93–104. https://doi.org/10.1037/1076-8998.12.2.93.

Zeng, C., & Chen, H. (2020). An exploration of the relationships between organizational dissent, employee burnout, and work-family balance: A cross-cultural comparison between China and Finland. *Communication Studies, 71*(4), 633–648. https://doi.org/10.1080/10510974.2020.1749864.

Zeng, C., Permyakova, T. M., Smolianina, E. A., & Morozova, I. S. (2020). Exploring the relationships between employee burnout, organizational dissent and work-family culture in Russian organizations. *Journal of Intercultural Communication Research, 49*(2), 119–132. https://doi.org/10.1080/17475759.2020.1719430.

Zhu, Y., & Dailey, S. (2019). Personal–organizational processes in workplace health promotion: Understanding wellness program participation in China. *International Journal of Communication, 13*(2). https://ijoc.org/index.php/ijoc/article/view/9548.

CHAPTER 10

Internal Crisis Communication

Alessandra Mazzei and Alfonsa Butera

Introduction

Crisis communication is progressively focusing on internal stakeholders, although coming from a tradition devoted towards the external ones (Frandsen & Johansen, 2011; Heide & Simonsson, 2014, 2019; Kim, 2018; Ravazzani, 2016; Strandberg & Vigsø, 2016; Taylor, 2010). The rising interest in employee communication before, during and after a crisis occurs is linked to the special relation employees have with their employer (Frandsen & Johansen, 2011) and their role as both receivers and senders in the crisis communication arena (Johansen et al., 2012; Mazzei et al., 2012). Furthermore, a lack or an inefficient internal crisis communication can lead to a double crisis (Frandsen & Johansen, 2017; Heide & Simonsson, 2020).

A. Mazzei (✉) · A. Butera
Università IULM, Milan, Italy
e-mail: alessandra.mazzei@iulm.it

A. Butera
e-mail: alfonsa.butera@iulm.it

L. R. Men and A. Tkalac Verčič (eds.), *Current Trends and Issues in Internal Communication*, New Perspectives in Organizational Communication, https://doi.org/10.1007/978-3-030-78213-9_10

This chapter starts by clarifying the perspective on internal crisis communication more suitable in the current competitive context. Therefore, it analyses the role of employee communication and relationship management in crisis prevention, management and recovery. Finally, it concludes with some reflections on future developments.

Definition and Relevance of Internal Crisis Communication

A contemporary comprehension of internal crisis communication embraces the social constructionist approach and is based on the broad vision of crisis as a dynamic process including three phases: pre-crisis, crisis response and post-crisis, instead of an episodic event (Coombs, 2015; Frandsen & Johansen, 2011; Heide & Simonsson, 2015; Sturges, 1994). In this vein, internal crisis communication is "the communicative interaction among managers and employees, in a private or public organization, before, during and after an organizational or societal crisis" (Johansen et al., 2012, p. 271). Underlining the employee perspective, it is worth adding that "internal crisis communication is the continuous communicative processes that take place between managers and co-workers and co-workers and co-workers" (Heide & Simonsson, 2019, p. 40).

The relevance of understanding how communication interactions occur within an organization in connection to a crisis is related to the particular status of employees. According to Frandsen and Johansen (2011, 2017), employees have a more complex psychological linkage with their organization compared to external stakeholders. First, they have a *legal relationship* through an employment contract. Second, their *set of stakes* includes salary, job security, working hours and working conditions, degrees of freedom and autonomy versus control, motivation and engagement. This set affects the perception of responsibility that employees tribute to their employer regarding a specific crisis. Third, employee *identification* to the organization is part of their personal *identity*, influencing their emotions and self-esteem.

Fourth, employees can act *both as receivers and senders* in crisis communication processes, acting as negative or positive ambassadors becoming either potential adversaries or advocates (Kim & Lim, 2020; Mazzei & Ravazzani, 2015; Mazzei et al., 2012). When acting as positive ambassadors, employees are willing to give their company the benefit of the doubt when its behaviour is questionable. Consequently, they commit to communicate their own trust to other people and to act as advocates for the company, contradicting false criticisms. Moreover, they avoid taking advantage or behaving opportunistically, they report to the management about dangers or threats, and they look for occasions to preserve or improve the reputation of the company (Mazzei et al., 2012).

In this stream, well-informed employees constitute a relevant channel of communication for reaching other stakeholders during a crisis (Coombs, 2015). Today a very relevant issue is related to the communicative role that employees play on social media, and companies should be cautious with employees who blog, as they can express or expand upon negative word-of-mouth (Austin & Jin, 2016).

Therefore, internal crisis communication involves all organizational members as communicators in the role of receivers, senders, and sense-makers in a dynamic and continuous communication process that takes place before, during and after a crisis (Coombs, 2015; Diers-Lawson, 2019; Heide & Simonsson, 2014; Johansen et al., 2012; Kim, 2018; Mazzei & Ravazzani, 2015; Mazzei et al., 2012).

Internal communication affect employees' sense-making and behaviours in connection to a crisis (Adamu & Mohamad, 2019; Frandsen & Johansen, 2011; Heide & Simonsson, 2014; Mazzei & Ravazzani, 2015; Mazzei et al., 2012). Another relevant aspect of the management of internal crisis communication is the link to its external management (Heide & Simonsson, 2019). The borders between what is internal and external to an organization are blurred. For example, employees can communicate through their personal networks and social media accounts what they know internally. Moreover, often crises are complex events that involve various organizations that interact to overcome them.

To sum up, the comprehension on internal crisis communication requires a dynamic and broad vision on the crisis, meant as a process instead of an episodic event; the awareness of the role of employees as both receivers, senders and sense-makers in the communication arena; the understanding of its interplay with its external management and communication.

Over the three dynamic stages of a crisis, internal communication plays different roles. Before a crisis occurs, prevention is key, since it helps to enhance employee engagement, the quality of internal relationships, the organizational preparedness and crisis awareness.

During the management of a crisis, the adoption of effective internal crisis communication strategies is capable to support the exit from the crisis and the protection of the relational capital based on relationship quality and employee engagement. Particular attention should be devoted to the multicultural context and to the crises highlighted by news media.

After a crisis, internal communication is required to sustain the recovery and relaunch of the organization.

The following pages examine each phase and related implications for communication among and with employees in depth.

Pre-Crisis: Internal communication for Crisis Prevention

The pre-crisis phase is crucial for an effective reaction of the organization to the crisis when it occurs, and to limit the damage that the organization itself can have as a cause of it. Internal communication is key for crisis prevention together with managerial effort. In fact, it helps to enhance the quality of internal relationships, thus supporting positive employee communication behaviours such as advocacy, and lessening negative ones such as badmouthing (Kim & Lim, 2020; Mazzei & Ravazzani, 2015; Mazzei et al., 2012).

Specifically, internal communication plays a fundamental role in the pre-crisis phase since it contributes to create the foundations for an effective reaction to the crisis when it occurs. The following pages analyse how internal communication influences: (a) the level of employee engagement; (b) the quality of internal relationships; and (c) the crisis preparedness and awareness.

(a) *Level of employee engagement*

Engaged employees are keener to perform communication behaviours in favour of their company, such as employee advocacy and information protection and therefore nurturing employee engagement is key before a crisis (Heide & Simonsson, 2019). In order to nurture employee engagement, managers have in their hands some levers to shape an engaging workplace context (Mazzei, Butera et al., 2019). These levers help to build an inclusive employee relations approach, which encourages employee voice through the means of planned internal communication and managerial practices; a developmental human resources management approach, which focuses on valuing people going beyond the mere accommodative management of human resources; a fair organizational justice approach, which is related to the perceived fairness and consistency of procedures related to evaluating employee performance, disciplining and terminating employees and giving promotions and pay raises. Empirical studies confirm that engaged employees are more inclined to highlight possible weak signals of a potential crisis, i.e. problems that can be solved in time, and to contribute to effective organizational decision-making.

(b) *Quality of internal relationships*

A positive relational history with stakeholders operates as a shield, protecting a company from the attribution of responsibility in a crisis situation, with the so-called halo effect (Coombs & Holladay, 2006). Specifically, in the case of a crisis, developing good relationships with employees can lead them to engage in megaphoning behaviours, acting as volunteer organizational advocates, with strategic advantages for organizations in both peaceful and turbulent times (Kim & Rhee, 2011).

Similar evidence is supported by the case of a manufacturing company dealing with a severe accident at a plant that caused the death of a worker (Mazzei et al., 2012). When the fatal accident occurred, employees actively defended their company in media interviews, diminishing the company's responsibility in the accident. At the origin of this advocating behaviour, the study showed the effort made by the company before the accident occurred: the company had invested a lot to enhance factory safety and made a continuous effort of internal communication to inform employees about these investments and concrete actions undertaken.

Also, perceived organization's authentic behaviour and employee empowerment, mediated by perceived relationship quality between an organization and its employees, increase the likelihood of positive megaphoning and reduce intentions of negative megaphoning regarding a corporate crisis (Mazzei, Kim et al., 2019).

(c) *Crisis preparedness and awareness*

Formal preparedness includes having constituted a crisis management team and developed a crisis management plan with a focus on crisis communication before a crisis becomes severe. Internal stakeholders should be considered key publics in this plan: this is related to the need of addressing the paradox of external-internal communication that seems to be crucial during crises (Heide & Simonsson, 2015; Strandberg & Vigsø, 2016).

Crisis awareness is part of organizational crisis preparedness (Frandsen & Johansen, 2011; Johansen et al., 2012). Each and every organization should in fact prepare itself to manage possible crises, adopting a strategic approach to crisis management. This approach begins with signal detection, issue management and risk assessment (Coombs, 2015).

Considering employees as receivers, internal crisis communication should be focused on risks, issues and stakes, and aimed at strengthening psychological crisis preparedness and at making employees aware about the crisis management plan in terms of policies and guidelines (Frandsen & Johansen, 2011). In organizations that have established a crisis management team or a crisis manager, employees seem to be less frustrated, insecure and afraid in a crisis situation, with a lower loss of motivation and engagement, compared to employees working in organizations not so well prepared (Johansen et al., 2012).

In terms of organizational crisis preparedness, specific internal communication actions and training initiatives could be undertaken in order to increase employees' awareness about the role that they can play in the first person to prevent and address crises. Alike, internal communication can be useful to increase employees' awareness about the possible crises generated by their improper behaviour.

Considering employees as senders, internal crisis communication in the pre-crisis stage involves them in a flow of upward communication in which they can play the role of whistleblowers, dissenters or detectors of weak signals of an impending problem that come from the bottom (Frandsen & Johansen, 2011; Heide & Simonsson, 2015, 2019; Mazzei & Ravazzani, 2020).

Regarding whistleblowing, it can be formal, through official arrangements implemented by an organization, or informal, through trusted colleagues and managers; moreover, it can be internal, directed to audiences inside the organization, or external (Frandsen & Johansen, 2017). An efficient internal whistleblowing arrangement and an organizational culture promoting a frank and open dialogue with employees, can be decisive in making employees disclose potential corporate wrongdoing internally, and consequently decreasing the possibilities that this leads to a crisis involving external stakeholders (Mazzei & Ravazzani, 2020).

In terms of crisis preparedness, a relevant issue today is also increasing employees' awareness of the role they can play to prevent and address crises on social media. Indeed, employee behaviour on social media is an opportunity for companies, since stakeholders perceive it as highly authentic when it supports the organization. However, employee online behaviours can also be very risky for companies. Therefore, social media policies (SMP) addressed to employees, and related internal communication and training initiatives, can be a key move for both brand building and crisis prevention (Mazzei & Butera, 2016).

SMP are issued to prevent the risks related to breaking laws, such as on property rights; violating ethical norms, such as transparency and honesty; or damaging the company's reputation by spreading negative messages. However, an internal SMP could also boost online communication behaviours of employees that strengthen reputation and positive dialogue with stakeholders. Used as an internal communication tool, SMP can help employees to avoid the above-described risks and encourage them to actively contribute to reputation building and advocacy efforts in crisis situations. SMP should be exploited as part of crisis prevention and integrated in the internal communication strategy to be effective in enhancing consistent and authentic voluntary employee communication behaviours on social media.

Enabling employees to be effective communicators on social media during a crisis, can boost organizational efforts to face the reputational challenges generated by the crisis itself. Crisis preparedness efforts undertaken by an organization should therefore take these aspects into account, not just focusing on preventing the risks that employees can generate through their online behaviours, but also on making them aware that they can actively support their company during a crisis.

During a Crisis: Internal Communication for Crisis Management

The acute phase of a crisis generates a series of communicational challenges for an organization, both with internal and external stakeholders. Managing internal communication during a crisis implies a series of aspects that managers should be aware of. The following pages are dedicated to: (a) possible internal communication strategies, as a paramount framework; (b) the management of internal crisis communication in multicultural organizations and (c) the management of employees' reaction to negative news coverage.

(a) *Internal communication strategies*

Having in mind the need of sustaining employees' sense-making with the ultimate aim of activating employee behaviours that support the organization to overcome the crisis, a relevant topic is related to the response strategies that can be more effective to target these objectives.

Regarding responding strategies, Kim and Lim (2020) indicated that positive employee communication behaviours are directly affected by stealing thunder strategies, that is proactive self-disclosure communication strategies about the crisis towards employees. They also showed that accommodative response strategies positively affect employee voice behaviours.

In managing a crisis, a company should show towards employees a very high level of concern and closeness to sustain their special psychological contract, their need for protection, their identification, and their attitude to communicate in favour of their company. In other words, accommodative communication strategies are in principle the most desirable for internal crisis communication (Coombs, 2015; Pang et al., 2009).

Those kinds of internal communication strategies can be grouped into three main categories (Mazzei & Ravazzani, 2015; Mazzei et al., 2020): *creating a sense of security, sustaining a sense of belonging, activating employees as allies of the organization*.

The first strategy is *creating a sense of security*. The rising of a crisis causes the perception of a lack of information about the current situation and the future of the organization and its employees (Mazzei & Ravazzani, 2015).

Once a crisis has occurred, employees should actually be advised early in the notification process and included in the initial response (Coombs, 2015; Fearn-Banks, 2010). In the acute phase of a crisis *providing instructions to employees* is a priority, in order to reduce the potential harm to people and objects (Heide & Simonsson, 2019). Instructing information is key to ensure public safety, which should be the primary concern in a crisis, before reputation and financial issues (Coombs, 2015). To be useful, instructing information should be quick and accurate. However, organizations should be careful that speed could be counterproductive if the information is inaccurate, increasing rather than decreasing the threat to public safety. Managing the balance between information accuracy and quickness is even more relevant considering that employees resort to informal communication with peers and colleagues when the corporate internal information flow is not quick enough, and informal communication is often inaccurate (Shaia & Gonzenbach, 2007).

The second strategy is *sustaining a sense of belonging*. Internal stakeholders during a crisis may feel anger and fear related to the individual impact of the crisis (Mazzei & Ravazzani, 2015; Pang et al., 2009), which affect their morale and loyalty. In this context, an organization needs to take corrective actions and communicate them also to sustain employees' sense of belonging.

The third strategy is *activating employees as allies of the organization*. A crisis may produce behavioural reactions such as immobility to action (Mazzei & Ravazzani, 2015) or negative reactions as argued before. Therefore, internal communication during a crisis should *activate employee behaviors that support the organization to overcome the crisis* (Frandsen & Johansen, 2011; Heide & Simonsson, 2014; Kim, 2018; Kim & Lim, 2020; Mazzei & Ravazzani, 2015).

(b) *Internal crisis communication in multicultural organizations*

The cultural background of employees affects message framing and sense-making, and this aspect can become salient during crisis situations intensifying communication problems: actually, stakeholders with culturally different and conflicting stakes perceive, react to and make sense of critical situations in different ways (Ravazzani, 2016). This issue becomes even more relevant when it comes to multinational companies, whose employees are located in different countries. Communicators should be attentive to the adaptation of verbal and non-verbal communicative dimensions with reference to the cultural features of employees. To adapt communication in multinational organizations, local communicators and leaders who act as cultural interpreters can play a key role, adapting messages and channels of communication.

(c) *Employees' reaction to negative news coverage*

To sustain employees' sense-making during a crisis, an organization should take into consideration also the information that employees receive from external sources and use to gain understanding. Einwiller and Korn (2020) suggest that negative media coverage about an organization can cause strong cognitive and emotional reactions to employees. Reactions can be particularly negative when employees receive first knowledge about the crisis affecting their organization from external media. Employees address to colleagues and line managers to make sense of the information they found through media, but the role of internal corporate communication plays a crucial role too in these situations. If employees evaluate internal corporate communication positively, they enact positive communication behaviours when they interact with outsiders addressing negative news topics. Conversely, employees try to evade interactions with outsiders when they do not consider internal communication positively.

Post-Crisis: Internal Communication for Recovery and Renewal

Crises force organizations to change and some of these changes can also have direct and harmful consequences on employees' lives: downsizing, changes in roles, re-organizations of functions and departments and benefit cuts (Seeger et al., 2005). After a critical event, the future development and the possibilities of success of a company rely on the engagement and the well-being of employees that remain with the organization. But a critical event usually causes stress and fatigue for these employees, as well as dissatisfaction with internal communication and measures undertaken by the company, a lower propensity to take risks, absenteeism, a higher sense of uncertainty, lower performances and loss of talents.

Following a period of crisis, communication can contribute to process the crisis itself on the employees' psychological level, in order to reduce their stress, and is crucial for organizational learning and resilience (Heide & Simonsson, 2019). In fact, it can help build a perspective vision shared by all the stakeholders involved, with the aim of activating a process of renewal (Seeger et al., 2005).

From a communicational point of view, a critical event induces the loss of all or part of the shared meanings in an organization. For example, following a crisis, disorientation may occur regarding the distinctive organizational identity, key competences, reference values and desirable behaviours. Exiting from a critical situation, the established interpretative schemes in an organization could be broken. Communication can play a decisive role in rebuilding a positive shared background and in activating a new vision of the organization, allowing to overcome the unstable condition generated by the crisis (Seeger & Ulmer, 2002).

This is why according to Heide and Simonsson (2019), the main objective of internal communication in the post-crisis phase is contributing to processing the crisis, thus reducing uncertainty.

The necessary premise of a process of recovery and renewal of positive perspectives is that the company explicitly and rapidly implement actions that can remedy the problems that have arisen due to the crisis. This can be useful to divert conversations about the causes of the problems and responsibilities and to make people concentrate on overcoming the situation.

The first characteristic of a communication aimed at renewal (Seeger et al., 2005; Ulmer et al., 2007) is the *perspective orientation*. This means that it is desirable that the organizational discourse avoids returning to retrospective discourses centred on the explanation and interpretation of what happened. On the contrary, it should be focused on the description of the actions aimed at achieving the next objectives. This kind of discourse builds the foundations for a new organizational reality.

The second characteristic of a communication aiming at renewing the organization is the focus on *representing its potential to seize the opportunities* that arise from the crisis. Actually, employees are inspired by optimism and a positive vision.

The third characteristic of a communication that can effectively sustain a renewal is giving an *honest and frank speech* based on the values expressed by management, rather than strategically aimed at preventing recriminations by stakeholders, including internal ones. Of course, the two needs should however be balanced.

Finally, the fourth characteristic of a communication aimed at renewing the organization is the *contribution of top management*, which interprets and rebuilds the overall picture. In fact, top managers express the vision about the future of the organization and elaborate the agenda to reach this vision.

Communication aimed at activating a renewed shared reality depends on some context conditions. Firstly, the type of crisis: natural disasters open up more space for a discourse of renewal than other types of crises. Secondly, companies that own a positive relational capital can more easily reconstruct their future building on this foundation. A well-managed communication and relationship management system available is also useful. Thirdly, the construction of a new shared reality based on renewal is facilitated by the implementation of corrective actions and operational changes.

Conclusions and Future Directions

Any crisis generates a loss of tangible and intangible assets of the victim organization. One of the most valuable resources at stake in case of a crisis is the human capital: employees. Their engaged behaviour is crucial in order to protect the reputation of the company from false criticism, to spread correct information, to sustain the corrective actions the organization is implementing to face the crisis and to relaunch the organization when the crisis is over. In order to reach these vital aims, an organization should invest in normal times to nurture employee engagement and relationship quality, showing concern during the crisis, and focusing on renewal after the crisis.

Internal crisis communication is in rapid development and there are several areas that will need further attention: the role of leaders in internal crisis communication, how to sustain engagement when the crisis is prolonged over time, the impact of social media on employees' perceptions and communication behaviour, the multicultural context for crisis management, the issue of diversity and inclusion in crisis situations. A great number of avenues for future studies in a field increasingly at stake in our era.

Professional Interview

The Main Approaches to the Recovery Phase

Interview to Andrea Notarnicola, partner of the consultancy company Newton and author of the book *L'impresa spezzata* (The broken enterprise, 2019).

How should managers approach a recovery phase?

Traditional management approaches often prove to be useless or harmful after a serious event. Any emergency produces a period of dysfunctionality, upsetting the organizational routines and balances. Without a recovery programme able to overcome organizational orthodoxies, the company risks falling into a persistent dysfunctionality, that is a permanent vulnerable state in terms of culture and mental attitudes.

In the reconstruction and renewal phase, employee engagement will be the essential goal. The sense of belonging to the company and organizational citizenship behaviours will make the difference. The sense of community implies the capability of mutual commitment around shared values, an experience of connection and sharing, a spirit of service and respect: all priorities to be cultivated. For a community, dying and being reborn means elaborating the meaning of an organizational culture: attitudes, actions, situations and ways of thinking.

Which are the main areas of intervention for management during a renewal phase?

In the managerial practice, the common areas of intervention after an external and internal emergency are the creation of a recovery team and an extraordinary employee communication plan, management's activation, organizational listening to read the new context, restructuring of the internal history, stakeholders' engagement, redefinition of the daily experience of employees, improvement of the customer experience and innovation processes for sustainability.

Renewal after a crisis implies changing perspectives. How can managers approach this change of perspectives?

Contradicting the historical need of a dictator in times of crisis, research and experience demonstrate the vital role of diversity of opinions to manage the most acute phases of an emergency as well as moments of recovery. Only inclusiveness and the overcoming of a single mindset allow an organization to find the energy and ideas necessary to restart. In many scenarios, management will have to ask employees to do different jobs because the disaster forced some of the population to leave. Restructuring means first of all opening up to the diversity of perspectives and sensibilities.

Specifically in extreme situations, a company's management can grasp the capabilities and potential of employees which were not evident in routine conditions. During a crisis, people can be seen in a different light and thus it can be discovered that some employees and some groups, who expressed a natural leadership in the heart of the event, are able to generate innovative solutions. This is why talent management programmes are so vital in a phase of corporate recovery.

The whole construction of an organization after a crisis rests on the transformation of traditional professional families into open learning communities. The best projects imply the overcoming of a hierarchical and self-referential organizational model in favour of a reticular system of interconnected communities. A new company emerges from the recovery and the renewal after a serious crisis. It may be better than the previous one.

Professional's bio

Andrea Notarnicola is partner of Newton, where he works as a cultural change management consultant for primary global businesses. He has been lecturer at various universities and schools, including Università IULM. He recently (2019) authored the book *L'impresa spezzata* (The broken enterprise), focused on the recovery phase after an emergency.

References

Adamu, A. A., & Mohamad, B. (2019). A reliable and valid measurement scale for assessing internal crisis communication. *Journal of Communication Management, 23*(2), 90–108. https://doi.org/10.1108/JCOM-07-2018-0068.

Austin, L., & Jin, Y. (2016). Social media and crisis communication: Explicating the social-mediated crisis communication model. In A. Dudo & L. A. Kahlor (Eds.), *Strategic communication: New agendas in communication* (pp. 163–186). Routledge.

Coombs, W. T. (2015). *Ongoing crisis communication: Planning, managing, and responding*. Sage.

Coombs, W. T., & Holladay, S. J. (2006). Unpacking the halo effect: Reputation and crisis management. *Journal of Communication Management, 10*(2), 123–137. https://doi.org/10.1108/13632540610664698.

Diers-Lawson, A. (2019). *Crisis communication: Managing stakeholder relationships*. Routledge. https://doi.org/10.4324/9780429437380.

Einwiller, S., & Korn, C. (2020). Employee reactions to negative media coverage. In F. Frandsen & W. Johansen (Eds.), *Crisis communication* (pp. 299–318). Mouton de Gruyter. *Handbooks of Communication Science* (Vol. 23). https://doi.org/10.1515/9783110554236-014.

Fearn-Banks, K. (2010). *Crisis communications: A casebook approach* (4th ed.). Routldege. https://doi.org/10.4324/9780203849521.

Frandsen, F., & Johansen, W. (2011). The study of internal crisis communication: Towards an integrative framework. *Corporate Communications: An International Journal, 16*(4), 347–361. https://doi.org/10.1108/13563281111186977.

Frandsen, F., & Johansen, W. (2017). *Organizational crisis communication: A multivocal approach* (4th ed.). Sage. https://doi.org/10.1515/commun-2018-2010.

Heide, M., & Simonsson, C. (2014). Developing internal crisis communication: New roles and practices of communication professionals. *Corporate Communications: An International Journal, 22*(4), 451–475. https://doi.org/10.1108/CCIJ-09-2012-0063.

Heide, M., & Simonsson, C. (2015). Struggling with internal crisis communication: A balancing act between paradoxical tensions. *PR Inquiry, 4*(2), 223–255. https://doi.org/10.1177/2046147X15570108.

Heide, M., & Simonsson, C. (2019). *Internal crisis communication: Crisis awareness, leadership and coworkership*. Routledge. https://doi.org/10.4324/9780429425042.

Heide, M., & Simonsson, C. (2020). Internal crisis communication: On current and future research. In F. Frandsen & W. Johansen (Eds.), *Crisis communication* (pp. 259–278). Mouton de Gruyter. *Handbooks of Communication Science* (Vol. 23). https://doi.org/10.1515/9783110554236-012.

Johansen, W., Aggerholm, H., & Frandsen, F. (2012). Entering new territory: A study of internal crisis management and crisis communication in organizations. *Public Relations Review, 38*(2), 270–279. https://doi.org/10.1016/j.pubrev.2011.11.008.

Kim, J. N., & Rhee, Y. (2011). Strategic thinking about employee communication behavior (ECB) in public relations: Testing the models of megaphoning and scouting effects in Korea. *Journal of Public Relations Research, 23*(3), 243–268. https://doi.org/10.1080/1062726X.2011.582204.

Kim, Y. (2018). Enhancing employee communication behaviors for sensemaking and sensegiving in crisis situations: Strategic management approach for effective internal crisis communication. *Journal of Communication Management, 22*(4), 451–475. https://doi.org/10.1108/JCOM-03-2018-0025.

Kim, Y., & Lim, H. (2020). Activating constructive employee behavioural responses in a crisis: Examining the effects of pre-crisis reputation and crisis communication strategies on employee voice behaviours. *Journal of Contingencies and Crisis Management, 28*(2), 141–157. https://doi.org/10.1111/1468-5973.12289.

Mazzei, A., & Butera, A. (2016). Brand consistent behavior of employees on social media: The role of social media governance and policies. *Mercati & Competitività: The Journal of the Italian Society of Marketing, 2016*(4), 85–106. https://doi.org/10.3280/MC2016-004006.

Mazzei, A., Butera, A., & Quaratino, L. (2019). Employee communication for engaging workplaces. *Journal of Business Strategy, 40*(6), 23–32. https://doi.org/10.1108/JBS-03-2019-0053.

Mazzei, A., Kim, J. N., & Dell'Oro, C. (2012). Strategic value of employee relationships and communicative actions: Overcoming corporate crisis with quality internal communication. *International Journal of Strategic Communication, 6*(1), 31–34. https://doi.org/10.1080/1553118X.2011.634869.

Mazzei, A., Kim, J. N., Togna, G., Lee, Y., & Lovari, A. (2019). Employees as advocates or adversaries during a corporate crisis: The role of perceived authenticity and employee empowerment. *Sinergie Italian Journal of Management, 37*(2), 195–212. https://doi.org/10.7433/s109.2019.10.

Mazzei, A., & Ravazzani, S. (2015). Internal crisis communication strategies to protect trust relationships: A study of Italian companies. *International Journal of Business Communication, 52*(3), 319–337. https://doi.org/10.1177/2329488414525447.

Mazzei, A., & Ravazzani, S. (2020). Whistleblowing in organizations. In F. Frandsen & W. Johansen (Eds.), *Crisis communication* (pp. 279–298). Mouton de Gruyter. *Handbooks of Communication Science* (Vol. 23). https://doi.org/10.1515/9783110554236-013.

Mazzei, A., Ravazzani, S., & Quaratino, L. (2020). *Internal crisis communication and the Covid-19 emergency*, CERC @ Department of Business & LECB, Università IULM, April 2020.

Pang, A., Jin, Y., & Cameron, G. T. (2009). Final stage development of the integrated crisis mapping (ICM) model in crisis communication: The myth of low engagement in crisis. *Proceedings of the 12th International Public Relations Research Conference: Coral Gables, Florida, March 11–15 2009*, 449–468.

Ravazzani, S. (2016). Exploring internal crisis communication in multicultural environments: A study among Danish managers. *Corporate Communications: An International Journal, 21*(1), 73–88. https://doi.org/10.1108/CCIJ-02-2015-0011.

Seeger, M., & Ulmer, R. (2002). A post-crisis discourse of renewal: The cases of Malden Mills and Cole Hardwoods. *Journal of Applied Communication Research, 30*(2), 126–142. https://doi.org/10.1080/00909880216578.

Seeger, M., Ulmer, R., Novak, J. M., & Sellnow, T. (2005). Post-crisis discourse and organizational change, failure and renewal. *Journal of Organizational Change Management, 18*(1), 78–95. https://doi.org/10.1108/09534810510579869.

Shaia, J. S., & Gonzenbach, W. J. (2007). Communications with management in times of difficulty and crisis: Silence explained. *International Journal of Strategic Communication, 1*(3), 139–150. https://doi.org/10.1080/15531180701434777.

Strandberg, J., & Vigsø, O. (2016). Internal crisis communication: An employee perspective on narrative, culture, and sensemaking. *Corporate Communications: An International Journal, 21*(1), 89–102. https://doi.org/10.1108/CCIJ-11-2014-0083.

Sturges, D. L. (1994). Communicating through crisis: A strategy for organizational survival. *Management Communication Quarterly, 7*(3), 297–316. https://doi.org/10.1177/0893318994007003004.

Taylor, M. (2010). Towards a holistic organizational approach to understanding crisis. In W. T. Coombs & S. J. Holladay (Eds.), *Handbook of crisis communication* (pp. 698–704). Wiley-Blackwell. https://doi.org/10.1002/9781444314885.ch36.

Ulmer, R. R., Seeger, M. W., & Sellnow, T. L. (2007). Post-crisis communication and renewal: Expanding the parameters of post-crisis discourse. *Public Relation Review, 33*(2), 130–134. https://doi.org/10.1016/j.pubrev.2006.11.015.

CHAPTER 11

Strategic Change Communication

Aniisu K. Verghese

Globally, organizations face a changed competitive landscape that expects organizational designs and processes to continually renew. Enabling and implementing change with communications has received scholarly attention over the years (Barrett, 2002; Bersin, 2020; Graamans et al., 2020; Klein, 1996; Lewis, 2007; Lewis et al., 2013; Strebel, 1996). However, the gap between the scale of change and the ability of organizations to manage it continues to widen. According to Gallup's State of the Global Workforce Report (2017), a staggering 85% of employees worldwide are not engaged or are actively disengaged in their job. One key underlying reason is the resistance to change—the inability to adapt to the ascent of information technology, globalization of markets for products and labor, the rise of the gig economy, stagnant management practices, and evolving expectations of the younger workforce.

Managing change is considered an integral part of a manager's job. In a study among HR professionals, 82% of organizations were involved in a change management initiative. These included introducing or renewing performance management processes and facilities and organizational

A. K. Verghese (✉)
Bangalore Urban, Karnataka, India

L. R. Men and A. Tkalac Verčič (eds.), *Current Trends and Issues in Internal Communication*, New Perspectives in Organizational Communication, https://doi.org/10.1007/978-3-030-78213-9_11

culture changes (Austin, 2015). It is estimated that considering the pace and scale of change and that 9.9% of every dollar is wasted due to poor project performance, there is a need for more attention to lead change within organizations (Project Management Institute, 2018). In addition, agility to sense and adapt to change can result in organizations achieving increased productivity and efficiency and helping them stay competitive (Project Management Institute, 2018).

Keeping employees informed, helping them appreciate messages and take appropriate action on key initiatives are crucial for successful change. However, change can create stress and uncertainty among staff. According to the 2019 Gartner Change Fatigue Survey, an average employee experienced 12 changes in a year. Furthermore, change is creating stress which impacts an organization's topline. Stressed employees underperform than those who aren't by 5%, reducing the topline by USD 32.5 million at an average company (Bryan, 2019). Therefore, the value of managing and communicating organizational change is considered more important than ever (Bersin, 2020).

Understanding Change

Change is considered as an organizational phenomenon within the context of human social interactions with communication serving as a medium. Organizational change relates to disordered and modified states, often complicated and unsettling for stakeholders (Lewis & Sahay, 2019). Change is classified as first order and second-order changes (van Vuuren & Elving, 2008). First-order changes are minor, state van Vuuren and Elving (2008), incremental in nature and needed to avoid second-order changes. On the other hand, second-order changes are adjustments within the organization where the end state is unknown. Examples of change include scenarios such as downsizing, introducing an internal process, or implementing important technology. Actively managing change can increase the success rate of such initiatives. Organizations that have highly effective change and communication practices are known to out beat competition by 3.5X. On the other hand, low effectiveness organizations aren't adept in managing change (Towers Watson, 2013). High performing organizations are known to address change as a manageable opportunity, stay resilient, believe that their change capabilities are ahead of competition, communicate their purpose and invest in training employees to be change-ready (Austin, 2015).

There is a difference between information and communication in relation to change management. The former relates to steps taken on change actions while communication is about establishing mutual understanding and improving the quality of interactions (van Vuuren & Elving, 2008). The process of change is understood as a successive series of steps which requires interventions with resources, communications, and culture inputs (Kotter, 1995).

Despite organizations spending millions of dollars on change management and systems, there is limited evidence of the impact because employees are often in the dark and people aren't clear on how to use the infrastructure organizations possess (Bersin, 2020). Also, the success of change management has been less than optimal with accountability and operational efficiencies inappropriately managed. Only less than half indicated they achieved desired operational goals from change initiatives. Likewise, 44% were able to stay on schedule, and just 47% hold team members accountable for deadlines. Just 48% of those surveyed indicated they stayed on or under budget (Towers Watson, 2011). Kotter (1995) explains that strategic change needs to go through a series of phases, and it takes a considerable amount of time. Skipping stages to speed up change doesn't work and can cause unrepairable damage. Therefore, paying attention to embedding change is essential for organizational success.

Embedding Change

Strategic change is a "difference in the form, quality, or state over time in an organization's alignment with its external environment" (Rajagopalan & Spreitzer, 1996, p. 50). Change management is defined "as a structured approach to transitioning individuals, teams and organizations from a current state to a desired future state" (Austin, 2015, p. iii). Strategic change management involves a series of successive steps each having definite objectives, activities, and communication needs (Klein, 1996). Making change work expects organizations and individuals to shift their mindsets and behaviors. According to the IBM's Change Study (2014), there are five maturity stages of managing change—informal (without a standard plan for driving change), emerging (change capabilities are emerging yet do not use a formal approach to change management), formalizing (specific projects have consistent change management practices), scaling (mature standards are applied companywide and leaders as well as managers are held accountable for change) and embedded (the highest stage of change maturity with all parts of the organization enabled with skills and capacity); each stage builds on the other in a continuous process of growth and development.

Among the models of change management, the Kurt Lewin's three-stage approach of unfreezing, changing, and refreezing serves as a useful framework for understanding the process (Schein, 1996). During the unfreezing stage, the organization prepares for change, challenges the current situation, and provides the rationale for change. Activities practiced include planning, investing in resources, training and preparing the structure. The communication needs during this phase include identifying the audiences, explaining the change, and reassuring stakeholders. In the changing stage, the goals include starting the progress, creating momentum, and testing progress in some areas of the business. The activities include implementing, evaluating, and modifying the change needs. Communication focuses on taking feedback, challenging and reassuring staff. In the refreezing stage, the goals are to reinforce change, supporting the process and correcting any gaps. The activities include broadening the extent of change, recognizing successes, and monitoring impact. On the communication needs, the focus is to showcase the impact and cascade the message widely (Klein, 1996).

Extending this direction, the Change and Communication ROI Study Report (Towers Watson, 2011) identifies three stages of change: (a) to understand and segment (gauging the environment, appreciating what's evolving, what matters to stakeholders and which audiences get impact), (b) to design and build (create customized strategies and approaches which includes tools and resources to create awareness and drive behavioral change), and (c) to implement and improve (deliver on change goals, measure impact and recognize progress and improvements).

Only when organizations align activities with the appropriate phases will change outcomes be most acceptable.

Austin (2015) suggests that change is facilitated in three phases—designing, enacting and sustaining with key moments where ideas are translated into action. Six activities influence overall change success—leading, communicating, learning, measurement, involving and sustaining. Those organizations who have been able to sustain change over time focused on leadership, communication, involvement, training/learning and measurement (Towers Watson, 2011). Three actors in the change management process from the viewpoint of senior leaders are change strategists—who create the framework of change; the change implementers—those who help influence and land change and change recipients—those who are the beneficiaries of change.

The first has the power to make decisions while the other two groups have no decision-making authority (Stoyanova, 2011). Lewis (2007) believes expanding the change stakeholder group beyond employees can benefit change implementation while considering key components such as alignment, consistency and genuineness in change communication. Understanding the barriers to change and the underlying motivators can enhance an organization's ability to drive progressive initiatives.

Change Impact

Among the key barriers to implementing change are uncertainty (Redmond, 2015), lack of buy-in (Project Management Institute, 2018), change fatigue (Baker, 2020), rumors (DiFonzo & Bordia, 1998) and resistance from staff (Strebel, 1996). Uncertainty is defined as having an inadequate state of knowledge due to multiple explanations and possibilities. As the number of options increases, so does confusion. It ranges from self, other, and partner uncertainty to cognitive and behavior uncertainty. Organizational and personnel changes lead to uncertainty and stress among employees (Redmond, 2015).

According to the Uncertainty Reduction Theory, improving our ability to comprehend the motives of others can help improve predictability and therefore certainty. Making sense of the situation can take the form of proactive, explanatory and descriptive approaches (Redmond, 2015). The inability of organizations to share timely information results in employees seeking insights from informal channels that cause stress, job dissatisfaction, and erode trust (Schweiger & Denisi, 1991). When employees don't receive timely communication from reliable sources, they resort to gathering information from informal channels such as rumors. "Rumors are a symptom of the uncertainty that often accompanies organizational change and persist or even flourish when poor communication strategies fail to adequately assuage this uncertainty" (DiFonzo & Bordia, 1998, p. 297).

Sensemaking is another way in which people infer meaning by interpreting themselves and the world around them. It is based on interruptions, anomalies, and disturbances. Through an ongoing process that covers location, meaning making and becoming, conversation and nonverbal behaviors help shape meaning (Weick, 2012). Sensemaking, communications, and change hold organizations together as they navigate ambiguity and pace of progress (van Vuuren & Elving, 2008).

Language plays an influential role in the comprehension of change (Ford & Ford, 1995). Understanding change from the context of communication means appreciating conversations. Ford and Ford (1995) refer to four types of conversations that can allow change to take shape through communications: initiative (a change starting exercise that focuses listeners' attention on what could or should be done), understanding (helping gain consensus), performance (interplay of requests and promises between parties involved), and closure (interactions that bring an end to the change process). The Speech Act Theory refers to business conventions within the realm of discourse. Since communication emerges from three levels within the context of language—the literal meaning, the intent of the act, and the outcomes, the message, channel, and timing matter most for effective change communication (Smeltzer, 1991). The approach in which organizations communicate impacts the success of change initiatives, especially on individual's commitment, morale, and retention. Studying two organizations, Goodman and Truss (2004) emphasize that both process and content of the communications strategy were important. The timing, personalization, methodology, and flexibility led to better change results.

Employee change fatigue is a serious concern with organizations unsure how to keep them engaged while progressing with change. Managing change fatigue is considered a critical priority for organizations (Gartner, 2020). Gaining employees' trust leads to change acceptance. Baker (2020) recommends engaging employees at all levels by focusing on two key aspects—building trust and improving team cohesion. Those employees who reported higher trust were 2.6 times more adaptable to change than those with lower trust. Likewise, those teams who felt they were in it together were more connected and committed, up to 1.8 times more than those with lower team bonding.

Effective Change Communications Strategies

Internal communication is an essential element of change management. One of the roles of the internal communication function is as a change agent (Vercic et al., 2012). The role of internal communication in employee relations and improving trust especially in times of change and stress is valuable (Dolphin, 2005). Effective employee communication is considered as a glue that holds an organization together, and during major change, it allows the smooth operation of the organization and links all other processes of the organization, such as the strategic and business planning processes (Barrett, 2002). One among the 8-step model proposed by Kotter (1995) is the crucial role of internal communication.

Change communication is more effective when related to the company's culture and workforce. Trained and informed managers can influence how change is conducted especially engaging the workforce to direct discretionary effort and pace (Towers Watson, 2013).

Transformational leadership and transparent communications provide clarity, reduces uncertainty, and enhances employees' trust in organizations (DiFonzo & Bordia, 1998; Yue et al., 2019). In a study among employees experiencing change, Yue et al. (2019) discovered that transformational leadership and transparent communication influenced how employees trusted their organizations by increasing their openness to change. Leaders can influence employees' organizational identification during change. Effective communication is one of the key leadership approaches that help staff cope during business disruptions and create deep connections with the organization during uncertainty (Aitken & von Treuer, 2020).

Honest and timely communications are among the top soft factors for change. When leaders personally demonstrate change behaviors, create a compelling reason for change and involve change catalysts at all levels, there is more acceptance for change (IBM, 2014). Employees reacted negatively when messages were indirect and sounded overtly positive (Smeltzer, 1991). Change is embedded when it seeps into the organization's culture. Communication plays a role in demonstrating the new approaches, behaviors, and attitudes that impact the organization as well as providing a line of sight (Kotter, 1995).

Employee alignment is crucial for change success. When an individual's psychology and the organizational strategy synchronize there is improved alignment. During the initial stages of change, training and communications are important to be established to accelerate knowledge and trust (Gagnon et al., 2008). Another aspect to consider is employees' personal compacts with their organizations. The dimensions of personal compacts are formal, psychological, and social which influence how employees accept change (Strebel, 1996). Strebel (1996) opines that formal compact covers the basic tasks and performance expectations on the job—compensation, performance evaluation among others.

The psychological dimension covers trust and relationship-based understanding which are mostly implicit. This is viewed in relations to their manager and covers new performance standards and goals—from the intensity of work needed to recognition and financial rewards. The social dimension is related to the culture—how the values are lived and if leaders walk the talk. It considers if the company really works including resource allocation, decision-making, conflict management and risk taking. Similarly, Barrett (2002) argues that when a culture of communication spreads to all parts of the company and management accepts it as a role they have to play, change is easier to implement.

Seeking feedback and including employees in the change communications process leads to improved results. Highly effective organizations consider and act on employee suggestions (IBM, 2014). Inviting views from stakeholders as they go along the change journey values their knowledge and skills and makes change a participatory process (Graamans et al., 2020; van Vuuren & Elving, 2008). A crucial aspect of change communication is appreciating the emotions and feelings of participants and using a mix of channels while engaging audiences. In a study involving hospital staff related to procuring sutures for surgery resulted in change rejection as doctors believed their sentiments weren't considered (Graamans et al., 2020). Similarly, while introducing change in a large public organization, when communication was poor, employees felt their feelings weren't considered, leading to a deterioration in senior management trust (Proctor & Doukakis, 2003). Such challenges can destabilize change movements and gaining perspectives on potential resistances can help organizations and change leaders.

Implementing Successful Change Communication

To successfully implement change, Kotter (1995) cites an eight-step model: creating a sense of urgency, forming a powerful guiding coalition, creating a vision, communicating the vision, empowering others to act, planning for and creating short-term wins, consolidating improvements and creating still more change and institutionalizing new approaches. Errors while following these steps can lead to a breakdown of trust, missed expectations and erosion of organizational effectiveness, opines Kotter (1995). In a longitudinal study among blue-collar workers at production plants, change communications and training that focused on sharing strategic knowledge and gaining commitment led to aligned behaviors (Gagnon et al., 2008). Kotter and Schlesinger (1989) highlight the importance of communication and education in situations where there is a lack of information or disinformation and rumors. Once convinced, employees will participate in implementing change although this approach can be time-consuming and involves many people. Among the strategies to progress through change, organizations can consider revisiting and revising the employer–employee compact. Revision of the compact can be done in three phases. First, leaders can draw attention to the need to change and establish connect for revision. Following that, they need to initiate a process for revising the compact and lastly, confirm commitment with the revised agreements (Strebel, 1996).

Involving stakeholders in the process of change matters. 74% of organizations have a top-down approach to change communications with few channels for employee feedback (IBM, 2014). Effective change takes place when the process is collaborative (Towers Watson, 2013). Involving stakeholders in the development process of change is believed to be more effective than a top-down approach that mandates participation and alignment (van Vuuren & Elving, 2008). When considering a deficit-based approach (review mistakes in change management) versus a constructionist approach (that positively reinforces improvements), having a blend of these approaches helps because individuals are irrational in their behavior and are risk-averse (Keller & Aiken, 2009).

Timing of change communication is critical to the success of initiatives. Providing timely information and even a preview communication helped alleviate fears and reduced uncertainty. In a study among employees to gauge the impact of communication during a merger between two plants, it was found that timely communication prevented informal channel messages from increasing uncertainty and stress. Employees in one plant were provided a preview communication while the control plant didn't receive the information on time. The preview communication helped give employees a realistic picture of the changes faced (Schweiger & Denisi, 1991). In another study that reviewed change communication in 43 organizations, the timing of messages was the biggest differentiator between effective and ineffective companies (Smeltzer, 1991). Exploring the themes that popular press books highlight on the role of communications in effective change, participation and empowerment, purpose, and vision, and creating a changed culture emerged as key approaches for success (Lewis et al., 2006).

While directly reaching employees with key organizational messages rather than cascading communication helps in timebound situations (Proctor & Doukakis, 2003), involving supervisors can enable deeper appreciation of the change goals (Salem, 2008). Salem (2008) argues that the valuable role of managers in transformational change is discounted and that management believes in the wrong assumption that producing communication with the right words brings about commitment to changes. Likewise, considering communication skills while hiring is a good practice because social interactions at the workplace make sense of change. Investing in training people on interpersonal communications helps. The use of technologies such as intranet and e-mail work best for change communication although conventional approaches to change management do work in influencing employee attitudes and management behaviors. Tapping into human psychology is an important strategy which most organizations fail to grasp (Keller & Aiken, 2009).

Studying the role of internal communications in a large-scale change in a multinational organization, it was found that meetings in small groups helped to explain and reinforce change. On the other hand, large meetings resulted in a lack of dialogue and two-way communications. Written communication was best for delivering data and information, although they were inappropriate while disseminating knowledge, skills, and wisdom (Stoyanova, 2011).

Although social media use in organizations is nascent, it is considered important and has a consequence on organizational change. They influence socialization, information sharing, and power processes, essential for communicating, and embedding change (Treem & Leonardi, 2013). By connecting people and creating a forum of sharing information, communication serves as an important approach to meet employee demands and develop a conducive situation through dialogue, feedback and transparency (Stankovic-Rice, 2011). Social media helps to facilitate goodwill toward the organization leading to change and renewal. A study among executives across different industries discovered that about half of their companies had adopted social media initiatives and of these 60% had a positive impact on the surveyed organizations' internal communications. Social media can help influence change among employees by creating feelings of trust, playfulness, belonging, and pride (Huy & Shipilov, 2012).

Storytelling is another valued approach to help communicate change effectively. Framing communications helps to diffuse conflicts, diminish the value of informal channels of communications, and share a unified narrative, binding stakeholders (Keller & Aiken, 2009). Feedback is crucial for change acceptance and needs to be included in the process of framing (van Vuuren & Elving, 2008). By creating a memorable story and inviting stakeholders to tackle complex problems facing a healthcare facility in the United States, it turned around the center's fortunes. Not only did employee morale and engagement improve, it also rallied the community and raised funds for future expansion. (Adamson et al., 2006).

Measuring Strategic Change Communication

Measurement of strategic change and communications is less established among organizations. While internal communications influence how change is accepted among employees, there are limited tools and resources to gauge its effectiveness (Harkness, 2000). Of the six factors of facilitating change (leading, communicating, learning, measuring, involving, and sustaining), measurement had one of the biggest impacts on overall change success. Organizations that are highly effective at change management are much better at measuring progress against goals than are lower effectiveness organizations (Towers Watson, 2011).

The traditional measures of change success were scope, time, and cost. These are no more relevant in a fiercely competitive environment. The need to demonstrate how businesses matched their goals with tangible benefits is the need of the hour. Organizations that completed 80% or more of their projects on time, within budgets, mapped to objectives and helped realize business benefits were considered successful (Project Management Institute, 2018). This is corroborated by the IBM Institute for Business Value study (2014) that discovered that project completion is considered the top measure of change management (IBM, 2014). Change is also measured by the readiness of the organization, individual and group as well as their receptivity.

Ranging from negative to positive, receptivity is a measure of the openness to change (Armenakis & Harris, 2002; Frahm & Brown, 2007).

Demonstrating positive intent by taking the views of employees on board can improve how strategic change communication is received. There is still progress to be made. For example, while 71% of organizations consider and act on employee suggestions, only 8% encourage dialogue via collaboration tools (IBM, 2014). Another gap is that practitioners have scarce abilities to conduct thorough communication evaluation or the understanding of valuation methods, thereby limiting measuring organizational change impact (Zerfass et al., 2017).

Finally, measurement can be considered at all stages of the change management process and include the role of communications. For example, asking employees about the quality of the change communication, gauging the effectiveness of the different messages and media used to inform employees, and understanding the extent to which the knowledge of the objectives of the change was accepted, can help measure success (Elving, 2005).

Summary

Managing change is a complex process and there is no one-size, fits-all model. Every change brings unique challenges and expects specific change design and communication. Organizations who invest and implement effective communication and change management strategies are financially successful. Involving change and internal communications professionals early in the journey can create positive value and outcomes. Building trust, creating a culture receptive to change and influencing behaviors can help overcome resistances.

Interview

Mahul Brahma, Ph.D. and DLitt heads Communications, CSR and Branding at mjunction Services Limited. A former journalist, Mahul is an award-winning communicator, a renowned luxury commentator and an author. He is the alumnus of institutes such as Indian Institute of Management (India) and University of Cambridge (UK).

1. **How is strategic change communications and management understood in your organization?**

Any change that influences how an organization progresses on its strategy across all levels is strategic change management. For example, a change in management, repurposing the organization or an improved brand positioning exercise. Strategic change management is a journey and that's how the organization approaches the subject.

2. **What is the role of communication in change management?**

Communication plays a crucial role as strategic change needs buy-in from all stakeholders including those outside the organization. Communication helps accelerate how organizations convey the imperative for change and presents a strong narrative from senior management. Without communication, strategic change will be ineffective.

3. **What signs tell you that communication in change management works? How do you differentiate between effective or ineffective communications?**

Strategic change is effective when the organization is ready and there is a sense of alignment among stakeholders. It can fail to fructify if stakeholders don't understand the rationale and don't trust the motive. Effectiveness of change is an outcome of the degree of stakeholders' alignment. Ineffective communication can result in poor understanding. On the other hand, effective communication is inclusive, clear and takes stakeholders along the journey.

4. **Which channels work best while communicating strategic change?**

It is key that stakeholders hear directly from senior management to establish context and importance. Therefore, channels such as face-to-face Town Halls and open Q&A forums are essential as platforms for stakeholders to engage and clarify the change. Co-creating change alongside stakeholders means staying transparent and involving them early. Internal communication channels such as discussion forums and mailers help in conveying change.

5. **What are the key obstacles or challenges while going about strategic change management?**

The key challenge is when your stakeholders, internal and external, aren't in agreement with the change. Since change creates uncertainty and stakeholders can feel insecure, communication needs to address relevance and context. For example, if the change entails automation of roles at the workplace using machine learning and artificial intelligence, stakeholders may fear losing their jobs. By explaining how impacted employees will be retrained and rebadged for other critical roles in the organization can help improve change acceptance.

6. **How are employees included in change management and communications?**

Senior management needs to convince stakeholders that change is a win–win for all involved. By explaining how strategic change allows the organization to be resilient and overcome macroeconomic situations, leaders can involve employees to voice their thoughts, be change agents and support change. For example, when a company shuts down stores it is perceived to be bad news. However, if the organization explains that reducing loss making units can help keep the business running and turnaround fortunes in the future, it can alleviate the concerns.

7. **Please share a recent example of a strategic change management practice.**

When the pandemic swept across the globe, working from home became the norm. However, the strategic change of working remotely created opportunities for the leadership to communicate the benefits of collaborating virtually, saving time and improving efficiencies. Employees shared ideas to reduce costs, directed their energies on more fruitful projects and increased knowledge sharing. That dramatically resulted in productivity improvement across the organization.

References

Adamson, G., Pine, J., Van Steenhoven, T., & Kroupa, J. (2006). How storytelling can drive strategic change. *Strategy & Leadership.*

Aitken, K., & von Treuer, K. (2020). Leadership behaviors that foster organizational identification during change. *Journal of Organizational Change Management*. Vol. ahead-of-print No. ahead-of-print. https://doi.org/10.1108/JOCM-01-2020-0029.

Armenakis, A. A., & Harris, S. G. (2002). Crafting a change message to create transformational readiness. *Journal of Organizational Change Management, 15*(2), 169–183. https://doi.org/10.1108/09534810210423080.

Austin, J. (2015). Leading effective change: A primer for the HR professional. *SHRM Foundation's Effective Practice Guideline Series.*

Baker, M. (2020, October 14). *Gartner cautions HR leaders that the risk of change Fatigue among employees has doubled in 2020* [Press release]. https://www.gartner.com/en/newsroom/press-releases/2020-10-14-gartner-cautions-hr-leaders-that-the-risk-of-change-fatigue-among-employees-has-doubled-in-2020-this-year.

Barrett, D. J. (2002). Change communication: Using strategic employee communication to facilitate major change. *Corporate Communications: An International Journal, 7*(4).

Bersin, J. (2020). *The urgent need for change communications.* https://joshbersin.com/wp-content/uploads/2020/06/Employee-Communications-For-Change-Bersin.pdf.

Bryan, J. (2019). *Gartner change Fatigue survey.* https://www.gartner.com/smarterwithgartner/top-challenges-for-communicators-in-2020/.

DiFonzo, N., & Bordia, P. (1998). A tale of two corporations: Managing uncertainty during organizational change. *Human Resource Management: Published in Cooperation with the School of Business Administration, the University of Michigan and in Alliance with the Society of Human Resources Management, 37*(3–4), 295–303.

Dolphin, R. R. (2005). Internal communications: Today's strategic imperative. *Journal of marketing communications, 11*(3), 171–190.

Elving, W. J. L. (2005). The role of communication in organizational change. *Corporate Communications: An International Journal, 10*(2), 129–138. https://doi.org/10.1108/13563280510596943.

Ford, J. D., & Ford, L. W. (1995). The role of conversations in producing intentional change in organizations. *Academy of Management Review, 20*(3), 541–570.

Frahm, J., & Brown, K. (2007). First steps: Linking change communication to change receptivity. *Journal of Organizational Change Management., 20*(3), 370–387. https://doi.org/10.1108/09534810710740191.

Gagnon, M. A., Jansen, K. J., & Michael, J. H. (2008). Employee alignment with strategic change: A study of strategy-supportive behavior among blue-collar employees. *Journal of Managerial Issues*, 425–443.

Gallup. (2017). *State of the global workplace.* Gallup.

Gartner. (2020). *Change management communication: Develop an effective communications strategy to successfully manage change.* https://www.gartner.com/en/corporate-communications/insights/change-communication.

Graamans, E., Aij, K., Vonk, A., & ten Have, W. (2020). Case study: Examining failure in change management. *Journal of Organizational Change Management, 33*(220), 319–330. Emerald Publishing Limited.

Goodman, J., & Truss, C. (2004). The medium and the message: Communicating effectively during a major change initiative. *Journal of Change Management, 4*(3), 217–228.
Harkness, J. (2000). Measuring the effectiveness of change—The role of internal communication in change management. *Journal of Change Management, 1*(1), 66–73.
Huy, Q., & Shipilov, A. (2012). The key to social media success within organizations. *MIT Sloan Management Review, 54*(1), 73.
IBM. (2014). Making change work... while the work keeps changing. *IBM Institute for Business Value.* https://www.ibm.com/thought-leadership/institute-business-value/report/making-change-work.
Keller, S., & Aiken, C. (2009). *The inconvenient truth about change management.* McKinsey & Company.
Klein, S. M. (1996). A management communication strategy for change. *Journal of Organizational Change Management, 9*(2), 32–46. © MCB University Press, 0953–4814.
Kotter, J. P. (1995). Leading change: Why transformation efforts fail. *Harvard Business Review*, March–April 1995.
Kotter, J. P., & Schlesinger, L. A. (1989). Choosing strategies for change. *Readings in Strategic Management* (pp. 294–306). Palgrave.
Lewis, L. K. (2007). An organizational stakeholder model of change implementation communication. *Communication Theory, 17*(2), 176–204.
Lewis, L., & Sahay, S. (2019). Change and change management. In *Movements in organizational communication research: Current issues and future directions* (pp. 214–232). Taylor and Francis.
Lewis, L. K., Schmisseur, A. M., Stephens, K. K., & Weir, K. E. (2006). Advice on communicating during organizational change: The content of popular press books. *The Journal of Business Communication, 43*(2), 113–137.
Lewis, L. K., Laster, N., & Kulkarni, V. (2013). Telling'em how it will be: Previewing pain of risky change in initial announcements. *The Journal of Business Communication (1973), 50*(3), 278–308.
Project Management Institute. (2018). *Pulse of the profession: Success in disruptive times.* https://www.pmi.org/-/media/pmi/documents/public/pdf/learning/thought-leadership/pulse/pulse-of-the-profession-2018.pdf.
Proctor, T., & Doukakis, I. (2003). Change management: The role of internal communication and employee development. *Corporate Communications: An International Journal, 8*(4), 268–277. https://doi.org/10.1108/13563280310506430.
Rajagopalan, N., & Spreitzer, G. M. (1996). Towards a theory of strategic change: A multi-lens perspective and integrative framework. In *Academy of management proceedings* (Vol. 1996, No. 1, pp. 51–55). Briarcliff Manor, NY 10510: *Academy of Management.*

Redmond, M. V. (2015). Uncertainty reduction theory. *English Technical Reports and White Papers*, 3. http://lib.dr.iastate.edu/engl_reports/3.

Salem, P. J. (2008). The seven communication reasons organizations do not change. *Corporate Communications, 13*(3), 333–348.

Schein, E. H. (1996). Culture: The missing concept in organization studies. *Administrative Science Quarterly*, 229–240.

Schweiger, D. M., & Denisi, A. S. (1991). Communication with employees following a merger: A longitudinal field experiment. *Academy of Management Journal, 34*(1), 110–135.

Smeltzer, L. R. (1991). An analysis of strategies for announcing organization-wide change. *Group & Organization Studies, 16*(1), 5–24.

Stankovic-Rice, B. L. (2011). Social media strategies to advance organizational change. *Pepperdine University. Proquest Dissertations Publishing, 2011*, 3473384.

Stoyanova, T. (2011). *Strategic change management and the use of internal communication*. Aarhus School of Business, University of Aarhus.

Strebel, P. (1996). Why do employees resist change? *Harvard Business Review, 74*(3), 86.

Treem, J. W., & Leonardi, P. M. (2013). Social media use in organizations: Exploring the affordances of visibility, editability, persistence, and association. *Annals of the International Communication Association, 36*(1), 143–189.

Towers Watson. (2011). *Change and communication ROI study report*.

Towers Watson. (2013). *Change and communication ROI–How the fundamentals have evolved and the best adapt*.

van Vuuren, M., & Elving, W. J. (2008). Communication, sensemaking and change as a chord of three strands. *Corporate Communications: An International Journal, 13*(3), 349–435.

Vercic, A. T., Vercic, D., & Sriramesh, K. (2012). Internal communication: Definition, parameters, and the future. *Public Relations Review, 38*(2), 223–230.

Weick, K. E. (2012). Organized sensemaking: A commentary on processes of interpretive work. *Human Relations, 65*(1), 141–153.

Yue, C. A., Men, L. R., & Ferguson, M. A. (2019). Bridging transformational leadership, transparent communication, and employee openness to change: The mediating role of trust. *Public Relations Review, 45*(3), 101779.

Zerfass, A., Verčič, D., & Volk, S. C. (2017). Communication evaluation and measurement: Skills, practices and utilization in European organizations. *Corporate Communications: An International Journal, 22*(1), 2–18. https://doi.org/10.1108/CCIJ-08-2016-0056.

CHAPTER 12

Measuring and Evaluating Internal Communication

Julie O'Neil, Michele E. Ewing, Stacey Smith, and Sean Williams

Why Measure and Evaluate Internal Communication?

The question of how to measure internal communication had an easy answer for too many years. We don't. There were many reasons why, including the "too busy, too dumb, too hard" argument that the authors of this chapter heard first-hand in the practice of public relations for many years. Scholars echoed a more robust sentiment in that spirit; Meng and

J. O'Neil (✉)
Bob Schieffer College of Communication, Texas Christian University, Fort Worth, TX, USA
e-mail: j.oneil@tcu.edu

M. E. Ewing
School of Media and Journalism, College of Communication & Information, Kent State University, Kent, OH, USA
e-mail: meewing@kent.edu

L. R. Men and A. Tkalac Verčič (eds.), *Current Trends and Issues in Internal Communication*, New Perspectives in Organizational Communication, https://doi.org/10.1007/978-3-030-78213-9_12

Berger (2012), for example, identified a lack of money and staff, difficulty determining a direct link between communication initiatives and business results, and time constraints.

During the past decade, internal communication measurement became not only a must-have in a practical sense but a symbol of strategic thinking. Suppliers of internal communication services responded to client demands with proprietary measurement strategies and methods (Sanders, 2018; Smarp, 2019; Vaughan, 2017). This shift illustrates the old business adage that organizations invest in the things they find valuable.

Internal communication has an impact on organizational objectives, sometimes directly, sometimes indirectly. Measurement and evaluation approaches can include both financial indicators, such as ROI and financial outcomes (Dortok, 2006; Ehling et al., 1992; Grossman, 2013; Harter et al., 2002; Meng & Berger, 2012; Towers Watson, 2013) and non-financial indicators, such as trust, satisfaction, and advocacy (Meng & Berger, 2012; Meng & Pan, 2012). Indeed, as both scholars and practitioners believe, internal communication affects employee attitudes, beliefs, knowledge, and behavior. Impact on safety, quality and productivity often relies on the often-cited drive for employee engagement. This idea indicates that highly engaged employees advocate for the organization, be more readily retained, exert higher degrees of discretionary effort, and generally conduct themselves more like owners than workers (Kahn & Heaphy, 2014). Byrne et al. (2016) discussed the difficulty in determining effective methods of measuring employee engagement, and though engagement is just one potential measure, its relationship with internal communication has been studied frequently (e.g., Mishra et al., 2014; Ruck et al., 2017; Tkalac Verčič & Polški Vokić, 2017).

Many strategic planning methodologies align communication objectives with organizational objectives and create good opportunities for

S. Smith
Jackson Jackson & Wagner, Rye, NH, USA
e-mail: ssmith@jjwpr.com

S. Williams
School of Media and Communication, Bowling Green State University, Bowling Green, OH, USA
e-mail: sdwilli@bgsu.edu

measurement. Popular planning methodologies include the OGSM tool–Objectives, Goals, Strategies, Metrics (Lafley & Martin, 2013); RPIE–Research, Planning, Implementation, Evaluation (Escovedo, 2012); RACE–Research, Action, Communication, Evaluation (Begìn & Charbanneau, 2012); and AMMO–Audiences, Messages, Methods, Objectives (Williams, 2015). Each of these models connect internal communication activities to organizational impact, as long as the organization in question has articulated goals that can indeed be affected by internal communication. Measurement, therefore, is more than "proving value." It also is a diagnostic tool that reveals opportunities for planning.

Measurement can also be of immense value in assessing and building an effective organizational culture. Based upon data, communicators can direct resources to the areas most in need of attention, conserving those resources and supporting the desired culture. As Williams asks, "Is the work atmosphere the way that the people within the organization want it to be, or can it stand to be improved?" (Vaughan, 2017, para. 10).

As an ongoing strategic activity, measurement, and evaluation enable communicators to join other organizational functions in solid, research-based, data-driven strategy. Clear, measurable objectives and strong strategic plans designed to drive toward those objectives, with evaluative processes firmly in place, contribute to the perception of the value of the function and its leaders. Meanwhile, measurement-based campaigns provide ongoing data to either validate assumptions or enable corrective action. This, then, represents the main answer to the question, "Why measure internal communication?" Measurement acts as an informer to strategic planning, a cue as to current state and guide to campaign planning, and as a means of evaluating the value of campaigns and of programs as a whole. Measurement and evaluation can examine the impact on employees, the organization, and society at large. This multipart utility makes measurement an indispensable tool for any internal communicator and strategic manager.

How to Measure and Evaluate Internal Communication?

Measurement and evaluation infuse the entire internal communication process, from conducting formative research to assess the situation/identify problem or opportunity, setting objectives, identifying target audiences, formulating strategy and tactics, to evaluating results to identify feedback and make improvements (Gregory, 2000; Paine, 2011).

The Measurement and Evaluation Process

Step 1: Align Communication Objectives with Organizational Objectives

As with any communication process, internal communicators must first align their objectives with the organizational goals. Practitioners should secure leadership's buy-in to these objectives early on, as they may be the most important internal customer and their expectations will guide how the program's success is measured. If the buy-in is achieved upfront, then support through budgeting, advocacy, and silo-busting (when needed) should be available. When writing communication objectives, practitioners must ensure that they are relevant, achievable, and measurable. Whereas a goal is aspirational, an objective includes a measure of impact (AMEC, 2020), so that the practitioner can showcase whether and how they have met their communication objectives. The acronym "S.M.A.R.T." is often used to define the most effective goal and objective design (AMEC, 2020). Good objectives are:

- **Specific**: scope is narrow and well-defined.
- **Measurable**: metric clearly defines achievement.
- **Attainable**: realistic budget and resources (time) for plan implementation.
- **Relevant**: related to the overall goals and stakeholders.
- **Time bound**: within the period of the plan.

Ultimately, writing clear and relevant communication objectives helps to focus communication efforts, increase the efficiency of communication efforts, secure management buy-in and to build an accountability system, which provides value for the internal communicator (Institute for Public Relations, 2021). Below are examples of SMART communication objectives.

- Increase by 20% the frequency of discussions around economic goals and employee contribution toward revenue by respected and influential supervisors within six months.

- Raise employee participation in external volunteer opportunities by 5% within five months.

Step 2: Identify Target Stakeholders and Communication strategy
Internal communicators must next determine which stakeholder(s) are key to achieving their objectives and prioritize them. Due to limited time and budget, prioritization is key. For example, in the Walmart case previewed in this chapter, the company spent significant time researching their target employee audience. After conducting more than two years of research to identify innovative ways to reach associates around the world, Walmart identified three key audiences: (a) Entrenched Loyalists, (b) Opportunity Seekers, and (c) Daily Subscribers. Walmart ultimately decided to focus on Opportunity Seekers, and they sought to develop strategy and tactics to reach this prioritized target audience.

Step 3: Measure Communication Activity
Measurement and evaluative activities should be guided by the designated communication objectives. Common approaches to measuring internal communication effectiveness include outputs, outtakes, outcomes, or impacts (AMEC, 2020), which are explained in the next section.

Step 4: Evaluate and Make Improvements
Scholars and communicators recommend implementing ongoing evaluation during a campaign or program to assess effectiveness of communication strategies and tactics, as well as progress toward achieving objectives and goals (AMEC, 2020; Lindenmann, 1993; Watson, 2001). According to the Institute for Public Relations (2021) "the purpose of evaluation is not celebration but optimization." For example, do employees view content as relevant and useful and why? Which channels in the internal communication program are attracting the highest engagement and why? How do internal communication data align with data from other organizational departments? Asking good questions allows the practitioner to make timely improvements to audience segmentation, messaging, channels, and other communication elements.

Internal Communication Standards: What to Measure and Evaluate

Academics and communication practitioners have opined that internal communicators both grapple with knowing how to measure and evaluate internal communication as well as doing so in different ways (Mendez et al., 2013; Meng & Pan, 2012; Ruck, 2015; Ruck & Welch, 2012). The lack of a standardized approach to measuring internal communication adds to potential inefficiency, because practitioners and their organizational leaders do not have a shared vocabulary to compare and contrast results. To address these challenges, the Institute for Public Relations Measurement Commission created a task force committee in 2015, comprised of academics and practitioners, to identify industry standards for internal communication measurement. A standard provides a shared vocabulary for organizational leaders and communicators to compare and contrast results (Institute for Public Relations, 2013). Following a two-year comprehensive research process, the task force identified 22 standards for internal communication (O'Neil et al., 2018), which were organized into three categories: outtakes, outcomes and organizational impact (Table 12.1).

Outtakes

Outtakes involve the response and reactions of the target audience to the communicative activity. These standards, such as awareness, knowledge and retention of information, are designed to evaluate informational communication objectives. For example, measuring employees' awareness and understanding of organization's business goals, safety protocols and other topics that employees need to understand to effectively perform their jobs.

Outcomes

The most meaningful way to measure and evaluate is outcomes, which are the effects of the communication on the target audience (AMEC, 2020). Outcomes typically measure changes in attitude, opinion, and behaviors among target audiences as a result of the communication initiative or campaign. Motivational communication objectives can be measured using these standards including advocacy, empowerment, and collaboration. Some examples of how these standards can be used in evaluating the level of employees' discretionary efforts with defending the company's reputation, how employees feel empowered take initiative and make decisions to solve problems, and how are employees sharing ideas and collaborating across departments and divisions. Other examples of outcomes include increased job satisfaction, innovation, sales, and likelihood to recommend other people to work at the organization.

Table 12.1 Internal communication measurement standards and definitions (O'Neil et al., 2018)

Standard	*Definition*
Outtakes	
Awareness	Whether employees have heard of an organizational message, issue, or topic
Knowledge	Employees' level of comprehension about organizational messages, issues, or topics
Understanding	Employees' ability to relate their knowledge to their work in a way that helps the organization achieve its goals
Relevance	Degree to which employees communication from the organization meaningful and useful
Retention of Information	Degree to which employees can recall key messages or topics when asked after an x timeframe
Outcomes	
Attitude	A way of thinking or feeling about a subject (about an organization, topic, or issue) ranging from very positive to very negative
Advocacy	Employees' discretionary effort and time to promote or defend an organization and its products and services
Authenticity	Perception that an organization is transparent, honest, and fair, especially regarding the pursuit of its organizational objectives
Empowerment	Employees have the information, rewards, and power to take initiative and make decisions to solve problems and improve performance
Collaboration	The process of employees across different divisions and or units coming together to solve a problem and/or create something successfully
Teamwork	The process of employees within the same unit coming together to successfully achieve a common goal or objective under the leadership of an appointed manager
Discretionary Effort	The amount of effort employees give to an organization, a team, or a project, above and beyond what is required
Trust	A belief in the reliability, truth, and integrity of the organization's leadership, decision-making, and communication
Satisfaction	Extent to which employees are happy or content with their job or work

(continued)

Table 12.1 (continued)

Standard	*Definition*
Transparency	The willingness of the organization to share positive and negative information with employees in a timely fashion
Fairness	Employee perception that organizational processes that allocate resources and resolve disputes are impartial and just
Organizational impact	
Productivity	The quality and quantity of work output based on resources
Innovation	Thinking differently and experimenting with new approaches, ideas, or behaviors related to the organization
Continuous Improvement	The process by which employees offer small or large improvements to improve efficiency, productivity, and quality of a product or process in the work environment
Reputation	Stakeholders'—both internal and external—evaluation of an organization based upon personal and observed experiences with the company and its communication
Employee Retention	The number or percentage of employees who remain employed after X period of time
Safety	Employees' freedom from physical and emotional harm, injury or loss

The Barcelona Principles 3.0 (AMEC, 2020) recommend that communicators measure both outputs and outcomes. Outputs, those things that are visible to the eye, are typically the easiest but least useful way to measure, at least when measured in isolation. For example, an employee who clicks on email or newsletter story does not equate to the employee understanding, retaining, or applying the information shared. While outputs by themselves may not be meaningful to internal communicators, linking outputs to outcomes can provide a more holistic assessment of the communication initiative. For example, practitioners could track an employees' attendance (output) at a training meeting to learn about social media in the workplace and then analyze their use of social media to collaborate, share feedback, or advocate for the company (outcome).

Organizational Impact

The scope of these standards focuses on evaluating if and how communication initiatives influence organization performance—the ultimate measurement of communication success. Some examples include productivity, continuous improvement and employee retention. It is important to recognize the challenge of aligning internal communication efforts as the direct influence organization performance; however, using benchmark and post-measurement methods can be effective in isolating how communication influenced organizational performance.

Engagement wasn't included as an internal communication standard (O'Neil et al., 2018), because it is a function of several other standards, including knowledge, understanding, discretionary effort, trust, and satisfaction. Internal communicators may want to isolate issues related to engagement and develop more effective strategies to resolve the challenges. For example, if an organization recognized apathy among employees and a decline in discretionary effort, an analysis beyond poor "engagement" is needed. What specific factors influence change in employees' perceptions and behaviors? Is it uncertainty about roles in the organization? Confusion about the relevancy of information shared? Perceptions about a lack of transparency by organizational leadership? If communicators can better understand these influencers by independently measuring them, they can then more effectively address the root cause of the engagement problem. Further, a more in-depth analysis of specific attitudes and behaviors impacting engagement aligns with the creation of specific and relevant communication objectives.

In summary, internal communicators should identify and prioritize the standards that best align with evaluating communication objectives.

Ways to Measure and Evaluate Internal Communication More Holistically

In recent years, scholars (e.g., Buhmann et al., 2018; Northhaft & Stensson, 2019; van Ruler, 2019) have advocated that communicators adopt novel and more holistic approaches for measuring and evaluating in organizations. Northhaft and Stensson (2019) encouraged academics to move away from functional measurement and evaluation to enable richer and alternative explanations of communication phenomenon. Buhmann et al. (2018) recommended that practitioners focus on insight, listening, and learning to better understand the role of communicators in providing "counsel, education and training, coaching, strategizing and planning" (p. 117). van Ruler (2019) postulated that communicators should focus more on formative—not summative—research in order to remain agile and fluid as organizations adapt to rapid and often unforeseen changes and events. According to Volk (2016), one of the most pressing challenges related to measurement and evaluation is the need to develop a "conclusive, holistic theory of value creation through communication" (p. 974).

Both quantitative and qualitative approaches should be undertaken to measure and evaluate internal communication efforts (AMEC, 2020; Lindenmann, 2003; Macnamara, 1992). Qualitative research, such as focus groups, in-depth interviews, sentiment analysis, can help internal communicators to understand and describe how and why employees are engaging with content and responding. Qualitative approaches are particularly useful for uncovering intangible contributions of communication in organizations (van Ruler, 2019; Volk, 2016). Eiro-Gomes and Duarte (2008) recommended a case study approach to examine social and cultural change in order to holistically examine work processes and communication planning. Place (2015) suggested that communicators use case studies and scorecards to holistically measure and evaluate organizational communication. Place explained that the German Public Relations Association and the Association of Communications Consultancies use scorecards and audits to indicate how communication engenders value creation and aids decision-making, considering the organization's culture (Huhn et al., 2011). O'Neil and Ewing (2020) qualitatively examined how communicators working for large global companies identified intangible contributions of their internal communication efforts. Using social capital theory (Portes, 1998) as a framework, the researchers explored how internal communication builds and maintains employee relationships and creates social capital for the organization, which can be accrued and later expended for organizational benefit.

Quantitative approaches (e.g., surveys, digital metrics, readership numbers) can establish statistical baseline numbers or examine the relationship between variables or predictors of variables. Digital tools and developments have made it easy to capture real-time data and metrics. For example, practitioners might use Google Analytics to understand time and behavior spent on a website or social media analysis tools to examine usage, engagement, sentiment or conversation topics. Practitioners might conduct periodic or annual survey data to measure such variables as satisfaction, reputation, or commitment. Digital data can easily be correlated with survey data to analyze relationships between variables or predictors of dependent variables such as trust, satisfaction and commitment (Men et al., 2020b) or engagement (Men et al., 2020a).

Looking Ahead: New Ways to Measure and Evaluate Internal Communication

Fueled by the ubiquity of digital tools and developments in artificial intelligence (AI), internal communication measurement and evaluation continue to adapt accordingly.

Digital Channels and Analytics

The advancement of technology has expanded digital channels to inform, connect, collaborate, and motivate employees (Men & Bowen, 2017; Men et al., 2020b). For example, organizations are increasingly using internal social media for internal communication strategies (Cardon & Marshall, 2014; Haddud et al., 2016; Sievert & Scholz, 2017). Communicators can access and transform data into insights to define SMART objectives, drive strategy, segment target audiences, pinpoint affinities and behaviors, and identify influencers who can help amplify messages. For instance, if an employee team or unit is frequently and effectively using communication channels to collaborate, that team can serve as influencers to motivate other employees to access these channels. Further, digital analytics can help communicators create the right content in the right channels at the right time (Men & Bowen, 2017; Social Chorus, 2018; Zerfass et al., 2017).

Ultimately, communicators can use data to establish benchmark metrics to gauge performance and measure impact on the business. Monitoring engagement rates (clicks, reactions, and shares) of employees' behaviors when viewing digital materials is one example of a digital metric. Evaluating sentiment or the tone of social media posts and online conversations can also be analyzed. Open and click-through rates (rate of clicks divided by impressions) for apps, emails, e-newsletters, and other digital channels can be tracked and analyzed. Conversation rates (the number of desired behaviors divided by total visitors), like requesting information or signing up for a project, can be used to evaluate behaviors. Other metrics include social reach (number of followers), unique impressions (number of content views from single users), number of downloads, video views, site loyalty, as well as a range of other digital metrics (Austin, 2020; Chow, 2018; Duncan, 2010; Kaushik, 2020; Walters, 2019). These metrics can help answer many questions about internal communication efforts. For example: What channels are employees using? How often and when? What content is most viewed and generates more positive reactions in terms of likes, shares and comments? How does print compared to video? Are employees using computers or phones to access information? Regardless of the tool or metric, it is critical to view data from many sources to obtain a comprehensive understanding of actionable insights. If conducted appropriately, digital analytics provide an effective and robust way to measure internal communication.

Technological Developments Informing Measurement and Evaluation

Public relations practitioners are starting to use AI to enhance their capabilities. Defined as the "ability of machines to perform tasks that typically require human-like understanding" (Knowledge@Wharton, 2018, para. 1), AI is being applied to public relations tasks such as responding to consumer questions, monitoring social media, and conducting outreach with journalists and influencers (Galloway & Swiatek, 2018).

There are two primary AI-fueled developments relevant to internal communication: chatbots and gamification. A chatbot is a software application that mimics human conversation via text or voice and interacts with people via a digital interface (Thomaz et al., 2020). Often referred to as conversational agents or virtual assistants (Thomaz et al., 2020), chatbots can facilitate conversations with people via messaging services such as Facebook Messenger, WhatsApp, Slack, Skype, Viber, and WeChat.

Although chatbots have been used most frequently for external communication tasks, they also have potential value for internal communicators (Holtz, 2016; O'Brien, 2019). While some employees don't have access to email or computers (e.g., healthcare, retail, industrial), almost every employee has a smartphone and uses messaging services, which chatbots use. Chatbots also enable a push/pull internal communication strategy (McGrath, 2016). Organizations can tailor information to be disseminated at a designated schedule, and employees can request when and the type of information they are interested in via a chatbot, thereby increasing message relevance and the likelihood that they will read the information (Holtz, 2016). Employees can ask a chatbot a question or request additional information (McGrath, 2016). Finally, chatbots can be integrated with an enterprise messenger to facilitate the sharing of big data to engender workplace collaboration, as has been documented with software development businesses (Emanuel et al., 2020).

Since chatbots are facilitated by AI, measurement and evaluation may become easier as organizational data become even more digitally automated. As communicators measure and evaluate their impact, they can now also examine how chatbots contribute or correlate to other outcomes, such as employee productivity or innovation. Organizations may also need to measure employee satisfaction with the chatbot—what public relations practitioner Allen (2016) refers to as an experienced channel (in contrast to the paid, earned, shared and owned channels in the PESO model)—since internal communicators will assume a key role in developing and managing the chatbot. Moreover, employees' experience with the chatbot will indirectly shape their perceived trust and reputation with the organization, so internal communicators may also want to measure how employees' experience with chatbots contributes to perceived organizational trust and reputation. Communicators may also want to qualitatively examine how employees' interaction and satisfaction contribute to company culture and the organizational identity.

AI has also fueled the development and usage of gamification in organizations. Gamification involves using game design elements—badges, leaderboards, scoring, challenges, and rewards—to engage and motivate people to achieve future behaviors (Xi & Juho, 2019). Gamification has many possible applications for internal communication. Gamification can be used to motivate and direct employees to share knowledge across organizational units. For example, Mizuyama et al. (2019) analyzed a case study in which gamification incentivized comment aggregation and evaluation to facilitate relevant knowledge sharing. Araújo and Pestana (2017) suggested organizations use gamification to recognize and reward seasoned employees for sharing soft and hard skills with younger employees. Employees' engagement with gamification apps may facilitate dialogue and two-way symmetrical communication (Seiffert-Brockmann et al., 2018).

According to Hall (2017), gamification can be used to make electronic learning more interactive, to increase productivity and efficiency, and to fuel sales competitions. Hall explained that companies can virtually reward an employee who illustrated a company value when making a business decision. Companies can incorporate a virtual treasure hunt to motivate employees to learn how to use a new tool or platform. Organizations can award badges to employees who regularly contribute to company intranets or who answer a quiz based upon material presented in the intranet.

Regardless of the tactic, communication practitioners should ensure that gamification is well integrated into internal communication strategy to reach goals and objectives. Measurement and evaluation will accordingly align with that strategy, whether to analyze improvements in knowledge, knowledge sharing, sales, or productivity. Because gamification is often used to encourage and motivate employees to do something, communicators may also want to measure and evaluate motivation, satisfaction, or perceived sense of collaboration/teamwork that may result from participation with the game. Finally, similar to chatbots, gamification may contribute to company culture, so communicators can qualitatively examine how gamification elements contribute to the ethos of the organizational identity.

Conclusion

In summary, communicators have many approaches and tools to use when measuring and evaluating initiatives. Many exciting options exist for future research. One such avenue would be to examine the relationships among the internal standards reviewed in this chapter. Many of these standards—such as awareness and knowledge, collaboration and teamwork, and trust and satisfaction—are correlated with one another, perhaps even causal. Additional testing of the standards would map out the relationships among the standards (O'Neil et al., 2018). A second fruitful research avenue would be to qualitatively examine how internal communication creates value for organizations, both to inform practice and develop theory (Volk, 2016). Third, researchers could study how emerging technologies such as AI impact how employees engage and respond to internal communication as well as how new technology usage shapes organizational processes and culture.

Case Study: How Walmart Measures and Evaluates Internal Communication

Started in 1962 with one discount retail store, Walmart had grown into the world's largest retailer by 1990. During that time, communication with associates (employees) was very organic and largely unformalized. By 2010, a formal internal communication function was developed, and focused on effectively communicating to associates around the world.

Walmart then initiated a comprehensive, 30-month project to provide meaningful data and evaluative insights to better connect senior leadership with what was then approximately two million associates in 27 countries. According to Jenifer Bice, former senior director of internal communication and now director of event solutions, the project purpose was to "gain a more thorough understanding of Walmart's global associates in order to communicate in a way that creates dialogue and connection, developing advocates for the company that will ultimately result in viral content created by those associates."

Seeking to gather data to inform strategy, the research process consisted of four key phases: discovery, research immersion, ideation, concept development and testing. Upon conclusion of the research component, communicators identified two communication objectives:

1. Identify and implement innovative methods to connect associates around the globe based on topics relevant to them.
2. Develop well-developed and tested concepts that would enable Walmart associates to become:

- more connected to each other and to the Walmart purpose
- more engaged and effective in their current roles
- advocates and ambassadors for Walmart, with key metrics
- inspired to talk about Walmart's values, products/services and the associate experience to friends and family in a positive way, thereby enabling more sales and improved brand perception.

Internal communicators developed messaging, content, videos, events and programming to meet these objectives and later measured whether they met the project objectives, as described below.

- *Focus on Why:* This became a talking point of senior leadership and disseminated through the organization. Surveys, both quantitative and qualitative, showed notable changes in tone and approach by leadership, which helped associates feel greater connection and appreciation, both outcome measures. Moreover, Walmart used social media engagement metrics—an output measure to measure awareness and knowledge of messaging.
- *Share Walmart Opportunities:* A company effort was initiated to focus on highlighting associate opportunities; for example, the CEO promoted associates on stage, communication teams featured job opportunities, stories and videos about associates participating in community service, among other approaches. Communicators conducted qualitative and quantitative research to measure associates' level of connection with one another and the Walmart purpose—both outcome measures.
- *Show We Care:* Following a reorganization in China, internal communicators developed and trained human resource associates on how to share information with associates. Upon completion of the reorganization, 40% of Walmart China associates remained with the company, another outcomes measure, versus the less than 1% that was anticipated.

Walmart continues to measure and evaluate its internal communication efforts by tracking outputs, outtakes, and outcomes. According to Bice, "As communicators, it is up to us to continue to understand our audiences, seek insights and apply them in the ways that are most engaging and inspiring to them."

> "We believed the combination of quantitative and qualitative research, all conducted in the respective countries, gave us the most rounded data and insights from which to work. Core team members were on site in the countries to learn alongside the research being conducted. This provided an added layer of knowledge and cultural understanding to add to the data set." Jenifer Bice, senior director, event solutions, Walmart.

References

Allen, L. (2016). *Edelman's Lucy Allen on PR for startups*. https://www.intercom.com/blog/podcasts/edelmans-lucy-allen-on-pr-for-startups/.

AMEC. (2020, July). *Barcelona principles 3.0*. Retrieved November 8, 2020, from https://amecorg.com/2020/07/barcelona-principles-3-0/.

Araújo, J., & Pestana, G. (2017). A framework for social well-being and skills management at the workplace. *International Journal of Information Management, 37(*6), 718–725. https://doi.org/10.1016/j.ijinfomgt.2017.07.009.

Austin, C. (2020, January 9). *Measuring internal communications in the workplace: 11 metrics you need to track*. https://www.contactmonkey.com/blog/measure-communications.

Begìn, D., & Charbanneau, K. (2012). Rethinking the R.A.C.E. for a social media world. *Journal of Professional Communication. 2*(2), 109–132. https://pdfs.semanticscholar.org/4d99/7d8fb935ddaa8430858d0f63f792fd68449c.pdf.

Buhmann, A., Likely, F., & Geddes, D. (2018). Communication evaluation and measurement: connecting research to practice. *Journal of Communication Management, 22*(1), 113–119. https://doi.org/10.1108/JCOM-12-2017-0141.

Byrne, Z. S., Peters, J. M., & Weston, J. W. (2016). The struggle with employee engagement: Measures and construct clarification using five samples. *Journal of Applied Psychology, 101*(9), 1201–1227. https://doi.org/10.1037/apl0000124.

Cardon, P., & Marshall, B. (2014). The hype and reality of social media use for work collaboration and team communication. *International Journal of Business Communication, 52*(3), 273–293. https://doi.org/10.1177/2329488414525446.

Chow, C. (2018, August 20). *How to measure internal communications: Internal communications measurement glossary*. https://socialchorus.com/blog/how-to-measure-internal-communications-glossary/.

Dortok, A. (2006). A managerial look at the interaction between internal communication and corporate reputation. *Corporate Reputation Review, 8*(4), 322–338. https://doi.org/10.1057/palgrave.crr.1540258.

Duncan, S. (2010). *Using web analytics to measure the impact of earned online media on business outcomes: A methodological approach*. https://www.instituteforpr.org/wp-content/uploads/Seth_Duncan_Web_Analytics.pdf.

Ehling, W. P., White, J., & Grunig, J. E. (1992). Public relations and marketing practices. In J. E. Grunig (Ed.), *Excellence in public relations and communication management* (pp. 357–394). Lawrence Erlbaum.

Eiro-Gomes, M., & Duarte, J. (2008). The case study as an evaluation tool for public relations. In B. Van Ruler, A. T. Vercic, & D. Vercic (Eds.), *Public relations metrics: Research and evaluation* (pp. 235–251). Routledge.

Emanuel, S., Dremel, C., Faulk, U., & Brenner, W. (2020). How affordances of chatbots cross the chasm between social and traditional enterprise systems. *Electronic Markets, 30*(2), 369–403. https://doi.org/10.1007/s12525-019-00359-6.

Escovedo, R. (2012). *Let them eat RPIE: Communication planning*. http://nextcommunications.blogspot.com/2012/02/let-them-eat-rpie-communication.html.

Galloway, C., & Swiatek, L. (2018). Public relations and artificial intelligence. It's not just about robots. *Public Relations Review, 44*, 734–740. https://doi.org/10.1016/j.pubrev.2018.10.008.

Gallup. (2020). https://www.gallup.com/workplace/229424/employee-engagement.aspx.

Gregory, A. (2000). *How to plan and manage a public relations campaign* (2nd ed.). Kogan Page.

Grossman, D. (2013). How internal CEO communications shapes financial performance. http://cdn2.hubspot.net/hub/83405/file-354160721-pdf/CEO_Research_V.1.pdf?t=1484002301231.

Hall, B. (2017). *5 ways gamification could transform your internal communication*. https://www.interact-intranet.com/blog/gamification-transform-internal-comms/.

Haddud, A., Dugger, J. C., & Gill, P. (2016). Exploring the impact of social media usage on employee engagement. *Journal of Social Media for Organizations, 3*(1), 1–22.

Harter, J. K., Schmidt, F. L., & Hayes, T. L. (2002). Business-unit-level relationship between employee satisfaction, employee engagement, and business outcomes: A meta-analysis. *Journal of Applied Psychology, 87*(2), 268–279. https://doi.org/10.1037/0021-9010.87.2.268.

Holtz, S. (2016). The next big communication thing is plain text. *Communication World,* 1.

Huhn, J., Sass, J., & Storck, C. (2011). *Communication controlling*. http://www.communicationcontrolling.de/fileadmin/communicationcontrolling/sonst_files/Position_paper_DPRG_ICV_2011_english.pdf.

Institute for Public Relations. (2021). The communication executive's guide to communication research, analysis, and evaluation. https://instituteforpr.org/wp-content/uploads/IPR-Guide-to-Measurement-v13-1.pdf..

Institute for Public Relations. (2013, July 23). *What are standards?* http://www.youtube.com/watch?v=nDMobcQlpo4.

Kahn, W. A., & Heaphy, E. D. (2014). Relational contexts of personal engagement at work. In C. Truss, R. Delbridge, K. Alfes, A. Schantz, & E. Soanz (Eds.), *Employee engagement in theory and practice* (pp. 82–96). Routledge.

Kaushik, A. (2020). Digital Marketing and Measurement Model. *Occam's razor*. Retrieved: https://www.kaushik.net/avinash/digital-marketing-and-measurement-model/.

Knowledge@Wharton. (2018). *Knowledge@WhartonVishal Sikka: Why AI needs a broader, more realistic approach*. http://knowledge.wharton.upenn.edu/article/ai-needs-broader-realistic-approach/.

Lafley, A., & Martin, R. (2013). Playing to win: How strategy really works. *Harvard Business Review Press*.

Lindenmann, W. K. (1993). An effectiveness yardstick' to measure public relations success. *Public Relations Quarterly, 38*(1), 7–10.

Lindenmann, W. K. (2003). *Guidelines for measuring the effectiveness of PR programs and activities*. Institute for Public Relations.

Macnamara, J. (1992). PR metrics: Measuring and evaluating public relations. *International Public Relations Research Review*. https://www.academia.edu/830282/PR_Metrics_Measuring_and_Evaluating_Public_Relations.

McGrath, C (2016). *10 reasons why chatbots will save internal communications*. https://chatbotsmagazine.com/chatbots-internal-communications-5fc4223cd159.

Men, L. R., & Bowen, S. A. (2017). *Excellence in internal communication management*. Business Expert Press.

Men, L. R., O'Neil, J., & Ewing, M. (2020a). Examining the effects of internal social media usage on employee engagement. *Public Relations Review, 46*(2), 1–9. https://doi.org/10.1016/j.pubrev.2020.101880.

Men, L. R., O'Neil, J., & Ewing, M. (2020b). From the employee perspective: Organizations' administration of internal social media and the relationship between social media engagement and relationship cultivation. *International Journal of Business Communication, 26*(1), 1–28. https://doi.org/10.1177/2329488420949968.

Mendez, E., Casadesus, M., & Gimenez, G. (2013). Model for evaluating and improving internal communication in an organization according to the principles of TQM. In I. HerasSaizarbitoria (Ed.), *Shedding light on TQM: Some research findings* (pp. 145–165). University of the Basque Country UPV/EHU.

Meng, J., & Berger, B. K. (2012). Measuring return on investment (ROI) of organizations' internal communication efforts. *Journal of Communication Management, 16*(4), 332–354. https://doi.org/10.1108/13632541211278987.

Meng, J., & Pan, P.-L. (2012). Using a balanced set of measures to focus on long-term competency in internal communication. *Public Relations Review, 38*(3), 484–490. https://doi.org/10.1016/j.pubrev.2012.03.005.

Mishra, K., Boynton, L., & Mishra, A. (2014). Driving employee engagement: The expanded role of internal communications. *International Journal of Business Communication, 51*(2), 183–202. https://doi.org/10.1177/2329488414525399.

Mizuyama, H., Yamaguchi, S., Sato, M., Kikkawa, T., & Ohnuma, S. (2019). A prediction market-based gamified approach to enhance knowledge sharing in organizations. *Simulation & Gaming, 50*(5), 572–597. https://doi.org/10.1177/1046878119867382.

Northhaft, H., & Stensson, H. (2019). Explaining the measurement and evaluation statis. *Journal of Communication Management, 23*(3), 213–227.

O'Brien, J. (2019). 5 technology trends that are changing business communication. *Communication World*, 1–4.

O'Neil, J., & Ewing, M. (2020, March 6). *Listening, measuring and evaluating to identify intangible contributions of internal communication.* Presented to the 23rd International Public Relations Conference. Orlando, FL.

O'Neil, J., Ewing, M., Smith, S., & Williams, S. (2018). A Delphi study to identify standards for internal communication. *Public Relations Journal, 11*(3), 1–16.

Paine, K. D. (2011). *Measure what matters.* Wiley.

Place, K. R. (2105). Exploring the role of ethics in public relations Program evaluation. *Journal of Public Relations Research, 27*(2), 118–135. https://doi.org/10.1080/1062726X.2014.976825.

Portes, A. (1998). Social capital: Its origins and applications in modern sociology. *Annual Reviews, 24*(1), 1–24.

Ruck, K. (2015, October). Top tips: Internal communication measurement. Retrieved from http://www.ciprinside.co.uk/ic-measurement/.

Ruck, K., & Welch, M. (2012). Valuing internal communication: Management and employee perspectives. *Public Relations Review, 38*(2), 294–302. https://doi.org/10.1016/j.pubrev.2011.12.016.

Ruck, K., Welch, M., & Menara, B. (2017). Employee voice: An antecedent to organisational engagement? *Public Relations Review, 43*(5), 904–914. https://doi.org/10.1016/j.pubrev.2017.04.008.

Sanders, G. (2018). *4 easy ways to measure internal communication.* https://dynamicsignal.com/2018/08/16/how-to-measure-internal-communication/.

Seiffert-Brockmann, J., Weitzl, W., & Henriks, M. (2018). Stakeholder engagement through gamification. *Journal of Communication Management*, 22(1), 67–78. https://doi.org/10.1108/JCOM-12-2016-0096.

Sievert, H., & Scholz, C. (2017). Engaging employees in (at least partly) disengaged companies. Results of an interview survey within about 500 German corporations on the growing importance of digital engagement via internal social media. *Public Relations Review, 43*, 894–903.

Smarp. (2019). *How to measure internal communication (IC): Best practices & examples*. https://blog.smarp.com/how-to-measure-internal-communication-ic-best-practices-examples.

Social Chorus (2018, June 15). *The digital transformation in communication: Social Chorus' 2018 comms effectiveness survey*. https://socialchorus.com/ebooks/digital-transformation-in-communications-10-key-insights/.

Thomaz, F., Salge, C., Karahanna, E., & Hulland, J. (2020). Learning from the dark web: Leveraging conversational agents in the era of hyper-privacy to enhance marketing. *Journal of the Academy of Marketing Science, 48*(1), 43–63. https://doi.org/10.1007/s11747-019-00704-3.

Tkalac Verčič, A., & Pološki Vokić, N. (2017). Engaging employees through internal communication. *Public Relations Review, 43*(5), 885–893. https://doi.org/10.1016/j.pubrev.2017.04.005.

Towers Watson. (2013, December). *2013–2014 change and communication ROI study*. https://www.towerswatson.com/en-US/Insights/IC-Types/Survey-ResearchResults/2013/12/2013-2014-change-and-communication-roi-study.

van Ruler, B. (2019). Agile communication evaluation and measurement. *Journal of Communication Management, 23*(3), 265–280. https://doi.org/10.1108/JCOM-12-2018-0136

Vaughan, T. (2017). *IC standards and how to measure them: Your questions answered*. https://www.poppulo.com/blog/ic-standards-and-how-to-measure-them-your-questions-answered/.

Volk, S. C. (2016). A systematic review of 40 years of public relations evaluation and measurement research: Looking into the past, the present, and future. *Public Relations Review, 42*(5), 962–977.

Walters, K. (2019, May 29). *Top 5 ways to measure internal communication*. https://icthrive.com/blog/5-way-to-measure-internal-communication.

Watson, T. (2001). Integrated planning and evaluation. In R. L. Heath (Ed.), *Handbook of public relations* (pp. 259–268). Sage.

Williams, S. (2015, Summer). Present-tense measurement: With AMMO, you don't have to wait to have measurement influence planning. *The Public Relations Strategist*. https://apps.prsa.org/Intelligence/TheStrategist/Articles/view/11131/1113/Present_Tense_Measurement_With_AMMO_You_Don_t_Have#.X6Wx15NKjRY.

Xi, N., & Juho, H. (2019). Does gamification satisfy needs? A study on the relationship between gamification features and intrinsic need satisfaction. *International Journal of Information Management, 46*, 210–221. https://doi.org/10.1016/j.ijinfomgt.2018.12.

Zerfass, A., Verčič, D., & Volk, S. C. (2017). Communication evaluation and measurement: Skills, practices and utilization in European organizations. *Corporate Communications: An International Journal.*, *22*(1), 2–18. https://doi.org/10.1108/CCIJ-08-2016-0056.

CHAPTER 13

Internal Communication in a Cross-Cultural and Global Context

Ana Tkalac Verčič, Dejan Verčič, and Krishnamurthy Sriramesh

Culture is the bedrock of every society. Yet, this vital concept has not been given its due in most mass communication scholarship including public relations (Sriramesh, 2020). Almost three decades ago we had hoped that culture would be accorded its due importance by public relations practice and scholarship (Sriramesh & White, 1992). Yet, both parts of the discipline continue to pay scant attention to this vital concept—much to

A. Tkalac Verčič (✉)
University of Zagreb, Zagreb, Croatia
e-mail: atkalac@efzg.hr

D. Verčič
University of Ljubljana, Ljubljana, Slovenia
e-mail: Dejan.Vercic@fdv.uni-lj.si

K. Sriramesh
University of Colorado, Boulder, CO, USA
e-mail: ksriramesh@colorado.edu

L. R. Men and A. Tkalac Verčič (eds.), *Current Trends and Issues in Internal Communication*, New Perspectives in Organizational Communication, https://doi.org/10.1007/978-3-030-78213-9_13

their detriment. Practitioners are more likely to be forced into accepting its presence by the ground realities they face on a daily basis. Even so, it is a reluctant acceptance of the culture's role in every society. The *Excellence study* (Dozier et al., 1995; Grunig, 1992; Grunig et al., 2002; Sriramesh et al., 2013) gave significant focus to societal culture and its influence on public relations looking at the concept as an *environment* in which public relations is practiced. However, despite the popularity of the study's many contributions, culture has not been embraced as much as it deserves. It is disheartening that after about 50 years of public relations scholarship, there is only one book dedicated to culture and public relations (Sriramesh & Verčič, 2012) although the three editions of *The Global Public Relations Handbook* (Sriramesh & Verčič, 2020) have addressed culture (broadly defined) as being integral to sound scholarship in the field.

Why should culture be given primacy by communication scholars? The reciprocal relationship between culture and communication was propounded very eloquently by the anthropologist Edward T. Hall in his book *The Silent Language*: culture is communication and communication is culture. His theorizing of *polychronic* and *monochronic* cultures is most helpful to internal communication as are his *high context* and *low context* dimensions. Culture, a concept that is known to every individual, has been hard to define even in the field of anthropology. Kluckhohn (1953) listed over 164 accepted definitions and about 300 more variations of these definitions. The first comprehensive definition can be attributed to Tyler (1871) who saw culture as "that complex whole which includes knowledge, belief, art, morals, custom, and any other capabilities and habits acquired by man as a member of society" (p. 1). The expansive nature of the term, and its link to society, was also highlighted by Kroeber and Kluckhohn who defined culture as a "set of attributes and products of human societies, and therewith of mankind, which are extrasomatic and transmissible by mechanisms other than biological heredity" (Kluckhohn, 1953, p. 145).

The culture of a society influences, but can often be different from, the culture of organizations in that society (Sriramesh & White, 1992; Sriramesh et al., 1992). Each culture influences, and is influenced by the other. As social scientists, we strive to empirically study the relationships between two concepts of interest—in this case the relationship between societal/organizational culture and organizational communication activities. Making this link requires us to empirically study both sides of the equation by operationalizing each variable. Hofstede's (1984) work stands out as the most frequently used with regard to societal culture although the author himself admitted that the dimensions he had been able to empirically identify did not encompass the entirety of culture. His success may well also be a lacuna of the field. Hofstede's (1984) studies of culture in the organizational context lead to the identification of first four and then a fifth and later a sixth dimensions of culture. Almost 40 years on from his seminal study, his dimensions of culture continue to be used by scholars in public relations.

After a review of the studies linking culture with public relations, Sriramesh (2006) had critiqued the almost singular reliance on Hofstede's dimensions of culture in public relations scholarship. Hofstede had overlooked the distinction between societal culture and organizational culture in his early work where he sought to assess the cultural idiosyncracies among managers of a single organization who hailed from 39 countries. He had not really taken into account the acculturation of these managers to organizational cultural norms, a serious flaw that may have been caused by the lack of knowledge of organizational culture when he conceptualized his study. Further, his approach sought to study societal cultural characteristics common across a number of societies, a limitation in itself because, Sriramesh (2006) noted, some of the most critical influencers of communication in a society are cultural traits unique to that society. This has been confirmed by several studies in public relations (Sriramesh et al., 1999, Sriramesh & Enxi, 2004; Sriramesh et al., 2005, 2007). Studies conducted in societies with Chinese populations have posited the overwhelming influence that *Guanxi*—a manifestation of personal influence (Sriramesh, 1988)—plays in communication in organizations (e.g., Aw et al., 2002; Huang, 2000; Hung, 2004; Kipnis, 1997; Tan, 2000). Similarly, Sriramesh and Takasaki (1999) discussed the strong influence of *wa, amae, tatamae, honne*—idiosyncrasies unique to Japanese culture with public relations practice in that country. Anecdotal evidence suggests that such unique cultural characteristics are evident in every society but are largely under-reported because of the almost singular focus on Hofstede's dimensions.

A practitioner with wide cross-cultural professional experience offered a different, yet useful, perspective in cross-cultural differences through his discussion of what he calls "cultural types." Rather than pigeonholing cultures as Hofstede did with his cultural dimensions, Lewis offered a continuum on which he placed different countries based on three dimensions: linear-active (cool, factual, decisive planners), multi-active (warm emotional, loquacious, impulsive), and reactive (courteous, amiable, accommodating, compromiser, good listener). Although this model has been popular with practitioners, one does not find any public relations studies that have used this model to measure societal culture. One obvious explanation is that the Lewis Model does not offer the kinds of tools to measure culture quantitatively that Hofstede did making Hofstede's dimensions of culture easier to replicate.

The confluence of organizations, international communication, and culture can be found in scholarship on organizational culture. As previously stated, there is an innate link between societal culture and organizational culture. Employees, acculturated in society—at homes and schools—bring those values into the workplace largely crafting organizational culture (Sriramesh, 2020). Scholars began to take interest in studying organizational culture especially beginning in the early 1980s, primarily wanting to learn how Japanese corporations had become so successful in the 1970s. These early studies added many new dimensions to the discussion examining the interplay of cultures, subcultures, and countercultures within organizations. Based on the *Excellence study*, Sriramesh et al. (1996) offered one of the first empirical links between organizational culture and public relations based on the conceptual framework offered by Sriramesh et al. (1992). Sriramesh et al. (1996) found two primary streams of organizational culture: authoritarian and participative. Based on empirical evidence from the US, Canada, and the UK they reported that authoritarian organizational cultures had a more top-down communication pattern whereas more participative cultures had horizontal communication. As the CEO and dominant coalition often determine an organization's culture, authoritarian cultures also practiced lower levels of symmetrical communication both with internal and external publics. Scholars have also posited that "strong" organizational cultures are preferred over "weak" ones. The former are typified by greater cohesion and harmony among internal publics—often a result of more participative and symmetrical communication. Strong cultures also directly correlate with low employee turnover and low stress at the workplace.

Given the realities of the twenty-first century, typified by a very mobile workforce owing to globalization, it is evident that internal publics are more likely to be multicultural and even spread over multiple borders (multinational) than in the past. As a result, it is imperative that organizational managers be more aware of the interplay between both societal and organizational culture, which is the primary theme of this chapter.

Global Internal Communication

Culture is evolving from a latent to a manifest variable of organizational communication competence because of internal and external reasons. Internally, there is a growing cultural variety of associates/employees. Externally, there is a growing cultural variety on territories in which organizations operate. For example, a company may have headquarters in London which is a highly multicultural center where over three hundred languages are spoken. Their production may be in South America, Africa, or Asia, and their markets worldwide. United Nations have headquarters in New York, and UNESCO in Paris, highly multicultural towns, and both organizations serve nearly two hundred countries all over the globe. In Europe, research shows that 8 out of 10 professional communicators have international communication as a part of their daily business, with nearly a quarter of those reaching more than 20 countries in their daily work. This number increases for Chief Communication Officers—more than 90 percent of CCOs operate internationally on a daily basis (Verčič et al., 2015; Zerfass, Moreno, et al., 2013). "Global CCOs are aware of a need to rethink the whole concept of headquarters (core, home). They see developing a truly intercultural and globalized communication structure across the corporation as a significant challenge and expect positive effects both on a local and global level" (Zerfass, Verčič, et al., 2013, p. 34).

As the world has become a global village (McLuhan, 1962), it is impossible to escape globalization. Scholte (2008) proposes that we analyze globalization as *internationalization*, which is characterized by the intensification of cross-border movements of ideas, goods and services, capital, and people. When restrictions on movements of ideas, goods and services, capital, and people disappear, we can talk about *liberalization*. As a result of the increased movement of ideas, goods and services, capital, and people we can note convergence, or even homogenization of all these, and we can talk about *universalization*. Since the beginning of the industrial revolution in the West, there is a worldwide spread of rationalist modernization, so we can perceive *Westernization*. And recent developments in technology, media and communication is promoting *globality*, development of transplanetary connections between people developing social space in its own right that transcends territorial geography. Using our Apple or Android mobile devices we can communicate simultaneously and instantaneously, we can share our experience on social media and do that in no time.

These developments influence ways in which large organizations structure their internal communication. Understanding culture and multicultural nature of contemporary organizations drives divergence in approaches to internal communication. Understanding the universal need for effectiveness and efficiency, on the other hand, drives convergence (Stohl, 2001, p. 325). Interviewing communicators with international responsibilities Zerfass, Verčič, et al. (2013) found that global Chief Communication Officers have a strong tendency to keep communication in control in corporate headquarters, "with communication being responsible for vision, mission, values and other 'soft' building blocks of a corporation. Losing control over them could endanger corporate identity and consequently reputation" (p. 32). On the other hand, in European companies, local communication managers and their teams enjoy a great latitude to implement these standards adjusting them to local cultures and circumstance. In the words of one of the interviewees:

> Aligned Decentralisation: meaning headquarters responsible for the corporate story (vision, mission, values, global strategy, targets), corporate standards (global messages, policies such as corporate design and keywording), while regional / national communications units should ensure aligned transformation in regional / national / local statements. However, online communication remains global due to the 'flat world' we live in. (p. 33)

Enabling Technologies for Global Internal Communication

Technology has had a remarkable impact on internal communication within organizations. As Holtz (2006) noted, the internet offers tools to turn anyone into a publisher while connecting everybody to everybody else. In modern organizations, communication networks allow the exchange of messages between people across time and space (García-Morales et al., 2011). It is therefore vital for them to adopt strategies which allow internal communication to flow quickly (Jablin & Putnam,

2001). This is becoming even more important in a physically disconnected new reality.

The influence of technology changes the way organizations are structured and can reduce organizational complexity. Additionally, emerging communication technologies are speeding up decision-making and changing the nature of interactions in organizations (Ganapathy, 2016), as well as helping to change organizational processes, decision-making into an organization design (Herschel & Andrews, 1997). New technologies allow greater access to people and events around the world, as well as next door. They help overcome human barriers and create more transparency. Globally, technology increases the possibility of encounters where different cultures and races meet. On the other hand, it also creates certain barriers mostly connected with resistance to technological transformation or fear of change (Cowan, 2017). In a study of digital natives conducted in 2011 (Friedl & Tkalac Verčič) employees reported a preference to traditional media (emails and meetings) in comparison to social media, which proved to be the same in a study conducted in 2020 (Tkalac Verčič & Špoljarić)—"traditional" media were still relevant and affected satisfaction more than "new" media. Even though this doesn't imply that incorporating new technologies into mediating communication should be slowed down, it does suggest that certain information should still dominantly be conveyed via traditional media.

Nevertheless, the global pandemic has made the workplace (and employees) more technology savvy and has gotten almost everyone to incorporate technology in all their tasks (not only the new generation that has grown up in the digital era). Adopting technology, such as social media in an organization often means changing internal communication habits. The organization has to be culturally ready and employees need to understand the process. It can pose a challenge to start working and communicating in a new way and move from one approach to another (Lombardi, 2015).

Competencies for Intercultural/Multicultural Communication

Organizations are cultivating their human capital through education and training for intercultural communication competence (ICC), which is defined as "the ability to ensure a shared understanding by people of different social identities, and the ability to interact with people as complex human beings with multiple identities and their own individuality" (Byram et al., 2002, p. 10). Chen (2014) proposed a triangular model of ICC with an affective dimension labeled "intercultural sensitivity," cognitive dimension labeled "intercultural awareness" and a behavioral dimension labeled "intercultural adroitness." There is an identified need to increase intercultural competence or literacy, and organizations run programs for their employees being assigned to other countries. First, they are preparing people to "enjoy and benefit from the experiences with people from other cultures." Meeting other cultures enriches a person, but it also increases the complexity of potential social interactions. To enjoy other cultures, one has to understand that there are no "better" or "worse" cultures, that meanings can differ and misunderstandings are frequent. Second, they try to make "these positive feelings reciprocated by host nationals with whom sojourners work." Communication competence is enacted in producing expected outcomes and that is usually complicated when dealing with other cultures. Third, "sojourners should be able to manage the stress that is inherent in overseas assignments." Intercultural competence is not only in an ability to communicate with people from other cultures, but also to live in places that are culturally different from home. There are several levels at which intercultural competency can be studied and learned: interpersonal, group, organizational and societal. One can be faced with "otherness" in one or in all four variables. And finally, fourth, sojourners should be able to "accomplish the tasks called for in their work assignments" (Brislin, 2008, pp. 2331–2332). Intercultural competence is a value in itself, but in an organizational environment it has a function to fulfill and that is producing desirable results for the focal organization, as well as for individuals involved.

The internet and social media are making multicultural competency and the ability to enjoy work with people from other cultures even more important than before. Studies in the effects of digital communication for organizational life have identified the rise of employee as a gatekeeper for sharing information about the organization with the outside world as one of the most important change organizational leaders face today (Tench et al., 2017; Verčič & Tkalac Verčič, 2016). When we add that in the twenty-first century all kinds of organizations are transforming themselves into media companies through a process of strategic mediatization (Tench et al., 2017; Verčič & Tkalac Verčič, 2016), meaning that they produce more and more media, many of them communicating directly with larger audiences than traditional media houses, the need for multicultural competence or literacy becomes even bigger.

Increasing intercultural competence is not an assignment only for organizations. European Union as a whole is developing programs to increase intercultural communication competence of its citizens in Erasmus + program, which stands for European Community Action Scheme for the Mobility of University Students."Erasmus + is the EU's program to support education, training, youth and sport in Europe. Its budget of €14.7 billion will provide opportunities for over 4 million Europeans to study, train, and gain experience abroad" (https://ec.europa.eu/programmes/erasmus-plus/about_en). One of its expected impacts is to increase intercultural communication competence of European youth (Altuğ et al., 2019).

Future of Global Internal Communication

Contemporary organizations operate in a complex world that includes globalization, deregulation and economic crises, which all create an unpredictable environment full of potential opportunities and threats (Tkalac Verčič, 2020). The impact of globalization on public relations—practice and scholarship—has been propounded by Sriramesh and Vercic (2020) who make conceptual links between public relations and different cultural environments (broadly defining culture) while also rendering the global communication of key players and issues. Employee trust in organizational leadership is reducing globally (Jiang & Probst, 2015), while considerable employee reductions greatly affect how loyal they feel toward their organizations (Tkalac Verčič, 2016). In this evolving environment, a global crisis caused by an unprecedented pandemic presents a bigger challenge for internal communication than ever before. It is therefore difficult to predict what the future holds when it comes to internal communication, especially now, in the middle of the crisis. However, some of the major trends identified prior to the pandemic such as diversification in the workplace, digitization, downsizing of technology, increased accountability, a higher consideration of the work–life balance and globalization (Men & Bowen, 2017) still remain significant.

As organizations geographically diversify, the need to interact efficiently with wider groups becomes critical (Ashkanasy et al., 2002). Diversity in the workplace is greater than ever and includes differences in race, ethnicity, language, nationality, religion, and sexual orientation

(Amadeo, 2013). Understanding and incorporating those differences will be essential for organizations of the future. Diversity and inclusion bring challenges such as miscommunication, creation of barriers and dysfunctional adaptation behaviors (Coote Martin, 2014), but on the other hand contribute to organizations' adaptability, range of skills, innovation, and creativity (Men & Bowen, 2017). Today, even more than before, companies depend on innovation to support growth and long-term success and this makes diversity in the workforce both necessary and inevitable (DiTomaso et al., 2007).

Digitization, which involves deep changes taking place in society through the use of digital technology (Agarwal et al., 2011), has gotten a new meaning in recent months. Organizations have to find a way to innovate using technology and embrace digital transformation to reach better performance (Hess et al., 2016). The internal communication landscape has already been transformed by digital technologies adapted to organizational needs and workplace requirements. The pandemic has propelled this trend into an even faster gear. New media tools that have been shaping how content is created and shared, have now taken the central place in everyday communication for a large portion of the global workforce. Digitized employees provide new opportunities for organizations (Men et al., 2020). Public relations scholars and practitioners agree that internal social media help position employees as corporate ambassadors (Ewing et al., 2019) and help build internal communities and connections (Haddud et al., 2016). This new reality leads to huge potential for innovation and performance, but renders organizations more fragile as they control fewer element of their environment (Vial, 2019). Some of the issues of digitizing the workplace, such as lack of equipment, choice of tools and negative attitudes of employees have been resolved by sheer necessity. In spite of those issues, interactive digital tools help create a democratic, transparent environment that encourages sharing (Men & Bowen, 2017).

Another trend growing in strength globally, points toward an increased demand for ethical accountability and transparency, by state representatives, grassroots movements and organized consumers. As the publics everywhere become progressively sensitive toward organizational misconduct it becomes necessary for organizations to include corporate ethics in all of their management decisions (Huber et al., 2009; Jones et al., 2007; Kim & Krishna, 2017). Transnational organizations are increasingly presenting a vision of social responsibility together with their business vision. This discourse of accountability is an element of globality and a component of contemporary world culture (Garsten, 2003). In the future, organizations will need to demonstrate an even stronger social conscience and give their employees more power and influence, since millennials and generation Z value the organization's social responsibility.

The changing nature of work and work context is having an intense effect on how employees are managed (Fleetwod, 2007). They are increasingly becoming interested in flexibility and freedom at work (Boudreau et al., 2015). As the generational change in the workforce means there is a shift toward the new generation, Gen Z, the importance of work–life balance becomes even stronger. Generation Y is the first generation to set a strong emphasis on achieving work–life balance, while Gen Z (often called the "me" generation) is even more driven toward their self (Pulevska et al., 2017). The focus of this new generation is not so much on the company, but on what the company can offer them. The possibility of working from home, offered by many employers before the pandemic, has acquired new meaning and has completely reshaped the way work and work environment is perceived.

Finally, globalization has reached new meaning. For the successful management of internal communication in different cultural contexts it is important to recognize cultural diversity without judgment, as well avoiding cultural blindness (Adler, 2002). Among existing factors, openness of economies, migration, market liberalization, technology advancement, and forced limitation of movement has actually brought us together, in a way. It is safe to assume that the global pandemic has redefined the element of physical distance in doing business and that once the crisis is over, nothing will ever be the same. This is why internal communication departments have an important role in building strong bonds with all employees across transnational environments (Neil & Jiang, 2017). The workforce is going to become more globalized, diverse and multicultural than ever, even though the issue of balancing corporate culture with societal culture remains. For the organizations that manage to solve this successfully there is a greater opportunity for organizational success, innovation, and creativity (Men & Bowen, 2017). "The key to effective cross-cultural internal communication is to develop cross-cultural competence within the internal communication department, to make the team aware of the effect of culture on their work and to ultimately develop knowledge and skills designed specifically for an internal multicultural communication team" (Apud & Apud-Martinez, 2008).

In a Crisis, Communication is a Game Changer

Internal Communication in the Context of SARS-CoV-2

Katarina Klemenc, Country Head Communications Novartis Slovenia

In a crisis, it is often difficult to understand what is actually going on and to predict what the next hour and the next day will bring. The time at the beginning of the crisis is particularly uncertain, as only limited information is available, and it is crucial to inform employees about the evolving situation. Even good measures mean nothing if no one knows about them. Transparent, clear, and regular communication is an essential element of a successful organization, especially in times of crisis. Communication is a link that allows us to make even the most unpredictable situation more manageable.

We started with crisis communication even before our colleagues started working from home because things in the countries around us had already appeared to be critical and we understood that something similar could happen in our country. We were already looking for solutions on how to best inform employees about what was going on. We organized ourselves quickly and efficiently and began to communicate key information clearly and transparently. You can imagine what a challenge it is if almost a third of 5.000 associates start working from home overnight. How to keep them informed about all the key happenings? The situation once again showed how important it is that we have Novartis Emergency Management (NEM) in place. And that we had crisis communication trainings every year for all key stakeholders in our system. I am convinced that this was critical in enabling us to start successfully operating in a crisis, I could say almost in an instant.

When the new way of working was established, we wanted to leverage on the communication to help us maintain the motivation of employees, as well as to strengthen the sense of pride that we work in a company which is both highly responsible in taking care for its employees, and was also really fast in donating financial aid as well as protective equipment to organizations that are "on the front lines." Thus, we shared the stories of associates from different parts of the company through various internal communication channels, motivational videos were prepared by members of the company's top management, we have invited employees to share ideas and good practices, and made sure we stayed connected through virtual meetings at various levels. The key role in this was played by 500 leaders from across the company.

The power of communication was also shown by our survey, in which employees mentioned communication as one of the key factors in making them feel safe and motivated to work. They mentioned communication at all levels: personal communication of top management and more than 500 leaders in the company, as well as all other tools of internal and external communication. All of this builds confidence that together we can make it. That is why we all agree that we will emerge from these times of crisis even stronger.

Fun facts:

In the first two months of the pandemic, we have created:

- 30 e-Newsletters for all associates,
- 7 e-Newsletters for leaders
- more than 15 videos for associates (including a video address by President Pahor),
- 1 video for the external public
- more than 20 media responses directly related to COVID-19,
- 5 brochures for employees and business partners,
- 23 posters with different content,
- the first virtual Town Hall for all Novartis associates in Slovenia
- intranet site & sharepoint COVID-19,
- internet site COVID-19 at www.lek.si.

References

Adler, N. J. (2002). *International dimensions of organizational behavior*. South-Western.

Agarwal, U. A., Datta, S., Blake-Beard, S., & Bhargava, S. (2011). Linking LMX, innovative work behavior and turnover intentions—The mediating role of work engagement. *Career Development International, 17*(3), 208–230. https://doi.org/10.1108/13620431211241063.

Altuğ, S. A., Sezgin, E. N., & Önal, A. (2019). Does Erasmus+ programmer improve the participants" intercultural communicative competence? *SDU International Journal of Educational Studies, 6*(1), 1–17. https://doi.org/10.33710/sduijes.537034.

Amadeo, K. (2013). *Cultural diversity*. Retrieved from http://useconomy.about.com/od/suppl1/g/Cultural-Diversity.htm.

Apud, S., & Apud-Martinez, T. (2008). *Effective internal communication in global organizations*. Retrieved from https://www.iabc.com/effective-internal-communication-in-global-organizations/.

Ashkanasy, N. M., Härtel, C. E. J., & Daus, C. S. (2002). Diversity and emotion: The new frontiers in organizational behavior research. *Journal of Management, 28*(3), 307–338. https://doi.org/10.1177/014920630202800304.

Aw, A., Tan, S. K., & Tan, R (2002, July 15–19). *Guanxi and public relations: An exploratory qualitative study of the public relations-guanxi phenomenon in Singapore firms*. Paper presented to the *Public Relations Division of the International Communication Association*. Seoul, South Korea.

Boudreau, J. W., Jesuthasan, R., & Creelman, D. (2015). *Lead the work: Navigating a world beyond employment*. Wiley.

Brislin, R. W. (2008). Intercultural communication training. In W. Donsbach (Ed.), *International encyclopedia of communication* (Vol. VI, pp. 2331–2333). Blackwell.

Byram, M., Gribkova, B., & Starkey, H. (2002). *Developing the intercultural dimension in language teaching: A practical introduction for teachers*. Council of Europe.

Chen, G. M. (2014). Intercultural communication competence: Summary of 30-year research and directions for future study. In X. Dai & G. M. Chen, (Eds.), *Intercultural communication competence: Conceptualization and its development in cultural contexts and interactions* (pp. 14–40). Cambridge Scholars Publishing.

Coote Martin, G. (2014). The effects of cultural diversity in the workplace. *Journal of Diversity Management, 9*(2), 89–91. https://doi.org/10.19030/jdm.v9i2.8974.

Cowan, D. (2017). *Strategic internal communication: How to build employee engagement and performance?* Kogan Page.

DiTomaso, N., Post, C., & Parks-Yancy, R. (2007). Workforce diversity and inequality: Power, status, and numbers. *Annual Review of Sociology, 33*, 473–501. https://doi.org/10.1146/annurev.soc.33.040406.131805.

Dozier, D. M., Grunig, L., & Grunig, J. (1995). *Manager's guide to excellence in public relations and communication management (Lea's communication series)*. Lawrence Erlbaum Associates.

Ewing, M., Men, L., & R., & O'Neil, J. (2019). Using social media to engage employees: Insights from internal communication managers. *International Journal of Strategic Communication, 13*(2), 110–132. https://doi.org/10.1080/1553118X.2019.1575830.

Fleetwood, S. (2007). Why work–life balance now? *International Journal of Human Resource Management, 18*, 387–400. https://doi.org/10.1080/09585190601167441.

Friedl, J., & Tkalac Verčič, A. (2011). Media preferences of digital natives' internal communication: A pilot study. *Public Relations Review, 37*(1), 84–86. https://doi.org/10.1016/j.pubrev.2010.12.004.

Ganapathy, N. (2016). Internal communication in the international organizations - the influence of technology. *International Journal of Advanced Research in Management and Social Sciences., 5*(5), 52–58.

García-Morales, V., Matías-Reche, F., Verdu-Jover, A., & J. . (2011). Influence of internal communication on technological proactivity, organizational learning, and organizational innovation in the pharmaceutical sector. *Journal of Communication, 61*, 150–177. https://doi.org/10.1111/j.1460-2466.2010.01530.x.

Garsten, C. (2003). The cosmopolitan organization-an essay on corporate accountability. *Global Networks*, 3.

Grunig, J. E. (1992). *Excellence in public relations and communication management*. Lawrence Erlbaum Associates.

Grunig, L. A., Grunig, J. E., & Dozier, D. M. (2002). *Excellent public relations and effective organizations: A study of communication management in three countries*. Lawrence Erlbaum.

Haddud, A., Dugger, J., & Gill, P. (2016). Exploring the impact of internal social media usage on employee engagement. *Journal of Social Media for Organizations, 3*(1), 1–23.

Herschel, R., & Andrews, P. H. (1997). Ethical implications of technological advances on business communication. *Journal of Business Communication, 34*, 160–170. https://doi.org/10.1177/002194369703400203.

Hess, T., Matt, C., Benlian, A., & Wiesboeck, F. (2016). Options for formulating a digital transformation strategy. *MIS Quarterly Executive, 15*(2), 123–139. https://doi.org/10.7892/BORIS.105447.

Hesse, A. (2018). Digitalization and leadership—How experienced leaders interpret daily realities in a digital world. In: Hawaii International Conference.

Hofstede, G. (1984). *Culture's consequences: International differences in work-related values*. Sage.

Holtz, S. (2006). The impact of new technologies on internal communication. *Strategic Communication Management., 10*(1), 22–25. https://doi.org/10.1023/A:1009618920604.

Huang, Y. H. (2000). The personal influence model and *gao guanxi* in Taiwan Chinese public relations. *Public Relations Review, 26*(2), 216–239. https://doi.org/10.1016/S0363-8111(00)00042-4.

Huber, F., Vogel, J., & Meyer, F. (2009). When brands get branded. *Marketing Theory, 9*(1), 131–136. https://doi.org/10.1177/1470593108100069.

Hung, C.-J. (2004). Cultural influence on relationship cultivation strategies: Multinational corporations in China. *Journal of Communication Management, 8*(3), 264–281. https://doi.org/10.1108/13632540410807682.

Jablin, F. M., Cude, R. L., House, A., Lee, J., & Roth, N. I. (1994). Communication competence in organizations: Conceptualization and comparison across multiple level of analysis. In I. Thayer & G. A. Barnett (Eds.), *Organization-communication emerging perspectives IV* (pp. 114–140). Ablex Publishing Corporation.

Jablin, F. M., & Putnam, L. L. (2001). *The new handbook of organizational communication: Advances theory, research and methods*. Sage.

Jiang, L., & Probst, T. (2015). Do your employees (collectively) trust you? The importance of trust climate beyond individual trust. *Scandinavian Journal of Management, 31*(4). https://doi.org/10.1016/j.scaman.2015.09.003.

Jones, T. M., Felps, W., & Bigley, G. A. (2007). Ethical theory and stakeholder-related decisions: The role of stakeholder culture? *Academy of Management, 32*(1), 137–155. https://doi.org/10.5465/amr.2007.23463924.

Kim, S., & Krishna, A. (2017). Communication or action? Strategies fostering ethical organizational conduct and relational outcomes. *Public Relations Review., 43*(3), 560–567. https://doi.org/10.1016/j.pubrev.2017.03.009.

Kipnis, A. (1997). *Producing guanxi: Sentiment, self, and subculture in a North China village*. Duke University Press.

Kluckhohn, F. (1953). Dominant and variant value orientations. In C. Kluckhohn & H. Murray (Eds.), *Personality in nature, society, and culture* (pp. 342–357). Alfred A. Khopf.

Lombardi, G. (2015). Social media inside a large organization, in *Exploring internal communication: Towards informed employee voice*, 3rd ed. K. Ruck (ed.). Gower.

McLuhan, M. (1962/2011). *The Guttenberg Galaxy: The making of typographic man*.

Men, L. R., & Bowen, S. (2017). *Excellence in internal communication management*. Business Expert Press.

Men, L., R., O'Neil, J., & Ewing, M. (2020). Examining the effects of internal social media usage on employee engagement, *Public Relations Review*, *46*(2), 101880. https://doi.org/10.1016/j.pubrev.2020.101880.

Neill, M., & Jiang, H. (2017). Functional silos, integration & encroachment in internal communication. *Public Relations Review, 43*(5), 850–862. https://doi.org/10.1016/j.pubrev.2017.06.009

Pulevska Ivanovska, L., Postolov, K., Janeska Iliev, A., & Magdincheva Shopova, M. (2017). Establishing balance between professional and private life of Generation Z. *Research in Physical Education, Sport and Health, 6*(1), 3–9.

Scholte, J. A. (2008). Defining globalization. *The World Economy, 31*(1), 1471–1502.

Sriramesh, K. (1988, November). Toward a cross-cultural theory of public relations: Preliminary evidence from India. Presented at the annual conference of the *Association for the Advancement of Policy, Research and Development in the Third World*, Myrtle Beach, SC.
Sriramesh, K. (2006). The relationship between culture and public relations. In E. Toth (Ed.), *Excellence in public relations and communication management: Challenges for the next generation* (pp. 507–527). Lawrence Erlbaum Associates Inc.
Sriramesh, K. (2020). The *silent language* is also the *forgotten* language. In K. Sriramesh & D. Vercic (Eds.), *The global public relations handbook: Theory, research, and practice* (3rd ed). Routledge.
Sriramesh, K., & Enxi, L. (2004). Public relations practices and socio-economic factors: A case study of different organizational types in Shanghai. *Journal of Communication Studies, 3*(4), 44–76.
Sriramesh, K., Grunig, J. E., & Buffington, J. (1992). Corporate culture and public relations. In J. E. Grunig (Ed.), *Excellence in public relations and communications management: Contributions to effective organizations* (pp. 577–596). Lawrence Erlbaum Associates.
Sriramesh, K., Grunig, J. E., & Dozier, D. (1996). Observation and measurement of organizational culture: Development of indices of participative and authoritarian cultures. *Journal of Public Relations Research, 8*(4), 229–262. https://doi.org/10.1207/s1532754xjprr0804_02.
Sriramesh, K., Kim, Y., & Takasaki, M. (1999). Public relations in three Asian cultures: An analysis. *Journal of Public Relations Research, 11*(4), 271–292. https://doi.org/10.1207/s1532754xjprr1104_01.
Sriramesh, K., Rhee, Y., & Sung, M. (2013). Aligning public relations with the demands of globalization: Conceptual foundations for a theory of global public relations. In K. Sriramesh, A. Zerfass, & J. N. Kim (Eds.) *Public relations and communication management: Current trends and future directions.* Routledge.
Sriramesh, K., Saminathan, M., & Lim, D. (2007). The situational theory of publics in a different cultural setting: Consumer publics in Singapore. *Journal of Public Relations Research, 19*(4), 307–332. https://doi.org/10.1080/10627260701402424.
Sriramesh, K., & Takasaki, M. (1999). The impact of culture on Japanese public relations. *Journal of Communication Management, 3*(4), 337–352. https://doi.org/10.1108/eb023497
Sriramesh, K., & Verčič, D. (2012). *Culture and public relations.* Routledge.
Sriramesh, K., & Verčič, D. (2020). *The global public relations handbook: Theory, research, and practice.* Routledge.
Sriramesh, K., & White, J. (1992). Societal culture and public relations. In J. E. Grunig (Ed.), *Excellence in public relations and communications management:*

contributions to effective organizations (pp. 597–616). Lawrence Erlbaum Associates.

Stohl, C. (2001). Globalizing organizational communication. In F. M. Jablin & L. L. Putnam (Eds.), *The new handbook of organizational communication: Advances in theory, research, and methods* (pp. 323–375). Sage.

Tan, S. L. (2000). *Guanxi and public relations in Singapore: An exploratory study.* Master's Thesis, Nanyang Technological University, Singapore.

Tench, R., Verčič, D., Zerfass, A., Moreno, Á., & Verhoeven, P. (2017). *Communication excellence: How to develop.* Palgrave Macmillan.

Tkalac Verčič, A. (2016). *Odnosi s javnošću.* HUOJ.

Tkalac Verčič, A. (2020). *Odnosi z javnostmi*, PRSS.

Tyler, E. B. (1871). *Primitive culture.* Murray.

Verčič, D., & Tkalac Verčič, A. (2016). The new publicity: From reflexive to reflective mediatisation. *Public Relations Review, 42*(2), 493–498. https://doi.org/10.1016/j.pubrev.2015.07.008.

Verčič, D., Zerfass, A., & Wiesenberg, M. (2015). Global public relations and communication management: A European perspective. *Public Relations Review, 41*(5), 785–793. https://doi.org/10.1016/j.pubrev.2015.06.017.

Vial, G. (2019). Understanding digital transformation: A review and a research agenda. *Journal of Strategic Information Systems, 28*, 118–144. https://doi.org/10.1016/j.jsis.2019.01.003.

Zerfass, A., Moreno, Á., Tench, R., Verčič, D., & Verhoeven, P. (2013). *European Communication Monitor 2013: A changing landscape –Managing crises, digital communication and CEO positioning in Europe. Results of a survey in 43 countries* EACD/EUPRERA, Helios Media.

Zerfass, A., Verčič, D., Moreno, Á., Verhoeven, P., Tench, R., & Klewes, J. (2013). *European Chief Communication Officers Survey 2013. Managing CEO positioning and international communication: Insights from interviews with corporate communication leaders.* Ketchum / EUPRERA.

CHAPTER 14

Closing Thoughts and Future Directions

Ana Tkalac Verčič

This book is a result of a growing need for knowledge, models, information, and solutions in the area of internal communication, both in practice and in academia. The chapters were designed to give an overview of internal communication, an area that is increasingly gaining in importance. The authors, all experienced academics, provided insight into the most important current trends and issues. The first chapter of the book offers a summary of internal communication definitions, discusses recent developments and emerging trends which are shaping the practice, and introduces the topics that the book covers. In this final chapter, I will give my view of the current state of the field, review some of the questions still left open, and conclude with, as the title states, closing thoughts and future directions.

A. Tkalac Verčič (✉)
University of Zagreb, Zagreb, Croatia
e-mail: atkalac@efzg.hr

L. R. Men and A. Tkalac Verčič (eds.), *Current Trends and Issues in Internal Communication*, New Perspectives in Organizational Communication, https://doi.org/10.1007/978-3-030-78213-9_14

Scope of Internal Communication

There is no organization without communication. This reflects, to an extent, the rhetorical/hermeneutical approach to communication in which organizations are symbolic and communication makes them possible (Grunig, 1992). As Cheney (1983) concluded years ago, much of our time is spent communicating with, within, and for organizations. It is also clear that there is no management without communication (Carrière & Bourque, 2009). However, for years there was no real interest in internal communication by academics in fields other than speech communication, which is why they have been given the "almost exclusive privilege of colonizing the oasis of organizational communication" (Grunig, 1992, p. 537).

Today, things have changed, and various disciplines focus on internal communication. It is explored within organizational and managerial theories (Thompkins, 1987), organizational communication (Goldhaber, 1993; Jablin & Putnam, 2001; Jablin et al., 1987), organizational psychology (Drenth et al., 1998; Lowenberg & Conrad, 1998) and, obviously, public relations (Men & Bowen, 2017; Ruck & Welch, 2012; Tkalac Verčič et al., 2012; Welch, 2012). Even though internal communication is now increasingly recognized as a crucial topic (Zerfass et al., 2010) in which research has exponentially grown since 2011 (Lee & Yue, 2020), I believe the field of public relations has yet to take charge of internal communication completely. In practice, both human resources management and marketing claim internal communication as being within their remit/jurisdiction, but it is the public relations and corporate communication functions that have the best understanding of internal audiences (Tkalac Verčič, 2016).

In 1992, Grunig wrote a chapter on symmetrical systems of internal communication and reviewed the theories developed in the field of organizational communication—"the name used for internal communication in academic departments of speech communication" (p. 531). He uses the terms "organizational communication" and "internal communication" interchangeably, as do some others (Quirke, 2008; Tourish & Hargie, 2009; Zwijze-Koning & de Jong, 2007), even though there is still an "unhelpful continuous loop" in referring to organizational communication when talking about internal communication (Welch & Jackson, 2007).

Defining internal communication from a public relations point of view is important as it reflects the approach of authors in their studies of the field. Throughout the book, we have described internal communications and its elements. We started from basic definitions, where communication in organizations includes an exchange of information, ideas, attitudes and emotions from one person to another, commonly with the intention of changing behavior (Bahtijarević-Šiber & Sikavica, 2001). As Kalla established, "Internal communication is defined as integrated internal communication, i.e., all formal and informal communication taking place internally at all levels of an organization" (2005, p. 304). Internal communication creates and maintains communication systems between employers and employees (Tkalac Verčič, 2019), and is a requirement for organizational success, which is why it needs to be carefully assessed and managed (Ruck & Welch, 2012). Internal communication systems are a part of organizational culture and structure and at the same time create organizational culture and structure (Grunig, 1992). If it is carefully managed, internal communication can mean a higher awareness of opportunities and threats, or it can pose a risk when communication is poor (Tkalac Verčič, 2019). Good communication can add to an organization's productivity, performance, and external customer orientation (Downs & Adrian, 2004). However, it has to create clearer links to business objectives, and focus on strategies more than tools in order to "establish a clear raison d'etre" (Helsby, 2002, p. 3).

Considering the importance of internal communication, it is clear why organizations invest substantial financial and human resources in developing efficient internal communication systems, in order to achieve appropriate communication within the organization (Carrière & Bourque, 2009). Today, there is a growing body of evidence that links internal communication to various outcomes including the degree to which employees are informed, employee engagement, job satisfaction and performance (Gray & Laidlaw, 2004; Tkalac Verčič & Pološki Vokić, 2017; Zucker, 2002). Adding weight to this, the advantage of managing internal communication strategically is more than just employee satisfaction and productivity; it means employees are well informed which adds to various positive contributions (White et al., 2010). It is clear from research that there is a significant link between internal communication and organizational climate and productivity (Joshi & Sharma, 1997), as well as employees' ability, motivation, and commitment (Nakara, 2006).

Internal communication can help improve corporate reputation and credibility since employees represent a highly credible source for all external publics (Dawkins, 2005; Hannegan, 2004; White et al., 2010) and can add significant insight into leadership communication (Men, 2015; Men & Jiang, 2016; Men & Stacks, 2014).

It is important to investigate the scope and practice of internal communication so that theoretical definitions reflect the reality of practice. In this book, the starting definition of internal communication is managing relationships with internal publics. This involves all types of formal and informal communication happening internally (within the organization and on all its levels) including hierarchical communication, media and informal networks. However, one of the main goals of the book was to widen the scope and adjust the starting definition so that it reflects internal communication precisely and realistically within its organizational context.

Positioning Internal Communication

Where does internal communication belong in the organization? The principle of the informed employee voice works only if there are structures that facilitate it (Ruck, 2015). In organizational practice, there are many different versions of internal communication within an organizational setting. The position of internal communication is determined by the size of the organization, its culture, management style, financial resources, employee characteristics, organizational expectations, and changes in the organizational environment. Internal communication managers can report to the human resource manager, corporate communications manager or directly to the CEO. This sometimes means there can be potential overlaps and tensions (Ruck, 2015). Human resources and marketing both have a claim on internal communication (Yeomans & Carthew, 2014). Positioning internal communication within the human resources function often means focusing solely on employees, which in turn separates internal from external communication. This can break the coordination between internal and external messages and can leave the internal communication function without the external context. Marketing, on the other hand, can use internal communication to focus on the brand, customer service, and achieving sales (Quirke, 2008). As Quirke (p. 293) concludes, "corporate communications is often the natural home for internal communication". Internal communication is, however, still rarely an independent department (Tkalac Verčič, 2016).

While various activities within internal communication can be handled through the human resources department, communication strategies should originate within corporate communication. In a study we conducted in 2012 (Tkalac Verčič et al.), we found that European internal communication experts believe in the importance of strong connections between internal communication departments with human resources management, marketing and change management. According to the study, internal communication should be a part of corporate communication departments (positioned high enough in the organizational structure) for best organizational results.

In academic research, too, there are numerous disciplines that claim internal communication, such as human resources management, change management, organizational development, marketing, management, corporate strategy, public relations, and corporate communications. Internal communication, as an area of research, is closely interconnected to all of those academic areas, especially communication and human resources management. Grunig (1992) reported that organizational psychologists show an interest in communication (mostly because of its relationship to constructs that interest them, such as job satisfaction), while organizational sociologists often show no interest in the area of internal communication (with major textbooks having no chapters or references to communication). According to marketing academics, internal communication is a part of a wider, internal marketing concept, since internal marketing covers all contacts with internal stakeholders. Internal communication stemming from marketing should be the key to creating strong psychological contracts between employees and their organizations and should be responsible for promoting the brand to internal publics. However, in practice, this is rarely true (Sinčić Ćorić & Pološki Vokić, 2009).

Researchers and theorists in public relations have analyzed internal communication as a part of public relations for decades (Grunig, 1992; Grunig & Hunt, 1984; Pincus, 1986). The quality and volume of research and theory are constantly improving, and through this, it is becoming clear that public relations is the best academic host for internal communication research. In a study we conducted in 2012 (Tkalac Verčič et al.), internal communication experts agreed that management and psychological theories were most useful in internal communication, with some naming language studies, media studies, and marketing. Most experts stated that internal communication belongs in communication studies but under great influence by management and human resources theories. The methodology of internal communication measurement therefore stems primarily from these areas.

Channels of Internal Communication

In internal communication, as in all forms of communication, the success of communication depends, among other things, on choosing the right channel. The choice of a specific channel is a result of a communicator's attempt to achieve a message goal (Westmyer et al., 1998). In various situations, certain channels are more appropriate than others. Organizations' choice of channels for internal communication can vary depending on factors such as organizational profile, size, culture, employees' qualifications, or the level of technical development (Dévényi, 2016). Communication channels can range from traditional (print publications such as newsletters), phone calls and face-to-face communication, all the way to interactive web tools, such as internal social networking sites (Crescenzo, 2011). They have different levels of complexity, formality, cost, and capacity. It is key that the organization and its management consider the needs and preferences, resources, speed of data transfer, sender goals, and message and receiver characteristics in choosing the best channels to reach internal publics.

In choosing internal communication channels, communicators should consider employee preferences, and this depends on many things. These preferences are not simple and are contingent on more than just the type of media. Satisfaction is a result of a complex combination of content, media, situational, and personality factors. It can be managed and improved, primarily by asking employees what they think and how they feel about internal communication practices (Tkalac Verčič & Špoljarić, 2020). Even though positive attitudes towards media are a required precondition of successful internal communication (Welch, 2012), organizations often have a one-way approach to both communication in general as well as the choice and shape of internal communication media. I believe satisfied employees are a precondition of prosperous companies of the future. The expectation that it is employees' responsibility to adjust to organizations (or their choice of communication media) will have to become a thing of the past.

There is not nearly enough research on internal communication channels. Especially in the current climate where new technologies are completely reshaping our world. Even though there is a huge shift towards using digital technologies in daily communication, studies show that adoption of new technologies is neither easy nor straightforward (Tkalac Verčič & Špoljarić, 2020).

Different social media platforms, which can range from blogs to social networks, bring interactivity, the possibility of two-way communication and employee engagement (Crescenzo, 2011). Social media can create dialogue and through that have an indirect influence on traditional media (Berger, 2008; Lee, 2018). These "new" media channels could prove to be helpful in promoting listening skills and superior face-to-face communication (Rhee, 2004). Even though face-to-face communication usually represents the preferred channel, employees' choice can differ depending on the task (Reder & Conklin, 1988). It is important to explore whether the trend towards computer-mediated communication meets employees' own needs (Braun et al., 2019).

Reasons for Evaluating Internal Communication

Internal communication is comprised of different strategies and tactics which all have a main goal of improving communication within an organization. Evaluation and measurement have the most important role in showcasing the success of internal communication (Men & Bowen, 2017). As the field of internal communication has matured, different authors have underlined different approaches and methods of measurement. Grunig and Hunt (1984) included retention of key organizational messages, through conducting communication audits, through coorientational analyses, through internal communication satisfaction measurement, and through communication network analyses. Men and Bowen (2017) summarized internal communication measurement as outputs, outtakes, and outcomes, following a distinction made between these three communication methodologies by Lindenmann (1993) and Broom and Dozier (1990). However, equating internal communication research with measuring internal communication satisfaction is still very common (Ruck, 2015).

In exploring the approaches to communication measurement (and establishing what to measure), it is useful to examine why it is important to measure any aspect of internal communication at all. As Tourish and Hargie (2009, p. xv) nicely put it—"high quality communication inside organizations, and between them and their external publics produces many tangible benefits which include a sane internal atmosphere, where teamwork is the norm, more satisfied employees and customers, greater levels of productivity and innovation, and sustained competitive advantage."

There is abundant proof that links the different aspects of internal communication to positive outcomes. For example, Robson and Tourish (2005) concluded there is significant evidence that connects internal communication with a higher chance of organizational success. Hargie and Tourish (2002) stated that an increase in internal communication quality brings a series of useful organizational outcomes. Quinn and Hargie (2004) agreed that the key values of good organizational communication are organizational relationships that contribute to organizational efficiency. Dickson et al. (2003) stated there are numerous studies connecting an improvement in communication practices with various positive outcomes.

In their analysis, Clampitt and Downs (1993) concluded that good internal communication leads to increased productivity, reduced absenteeism, higher quality of services and products, increased levels of innovation, lesser strikes, and a reduction in total cost. Internal communication has been linked to employee trust (Men et al., 2020), employee advocacy (Men, 2014); organizational reputation (Men, 2014), organizational citizenship behavior (Men & Yue, 2019), and work–life enrichment (Jiang & Men, 2017). Snyder and Morris (1984) proved that two communication variables (quality of communication with superiors and exchange of information with peers) positively correlate with some measures of total organizational success. On the flipside, poor internal communication can lead to a number of negative consequences. For example, when people work in isolation or share only a minimum of information, positive change is slowed down (Hargie & Tourish, 2002). The same authors found that a lower quality of interdepartmental communication creates feelings of isolation and dissatisfaction and this correlates with lower levels of involvement in decision-making processes. Similarly, insufficient information exchanges can lead to insecurity and increased alienation for employees.

Research in and of internal communication should be rooted in communication and management theories but should also build its own body of knowledge. Incorporating research around engagement, reputation and employer branding into internal communication will help further develop the area and establish it more effectively both in academia and practice.

In contemporary organizations, engaged employees represent a competitive advantage (Macey & Schneider, 2008). According to Welch (2011), employee engagement falls into the internal communication domain, while Bakker et al. (2011) stated that internal communication is key in promoting employee engagement. Despite this, the relationship between internal communication and employee engagement is underexplored (Men et al., 2020; Tkalac Verčič et al., 2012; Tkalac Verčič & Pološki Vokić, 2017). It is internal communication that has the biggest potential in transferring organizational values to each employee, and through this, engaging them into organizational goals (Bindl & Parker, 2010; Pugh & Dietz, 2008; Wiley et al., 2010). Ruck and Welch (2012) have shown how employee engagement depends on internal communication and how organizations that have better internal communication have a four times higher chance of having engaged employees. In a recent study in which we explored this relationship further (Tkalac Verčič & Pološki Vokić, 2017), internal communication proved to be a precondition for effective employee engagement.

With regard to reputation, most authors would agree to define it as a combination of internal and external perceptions of an organization (Cheney & Christensen, 2001; Gummesson, 2000; Tkalac Verčič & Verčič, 2007). Some authors believe that reputation is an aggregation of identity and image (Fombrun, 1996; Fombrun & van Riel, 1997). From this perspective, communication directed toward internal publics is vital in reputation management (Ahmed & Rafiq, 2002; Tkalac Verčič & Verčič, 2007). The concept of employer brand is also closely connected to reputation (Ruiz et al., 2016), occasionally as a protector of it (Burke et al., 2011). Academic research aimed at exploring reputation and employer brands shows a certain overlap on the conceptual, methodological, and empirical levels (Hendriks, 2016). As a result, both reputation and employer brand should be important elements in the research of internal communication and should be placed within the remit of the internal communicator's responsibilities. This is particularly important since profitability and the future success of modern organizations depend on their readiness to put employees first and recognize them as the most important resource of organizational success (Aggerholm et al., 2011).

In practice, however, the use of research in internal communication is still rather uncommon. A study by Nelli (2018) showed that practitioners generally pay little attention to monitoring internal communication practices. His study shows that companies rarely measure costs, both financial and in terms of personnel, of internal communication projects. Most of the research is focused on intranet usage and on the satisfaction or engagement of employees, followed by measures of the quality of internal workflows and the effectiveness of communication channels. Measures that reveal the impact of communication at the outcome level are rarely conducted, while methods to evaluate the impact of internal communication on strategic and/or financial objectives are ranked last.

The Future of Internal Communication

The increasing complexity of modern organizations and significant changes in which they operate, as well as the major advances in information technologies, all lead to an increased interest in internal communication (Bélanger & Watson-Manheim, 2006). This fast-changing and connected modern society has made employees one of the most important publics for every organization (Kim & Rhee, 2011). A satisfying employee–employer relationship aids productivity, external relations and organizational reputation (Berger, 2008). In the past, internal communication has been viewed, quite basically, as the function of providing employees with information (McKenzie, 2007). This one-way approach was mainly concerned with regulating employee behavior and guaranteeing agreement. Today, organizations are moving toward creative involvement and participation. This contemporary approach should highlight organizations as an "…interconnected whole which needs to be focused on agreed objectives in order to go through organizational transformation without collapsing into internal strife" (Tourish & Hargie, 2009, p. 24).

As we stated in Chapter 13, there are certain trends which shape the future of internal communication. Globalization, deregulation, economic crises, and now a global pandemic, all create an unpredictable environment full of potential opportunities and threats (Tkalac Verčič, 2020). There is an overall decrease of trust in organizational leadership (Jiang & Probst, 2015) and loyalty toward organizations (Tkalac Verčič, 2016).

The future is not easy to predict, but some major trends seem clear (Men & Bowen, 2017).

Successful organizations depend on innovation for growth, and so incorporating differences that ensure diversity is becoming necessary (DiTomaso, 2007). Diversification in the workplace now includes differences in language, nationality, race, ethnicity, religion, and sexual orientation (Amadeo, 2013). Also, changes in society that are a result of digital technology are reshaping our world. Only innovating and embracing digital technologies in internal communication can lead to better performance (Hess et al., 2016) and a democratic, transparent environment that encourages sharing (Men & Bowen, 2017). Coupled with this, there is a bigger demand for ethical accountability and transparency, as the publics everywhere become increasingly sensitive toward organizational misconduct. As new generations become the majority of the workforce, companies will have to show an even stronger social conscience and give their employees more power and influence. New generations are also showing an increasing interest in flexibility and freedom at work (Boudreau et al., 2015), as the importance of work–life balance becomes even stronger. The focus of younger employees is not so much on the organization, but on what the organization can offer them. Finally, to ensure the successful management of internal communication, it is important to recognize cultural diversity without judgment, as well as to avoid cultural blindness (Adler, 2002). The workforce is becoming more globalized, diverse and multicultural than ever, which means there is a greater opportunity for organizational success, innovation, and creativity (Men & Bowen, 2017).

References

Adler, N. J. (2002). *International dimensions of organizational behavior* (4th ed.). South-Western Thomson Learning.

Aggerholm, H., Andersen, S. E., & Thomsen, C. (2011). Conceptualizing employer branding in sustainable organizations. *Corporate Communications: An International Journal, 16*(2), 105–123. https://doi.org/10.1108/13563281111141642.

Ahmed, P. K., & Rafiq, M. (2002). *Internal marketing: Tools and concepts for customer-focused management*. Butterworth-Heinemann.

Amadeo, K. (2013). *Cultural diversity*. Retrieved from http://useconomy.about.com/od/suppl1/g/Cultural-Diversity.htm.

Bahtijarević-Šiber, F. & Sikavica, P. (eds.) (2001). Leksikon menedžmenta [*Management lexicon*]. Masmedia.

Bakker, A. B., Albrecht, S. L., & Leiter, M. P. (2011). Key questions regarding work engagement. *European Journal of Work and Organizational Psychology, 20*(1), 4–28. https://doi.org/10.1080/1359432X.2010.485352.

Bélanger, F., & Watson-Manheim, M. B. (2006). Virtual teams and multiple media: Structuring media use to attain strategic goals. *Group Decision and Negotiation, 15*(4), 299–321. https://doi.org/10.1007/s10726-006-9044-8.

Berger, B. (2008). Employee/organizational communications. Institute for Public Relations. Retrieved from http://www.instituteforpr.org/topics/employee-organizational-communications/.

Bindl, U. K., & Parker, S. K. (2010). Feeling good and performing well? Psychological engagement and positive behaviors at work. In S. L. Albrecht (Ed.), *Handbook of employee engagement: Perspectives, issues, research and practice*. Edward Elgar.

Boudreau, J. W., Jesuthasan, R., & Creelman, D. (2015). *Lead the work: Navigating a world beyond employment*. John Wiley & Sons.

Braun, S., Hernandez Bark, A., Kirchner, A., Stegmann, S., & Van Dick, R. (2019). Emails from the boss curse or blessing? Relations between communication channels, leader evaluation, and employees' attitudes. *International Journal of Business Communication, 56*(1), 50–81. https://doi.org/10.1177/2329488415597516.

Broom, G. M., & Dozier, D. M. (1990). *Using research in public relations: Applications to program management*. Prentice-Hall.

Burke, G. Martin, & C. L. Cooper. (2011). (Ed.). *Corporate reputation: Managing opportunities and threats* (1–43). Gower.

Carrière, J., & Bourque, C. (2009). The effects of organizational communication on job satisfaction and organizational commitment in a land ambulance service and the mediating role of communication satisfaction. *Career Development International, 14*(1), 29–49. https://doi.org/10.1108/13620430910933565.

Cheney, G. (1983). The rhetoric of identification and the study of organizational communication. *Quarterly Journal of Speech, 69*, 143–158. https://doi.org/10.1080/00335638309383643.

Cheney, G., & Christensen, L. T. (2001). Organizational identity: Linkages between internal and external communication. In F. M. Jablin & L. L. Putnam (Eds.), *The new handbook of organizational communication: Advances in theory, research, and methods* (pp. 231–269). Sage.

Clampitt, P. G., & Downs, C. W. (1993). Employee perceptions of the relationship between communication and productivity: A field study. *The Journal of Business Communication, 30*(1), 5–29.

Crescenzo, S. (2011). Internal employee communications media. In T. Gillis (Ed.), *The IABC handbook of organizational communication* (2nd ed., pp. 219–230). Jossey-Bass.

Dawkins, J. (2005). Corporate responsibility: The communication challenge. *Journal of Communication Management, 9*, 108–119. https://doi.org/10.1108/13632540510621362.

Dévényi, M. (2016). The role of integrative strategies and tactics in HR negotiations. *Strategic Management, 21*(2), 32–36.

Dickson, D., Reiney, S., & Hargie, O. (2003). Communication sensitive business issues: Part 1. *Corporate Communications, 8*(1), 35–43. https://doi.org/10.1108/13563280310458902.

DiTomaso, N., Post, C., & Parks-Yancy, R. (2007). Workforce diversity and inequality: Power, status, and numbers. In K. Cook & D. Massey (Eds.), *Annual Review of Sociology, 33*, 473–501. https://doi.org/10.1146/annurev.soc.33.040406.131805.

Downs, C. W., & Adrian, A. (2004). *Assessing organizational communication: Strategic communication audits*. The Guilford Press.

Drenth, P. J. D., Thierry, H., & de Wolff, C. J. (Eds.). (1998). *Organizational psychology*. Psychology Press.

Fombrun, C. (1996). *Reputation: Realizing value from the corporate image*. Harvard Business School Press.

Fombrun, C., & van Riel, C. (1997). The reputational landscape. *Corporate Reputations Review, 1*(1), 5–13. https://doi.org/10.1057/palgrave.crr.1540008.

Goldhaber, G. M. (1993). *Organizational communication*. Brown & Benchmark.

Gray, J., & Laidlaw, H. (2004). Improving the measurement of communications satisfaction. *Management Communication Quarterly, 17*(3), 425–448. https://doi.org/10.1177/0893318903257980.

Grunig, J. E. (1992). Symmetrical systems of internal communication. In J. Grunig (Ed.), *Excellence in public relations and communication management* (pp. 531–576). Lawrence Erlbaum.

Grunig, J. & Hunt, T. (1984). *Managing public relations*. Harcourt Brace Jovanovich College Publishers.

Gummesson, E. (2000). *Qualitative methods in management research*. Sage.

Hannegan, C. (2004). Employees as reputation makers. *Strategic Communication Management, 8*(6), 5.

Hargie, O., & Tourish, D. (eds.) (2002). *Handbook of communication audits for organizations*. Routledge.

Helsby, N. (2002). *The rise of the internal communicator: A research report on the role of senior internal communication practitioners conducted in 37 major UK and US businesses*. Watson Helsby. Retrieved from http://www.watsonhelsby.co.uk/assets/files/TheRiseoftheInternalCommunicator%282002%29.pdf.

Hendriks, M. (2016). *Organizational reputation, organizational attractiveness and employer branding: Clarifying the concepts*. Master thesis. Faculty of behavioral, management and social sciences Master Business Administration.

Hess, T., Matt, C., Benlian, A., & Wiesboeck, F. (2016). Options for formulating a digital transformation strategy. *MIS Quart. Execut, 15*(2), 123–139. https://doi.org/10.7892/BORIS.105447.

Jablin, F. M. (1987). Formal organization structure. In F. M. Jablin, L. L. Putnam, K. H. Roberts & L. W. Porter (Eds.), *Handbook of organizational communication: An interdisciplinary perspective* (pp. 389–419). Sage.

Jablin, F. M., & Putnam, L. L. (2001). *The new handbook of organizational communication: Advance theory, research and methods*. Sage.

Jiang, L., & Probst, T. M. (2015). Do your employees (collectively) trust you? The importance of trust climate beyond individual trust. *Scandinavian Journal of Management, 31*, 526–535. https://doi.org/10.1016/j.scaman.2015.09.003.

Jiang, H., & Men, R. L. (2017). Creating an engaged workforce: The impact of authentic leadership, transparent organizational communication, and work-life enrichment. *Communication Research, 44*(2), 225–243. https://doi.org/10.1177/0093650215613137.

Joshi, R. J., & Sharma, B. R. (1997). Determinants of managerial job satisfaction in private organization. *Indian Journal of Industrial Relations, 33*(1), 331–337.

Kalla, H. K. (2005). Integrated internal communications: A multidisciplinary perspective. *Corporate Communications: An International Journal, 10*(4), 302–314. https://doi.org/10.1108/13563280510630106.

Kim, J. N., & Rhee, Y. (2011). Strategic thinking about employee communication behavior (ECB) in public relations: Testing the models of megaphoning and scouting effects in Korea. *Journal of Public Relations Research, 23*(3), 243–268. https://doi.org/10.1080/1062726X.2011.582204.

Lee, Y. (2018). Dynamics of symmetrical communication within organizations: The impacts of channel usage of CEO, managers, and peers. *Journal of Business Communication*. 232948841880366. https://doi.org/10.1177/2329488418803661.

Lee, Y., & Yue, C. A. (2020). Status of internal communication research in public relations: An analysis of published articles in nine scholarly journals from 1970 to 2019. *Public Relations Review, 46*(3), 1–10. https://doi.org/10.1016/j.pubrev.2020.101906.

Lindenmann, W. (1993). An 'effectiveness yardstick' to measure public relations success. *Public Relations Quarterly, 38*(1), 7–9.

Lowenberg, G., & Conrad, K. A. (1998). *Current perspectives in industrial/organizational psychology*. Allyn & Bacon.

Macey, W. H., & Schneider, B. (2008). Engaged in engagement: We are delighted we did it. *Industrial and Organisational Psychology, 1*(1), 76–83. https://doi.org/10.1111/j.1754-9434.2007.00016.x.

McKenzie, T. (2007). Lessons learned about change at sun microsystems. *Strategic Communication Management, 11*(1), 14–17.

Men, L. R. (2014). Internal reputation management: Effects of authentic leadership and transparent communication. *Corporate Reputation Review, 17,* 254–272.

Men, L. R. (2015). The internal communication role of the Chief Executive Officer: Communication channels, style, and effectiveness. *Public Relations Review. 41*(4), 461–471.

Men, L. R., & Jiang, H. (2016). Toward an integrated model of internal relationship management: Understanding the interplay between authentic leadership, organizational culture, and symmetrical communication. *International Journal of Strategic Communication., 10*(5), 462–479. https://doi.org/10.1080/1553118X.2016.1226172.

Men, L. R., & Bowen, S. (2017). *Excellence in internal communication management*. University of Toronto Press.

Men, L. R., O'Neil, J., & Ewing, M. (2020). Examining the effects of internal social media on employee engagement. *Public Relations Review, 46*(2). https://doi.org/10.1016/j.pubrev.2020.101880.

Men, L. R., & Stacks, D. W. (2014). The effects of authentic leadership on strategic internal communication and employee-organization relationships. *Journal of Public Relations Research, 26,* 301–324.

Men, L. R., & Yue, A. C. (2019). Creating a positive emotional culture: Effects of strategic internal communication and its impact on employee supportive behaviors. *Public Relations Review, 45*(3), 101764. https://doi.org/10.1016/j.pubrev.2019.03.001.

Nakara, R. (2006). Relationship between communication satisfaction and organizational identification: An empirical study vision. *The Journal of Business Perspective, 10*(2), 41–51. https://doi.org/10.1177/097226290601000206.

Nelli, R. P. (2018). *Internal Communication in Europe. Key success factors and managerial approaches*. Ascai: European Association for Internal Communication. Available at: http://www.ascai.it/uploads/files/RAPPORTI%20ASCAI/E_BOOK%20IC%20EUROPEAN%20REPORT%202018.pdf.

Pincus, J. D. (1986). Communication satisfaction, job satisfaction and job performance. *Human Communication Research, 12*(3), 395–419. https://doi.org/10.1111/j.1468-2958.1986.tb00084.x.

Pugh, S. D., & Dietz, J. (2008). Employee engagement at the organizational level of analysis. *Industrial and Organizational Psychology, 1*(1), 45–48. https://doi.org/10.1111/j.1754-9434.2007.00006.x.

Quinn, D., & Hargie, O. (2004). Internal communication audits: A case study. *Corporate Communication: an International Journal, 9*(2), 146–158. https://doi.org/10.1108/13563280410534348.

Quirke, B. (2008). *Making the connections: Using internal communication to turn strategy into action*, 2nd ed. Gower.

Reder, S., & Conklin, N. F. (1988). *Selection and effects of channels in distributed communication and decision-making tasks: A theoretical review and a proposed research paradigm.* Northwest Regional Educational Lab.

Robson, P. J. A., & Tourish, D. (2005). Managing internal communication: An organizational case study. *Corporate Communications: An International Journal, 10*(3), 213–222. https://doi.org/10.1108/13563280510614474.

Ruck, K. (ed.). (2015). *Exploring internal communication—Towards informed employee voice.* Gower.

Ruck, K., & Welch, M. (2012). Valuing internal communication: Management and employee perspective. *Public Relations Review, 38*(2), 294–302. https://doi.org/10.1016/J.PUBREV.2011.12.016.

Ruiz, B., García, J., A. & Revilla, J., J. (2016). Antecedents and consequences of bank reputation: A comparison of the United Kingdom and Spain. *International Marketing Review, 33*(6), 781–805. https://doi.org/10.1108/IMR-06-2015-0147.

Sinčić Ćorić, D., & Pološki Vokić, N. (2009). The roles of internal communications, human resource management and marketing concepts in determining holistic internal marketing philosophy. *Zagreb International Review of Economics & Business, 12*(2), 87–105.

Snyder, R., & Morris, J. (1984). Organizational communication and performance. *Journal of Applied Psychology, 69*(3), 461–466.

Thompkins, P. K. (1987). Translating organizational theory: Symbolism over substance. In F. M. Jablin, L. L. Putnam, K. H. Roberts, & L. W. Porter (Eds.), *Handbook of organizational communication: An interdisciplinary perspective* (pp. 70–96). Sage.

Tkalac Verčič, A. (2016). Odnosi s javnošću [*Public relations*]. HUOJ.

Tkalac Verčič, A. (2019). Internal communication with a global perspective. In K. Shriramesh & D. Verčič (Eds.), *The global public relations handbook theory, research, and practice* (pp. 270–296). Routledge.

Tkalac Verčič, A. (2020). Odnosi z javnostmi [*Public relations*]. PRSS.

Tkalac Verčič, A., & Špoljarić, A. (2020). Managing internal communication: How the choice of channels affects internal communication satisfaction. *Public Relations Review*. 46(3), 101926. https://doi.org/10.1016/j.pubrev.2020.101926.

Tkalac Verčič, A., & Verčič, D. (2007). Reputation as matching identities and images: Extending Davies and Chun's (2002) research on gaps between internal and external perceptions of the corporate brand. *Journal of Marketing Communications, 13*(4), 277–290. https://doi.org/10.1080/13527260701300151.

Tkalac Verčič, A., Verčič, D., & Sriramesh, K. (2012). Internal communication: Definition, parameters, and the future. *Public Relations Review, 38*(2), 223–230. https://doi.org/10.1016/j.pubrev.2011.12.019.

Tkalac Verčič, A., & Pološki, N. (2017). Engaging employees through internal communication. *Public Relations Review., 43*(5), 885–893. https://doi.org/10.1016/j.pubrev.2017.04.005.

Tourish, D., & Hargie, O. (2009). Communication and organizational success. In O. Hargie & D. Tourish (Eds.), *Auditing organizational communication: A handbook of research, theory and practice* (pp. 3–26). Routledge.

Welch, M. (2011). The evolution of the employee engagement concept: Communication implications. *Corporate Communications: An International Journal, 16*(4), 328–346. https://doi.org/10.1108/13563281111186968.

Welch, M. (2012). Appropriateness and acceptability: Employee perspectives of internal communication. *Public Relations Review, 38*(2), 246–254. https://doi.org/10.1016/j.pubrev.2011.12.017.

Welch, M., & Jackson, P. R. (2007). Rethinking internal communication: A stakeholder approach. *Corporate Communications: An International Journal, 12*(2), 177–198. https://doi.org/10.1108/13563280710744847.

Westmyer, S., DiCioccio, R., L. & Rubin, R. (1998). Appropriateness and effectiveness of communication channels in competent interpersonal communication. *Journal of Communication, 48*, 27–48. https://doi.org/10.1111/j.1460-2466.1998.tb02758.x.

White, C., Vanc, A., & Stafford, G. (2010). Internal communication, information satisfaction, and sense of community: The effect of personal influence. *Journal of Public Relations Research, 22*(1), 65–84. https://doi.org/10.1080/10627260903170985.

Wiley, J.W., Kowske, B. J., & Herman, A. E. (2010). Developing and validating a global model of employee engagement. In S. L. Albrecht (Ed.), *Handbook of employee engagement: Perspectives, issues, research and practice*. Edward Elgar.

Yeomans, L., & Carthew, W. (2014). Internal communication. In R. Tench & L. Yeomans (Eds.), *Exploring public relations* (3rd ed.). Pearson Education.

Zerfass, A., Tench, R., Verhoeven, P., Verčič, D., & Moreno, A. (2010). *European communication monitor 2010. Status quo and challenges for communication management in Europe. Results of an empirical survey in 46 countries*, EACD & EUPRERA, Brussels.

Zucker, R. (2002). More than a name change—Internal branding at pearl. *Strategic Communication Management, 6*(4), 24–27.

Zwijze-Koning, K. H., & de Jong, M. D. T. (2007). Measurement of communication satisfaction. Evaluating the Communication Satisfaction Questionnaire as a communication audit tool. *Management Communication Quarterly*, *20*(3), 261–282. https://doi.org/10.1177/0893318906295680.

Index

L. R. Men and A. Tkalac Verčič (eds.), *Current Trends and Issues in Internal Communication*, New Perspectives in Organizational Communication, https://doi.org/10.1007/978-3-030-78213-9

The manufacturer's authorised representative in the EU is Springer Nature Customer Service Centre GmbH, Europaplatz 3, 69115 Heidelberg, Germany. If you have any concerns regarding our products, please contact ProductSafety@springernature.com

Printed and bound by CPI Group (UK) Ltd, Croydon, CR0 4YY
22/09/2026
02221054-0012